Health Care UK 1997/98

The King's Fund annual review of health policy

Health Care UK 1997/98

The King's Fund annual review of health policy

Edited by Anthony Harrison

Published by
King's Fund Publishing
11–13 Cavendish Square
London W1M 0AN

First published 1998

ISBN 1 85717 218 3

A CIP catalogue record for this book is available from the British Library

Available from:
King's Fund Bookshop
11–13 Cavendish Square
London W1M 0AN
Tel: 0171 307 2591

Printed and bound in Great Britain

Cover illustration by Minuche Mazumdar Farrar

Contents

Contributors

Anthony Harrison
Fellow in Health Systems, King's Fund Policy & Development Directorate

Robert Hazell
Professor of Government and the Constitution, School of Public Policy, University College London

Paul Jervis
Visiting Professor in Organisation Development, Middlesex University Business School

Justin Keen
Fellow in Health Systems, King's Fund Policy & Development Directorate

Rudolf Klein
Visiting Fellow, King's Fund Policy & Development Directorate

Jack Kneeshaw
Visiting Fellow, King's Fund Policy & Development Directorate

Nicholas Mays
was, until Sept 1998: Director, Health Systems Programme, King's Fund Policy & Development Directorate

Jo-Ann Mulligan
Research Officer, Health Systems Programme, King's Fund Policy & Development Directorate

Bill New
Senior Research Officer, King's Fund Policy & Development Directorate

HEALTH POLICY REVIEW

Part 1 Main events

On 1 May 1997, Labour came to power after 18 years in Opposition. During that time, it had found little to praise in the health policies the Conservatives had pursued, but it came to office with only a small number of commitments of its own in relation to the NHS:

- to cut bureaucracy;
- to devote extra resources to breast cancer services;
- to cut waiting lists by treating 100,000 more patients;
- to end GP fundholding.

It was not until December 1997 that Labour unveiled its plans for what it termed 'The New NHS' and not until February 1998 before its full intentions towards the broader field of public health policy became clear. By the end of its first full Parliamentary session, however, a massive range of new policies had been announced which, on the surface at least, promised substantive change.

Parts 1 and 2 of the Review set these out within the same framework which we have used since 1991 to describe the Conservatives' policies. In Section 1.1 we look primarily at the proposals for

the structure of purchasing and providing which, in many respects, build on Conservative policies, but which abandon the rhetoric of competition for that of partnership and co-operation. Section 1.2 considers community care, which did not feature strongly in pre-election debate and where new ideas have proved particularly hard to find. Section 1.3 looks at the proposals for a public health policy where the new Government was confident that it did have a new approach to offer, one which placed greater emphasis on the wide economic and social content and which embodied an explicit commitment to the reduction of health inequalities. The White Paper proposals bearing on users, where no substantial innovations had been introduced by mid-1998, are discussed in Section 1.4, and those on clinical knowledge where a radically new direction was laid out, are set out in Section 1.5.

Part 2 of the Review begins by considering the Government's plans for spending on the NHS: out of office Labour had made a commitment to spending more in real terms each year but had inherited and stuck to the previous Government's plans. By July 1998 it was confident enough of the public finances to increase NHS spending by a substantial amount, but the familiar doubts about what is 'enough' nevertheless remained. Part 2 then goes on to consider equity, which features at the heart of *The New NHS*. It concludes with a description of the Government's proposals for extending the accountability of the services through the introduction of a new range of performance indicators, together with the proposals for clinical governance.

In Part 3 of the Review, we look at the full range of policies announced by the Labour Government up to the end of July 1998 and consider whether they do in fact amount to a 'third way' of running the NHS, as *The New NHS* claims, as well as the feasibility of implementing the vast range of innovations introduced by the middle of 1998.

We focus in our commentary on proposals for England, but each country has a White Paper of its own – see Box – refer forward to article – despite the emphasis in the English White Paper on a 'one-nation' NHS. Robert Hazell and Paul Jervis consider the implications for the NHS of constitutional change on pages 220–31.

Department of Health, *The New NHS: Modern, Dependable,* Cm 3807, The Stationery Office, London, 1997.

The Scottish Office Department of Health, *Designed to Care: Renewing the National Health Service in Scotland,* Cm 3811, The Stationery Office, Edinburgh, 1997.

The Welsh Office, *NHS Wales: putting patients first,* Cm 3841, The Stationery Office, Cardiff, 1998.

DHSS Northern Ireland, *Fit for the Future,* DHSS, Belfast, 1998.

1.1 Labour's New NHS

The New NHS: Modern, Dependable begins with a statement of its ambition for the NHS:

> *The Government is committed to giving the people of this country the best system of health care in the world.* (p.4)

Wisely, the White Paper did not contain any suggested timescale by which this would be achieved nor benchmarks which might indicate that it had. The Paper follows up this global target with a more specific commitment which had already appeared in the Labour Party Election Manifesto:

> *If you are ill or injured there will be a national health service there to help: and access to it will be based on need and need alone – not on your ability to pay, or on who your GP happens to be or on where you live.* (p.5)

In line with the second commitment, the Government announced in May 1997, before the publication of the White Paper that what would have been the sixth wave of fundholding would not be brought in, that hospitals should maintain common waiting lists, so as to make queue-jumping by the patients of fundholders impossible, and that GP fundholding itself would be abolished.

Ensuring equal access for equal need is a much more ambitious objective. Over the years, numerous reports have brought out the differences between areas in respect, for example, of the availability of the more specialised services and the quality of the services which are available. The White Paper contains a series of ambitious proposals explicitly designed to ensure that the NHS is equitable in practice. We consider both the precise meaning of the objective and the means proposed to pursue it in Section 2.2.

Equal access for equal need is a principle which the previous Government would also have accepted. However the White Paper makes clear that the Government's aim is to change the principles which guided policy-making under the Conservatives:

- *first, to renew the NHS as a genuinely **national** service. Patients will get fair access to consistently high quality, prompt and accessible services right across the country;*

- *but second, to make the delivery of health care against these new national standards a matter of **local** responsibility. Local doctors and nurses who are in the best position to know what patients need will be in the driving seat in shaping services;*

- *third, to get the NHS to work in **partnership.** By breaking down organisational barriers and forging stronger links with Local Authorities, the needs of the patient will be put at the centre of the care process;*

- *but fourth, to drive **efficiency** through a more rigorous approach to performance and by cutting bureaucracy, so that every pound in the NHS is spent to maximise the care for patients;*

- *fifth, to shift the focus onto quality of care so that **excellence** is guaranteed to all patients, and quality becomes the driving force for decision-making at every level of the service;*

- *and sixth, to rebuild **public confidence** in the NHS as a public service, accountable to*

patients, open to the public and shaped by their views.

(*The New NHS*, p.11)

While these objectives are intended to indicate a new direction, the White Paper asserts that the Government also intended to build on what has worked.

> *2.5 There are some sound foundations on which the new NHS can be built. Not everything about the old system was bad. This Government believes that what counts is what works. If something is working effectively then it should not be discarded purely for the sake of it. The new system will go with the grain of the best of these developments.*

(*The New NHS*, p.11)

Accordingly, it sets out three areas where it proposes to 'build on what has worked':

- the separation between the planning of hospital care and its provision – in other words, it accepts that the purchaser/provider split, introduced for clinical services with the 1990 Act, should remain;
- an increasingly important role for primary care, i.e. while rejecting fundholding because of the inequities it has produced, the Government accepts that it was right to locate the purchasing of most clinical services within primary care;
- decentralising responsibility to trusts for operational management. The creation of trusts was intended by the Conservatives to allow greater freedom of action at local level. The emphasis in Labour's White Paper is slightly different, focusing more on the role of

trusts and their staff in the development of local policies for health and health care as a whole and their corporate roles as accountable units for clinical quality.

The White Paper also lists seven areas where the intention is to discard what has failed (see Box).

Discarded policies

- Fragmented responsibility between 4,000 NHS bodies. Little strategic planning. Patients passed from pillar to post.

- Competition between hospitals. Some GPs get better service for their patients at the expense of others. Hospital clinicians disempowered.

- Competition prevented sharing of best practice, to protect 'competitive advantage'. Variable quality.

- Perverse incentives of Efficiency Index, distorting priorities, and getting in the way of real efficiency, effectiveness and quality. Artificially partitioned budgets.

- Soaring administrative costs, diverting effort from improving patient services. High numbers of invoices and high transaction costs.

- Short term contracts, focusing on cost and volume. Incentive on each NHS Trust to lever up volume to meet financial targets rather than work across organisational boundaries.

- NHS Trusts run as secretive commercial businesses. Unrepresentative boards. Principal legal duty on finance.

Source: *The New NHS,* p.16

The three features which the new Government accepts as worth preserving were central elements of the market in clinical services which the 1990 Act provided for and so in terms of the broad structure within which purchasing and provision are to take place, the emphasis is on continuity rather than change. Nevertheless changes are proposed for each element which, in the case of purchasing at least, are extremely far-reaching. Moreover, although the broad structure is to remain the same, the system as a whole is intended to work differently: competition is to be replaced by a series of partnership or collaborative arrangements. The rest of this section looks at each of the elements in more detail and concludes by considering how the various elements will be brought together.

Purchasing

In England the key change is the creation of primary care groups which are intended to take over nearly all the purchasing role – the other parts of the UK have taken a different approach. Their functions are to:

- contribute to the **Health Authority's Health Improvement Programme** on health and health care, helping to ensure that this reflects the perspective of the local community and the experience of patients;

- **promote the health of the local population,** working in partnership with other agencies;

- **commission health services** for their populations from the relevant NHS Trusts, within the framework of the Health Improvement Programme, ensuring quality and efficiency;

- **monitor performance** *against the service agreements they (or initially the Health Authority) have with NHS Trusts;*

- **develop primary care** *by joint working across practices; sharing skills; providing a forum for professional development, audit and peer review; assuring quality and developing the new approach to clinical governance; and influencing the deployment of resources for general practice locally. Local Medical Committees will have a key role in supporting this process;*

- **better integrate primary and community health services** *and work more closely with* **social services** *on both planning and delivery. Services such as child health or rehabilitation where responsibilities have been split within the health service and where liaison with Local Authorities is often poor, will particularly benefit.*

(*The New NHS*, p.34)

The groups are intended to be larger than most fundholding practices but smaller than existing health authorities:

> 5.16 *The intention is that Primary Care Groups should develop around natural communities, but take account also of the benefits of coterminosity with social services. Practices based close to the borders of a Group will be able to choose to join with others in the way which makes best sense locally. Primary Care Groups may typically serve about 100,000 patients. But there will be flexibility to reflect local circumstances and emerging evidence about the effectiveness of different size groupings. Primary Care Groups will generally grow out of existing local groupings, modified as needed to meet the criteria set out above.*

(*The New NHS*, p.37)

Recognising the large-scale nature of the changes that the introduction of Primary Care Groups will bring about, the White Paper acknowledges the need for 'an orderly transition'. It suggests that there will be a need to consider:

- *future arrangements for services currently funded through the fundholding scheme so that those that are cost-effective, including those in GP practices, can continue to be provided, and spread to others*

- *arrangements for fundholding staff, currently sponsored from the Practice Fund Management Allowance, so that those skilled in primary care commissioning are wherever possible retained at the practice, Primary Care Group or Health Authority level*

- *arrangements for winding up Practice Funds, including how savings can be used for the benefit of patients subject to appropriate value-for-money tests.*

(*The New NHS*, para 5.36)

Despite the introduction of primary care groups, health authorities retain a number of 'key tasks':

- **assessing the health needs** *of the local population, drawing on the knowledge of other organisations;*

- *drawing up a strategy for meeting those needs, in the form of a* **Health Improvement Programme,** *developed in partnership with all the local interests and ensuring delivery of the NHS contribution to it;*

- *deciding on the* **range and location of health care services** *for the Health*

Authority's residents, which should flow from, and be part of, the Health Improvement Programme;

- *determining **local targets and standards** to drive quality and efficiency in the light of national priorities and guidance, and ensuring their delivery;*

- *supporting the **development of Primary Care Groups** so that they can rapidly assume their new responsibilities;*

- ***allocating resources to Primary Care Groups;***

- *. **holding Primary Care Groups to account.***

(*The New NHS*, p.25)

Over and above these roles, the subsequent Green Paper, *Our Healthier Nation* – considered in more detail in Section 1.3 – emphasises primary care groups' roles in promoting the health of local populations in general and reducing health inequalities in particular.

The roles set out above are substantial ones, but health authorities will, like the rest of the NHS, be subject to the drive to cut management costs. The White Paper makes it clear that the expectation is that the number of health authorities will fall as a result of mergers. That may allow some pooling of scarce skills but overall the level of resources available for the demanding tasks remaining to them seem set to decline rather than to rise.

Despite the emphasis on primary care purchasing, the White Paper acknowledges that neither primary care groups nor health authorities may be the best vehicle for all forms of purchasing. It therefore proposes that so-called specialist services will be commissioned at regional level.

7.23 There is a further new function that will be central to the Regional Office role – providing the means to commission specialist hospital services. The internal market's fragmentation between multiple fundholders and Health Authorities made it difficult to ensure properly co-ordinated commissioning arrangements for these very specialised services. They are needed for highly complex treatments (such as bone marrow transplants and medium secure psychiatric services) where one centre covers the population of a number of Health Authorities.

(*The New NHS*, p.61)

This proposal is in line with the conclusions of the Audit Commission report *Higher Purchase* published in 1997, which found that the existing arrangements for commissioning specialised services were not effective. The previous Government had attempted to reduce the central role in favour of local consortia of health authorities. In practice, the Commission found that 'consortia arrangements were not as common as anticipated'. It went on to point out that:

131. Some consortia have fallen apart because of real differences between authorities in culture, priorities and financial position. (p.70)

In other words, the co-operation which this element of the internal market required was not generally forthcoming. Nevertheless, the Commission accepted the case for larger groupings, which make better use of existing expertise, reduce transactions costs and allow risk to be shared. It points out that:

> 135. Smaller players may be able to bear financial risks, but that does not necessarily make them good commissioners of specialised services. Commissioning includes the development of a strategic vision for services and assessment of the impact of changes on a large population ... The health authority will remain the key body responsible for these tasks, even if some purchasing activity is devolved to others.

(Higher Purchase, p.71)

The Audit Commission report suggests that the NHS Executive should identify models of care associated with good outcomes. Although the consultation document refers to collective planning it does not refer to care models. However, the White Paper itself sets out a programme of national service frameworks, which will embody models of care and which it describes as follows:

> 7.8 The Government will work with the professions and representatives of users and carers to establish clearer, evidence-based **National Service Frameworks** for major care areas and disease groups. That way patients will get greater consistency in the availability and quality of services, right across the NHS. The Government will use them as a way of being clear with patients about what they can expect from the health service.

> 7.9 The new approach to developing cancer services in the Calman-Hine Report, and recent action to ensure all centres providing children's intensive care meet agreed national standards, point the direction. In each case, the best evidence of clinical and cost-effectiveness is taken together with the views of users to establish principles for the pattern and level of services required. These then establish a clear set of priorities against which local action can be framed. The NHS Executive, working with the professions and others, will develop a similar approach to other services where national consistency is desirable. There will be an annual programme for the development of such frameworks starting in 1998.

(The New NHS, p.57)

In April 1998, a consultation document, The New NHS: Commissioning Specialised Services, was published designed to elicit views on how progress should be made. The stages of that process which was not complete at the time of writing are set out in the Box.

The role of the National Specialist Commissioning Advisory Group continues. This was established in 1996 following a review by the Chief Medical Officer of specialised services which superseded the Supra Regional Services Advisory Group. Its overall aim is to:

> ensure that the highest possible standard of care that can be delivered within available resources is available to all NHS patients requiring treatment or investigation of a very specialised nature, or for a very uncommon condition.

Set against the overall volume of purchasing, it is a minor player. The Group's report makes clear that it regards its role as a limited one, stating

Introduction of specialist service commissioning

7. Arrangements *must be in place* to commission specialised services effectively from 1 April 1999; but there will clearly only be time to carry out the full set of commissioning activities for a few services each year. By April 1999, therefore:

i.   a national list of specialised services will be agreed and published;

ii. each Regional Office will establish a regional specialised commissioning group (RSCG) representing all health authorities and accountable to the Regional Office;

iii. each RSCG will have established, by conducting a stocktake, under what arrangements these services are currently commissioned;

iv. each RSCG will have mapped and ensured the maintenance of funding flows, including those provided by extra-contractual referrals (ECRs). It should be exceptional for specialised services to be funded by the system which will replace ECRs from 1 April 1999;

v.   RSCGs will ensure that short term commissioning arrangements for these services are agreed and documented. These formalised commissioning arrangements will take responsibility for the status quo (unless changes have already been agreed); that is, they will take on all existing agreements for these services; and will be for development discussions in the short term;

vi. RSCGs will have agreed a programme of specialised services from the list to undergo full service review in the first year;

vii. machinery will be established, within the NHS Executive, for maintenance of the list; agreement of lead RSCGs across the country to conduct reviews; performance management.

Source: *The New NHS Commissioning Specialised Services*, Consultation Document, p.7

clearly that central funds are a scarce resource and that local purchasing should be the norm. In 1996/97 it placed contracts for just under £70 million for eight services funded from the central services levy. It recommended three more for central purchase and two more for further consideration. A large number of other services were rejected.

Allied to these changes in the structure of purchasing and service planning is a financial reform which is designed to allow greater flexibility between the elements of the NHS budget: the separate control totals for hospital and community health services drugs and the costs of practice staff and support services are to be merged. Those for general medical services themselves, however, will continue to be separately controlled.

The 1997 Primary Care Act had envisaged such a merger on a selective pilot basis: the White Paper proposes its general application. The greater financial flexibility will mean there will be no financial obstacle to moving services from one form of provider to another so that the scope for competition to provide services between secondary and primary care will actually be increased. That freedom is to be exercised within the local Health Improvement Programme (see below).

Before the publication of the White Paper, the Government had entered into a piloting process for service commissioning. In June 1997, applications were invited for 20 primary care-led commissioning pilots, which should: *'explore new approaches to securing high quality health services for all patients in their areas'*. (97/146) In September it was announced that 42 projects had been accepted to begin on 1 April 1998. In June 1998 a second wave was launched.

The first wave pilots are claimed to have led to:

- *New ways of working to providing a full range of local health services at greater convenience to patients.*
- *Community nurses taking the lead in shaping local services, including employing GPs.*
- *Local services being tailored for particular local groups with particular needs, such as children, the elderly, the mentally ill, ethnic minorities or the homeless.*
- *Greater fairness in access to services for local patients.*
- *More local health promotion and health education.*
- *More flexible working opportunities for GPs and members of Primary Care teams.*

(Department of Health 98/262, 29 June 1998)

Despite the widespread attainment of GP fundholding status on a voluntary basis and a strong lobby within that group for its retention, the proposals for primary care groups were initially welcomed by the medical profession. It became apparent that this initial response to the proposals for primary care groups did not properly reflect the views of those who would be involved in them. GPs raised a number of concerns with ministers, including their independent status, which they felt might be threatened, their clinical freedom to refer and prescribe, the implications of current health authority deficits and future overspend, and the amount of support for the development of primary care groups.

In a letter to John Chisholm, Chair of the GMSC, dated 17 June 1998, the Minister of Health Alan Milburn offered a series of reassurances on these matters, stressing in particular that the status of GPs as independent contractors would remain and that they would continue to enjoy full freedom to prescribe and refer, in particular stressing that a patient will not need to 'go without' because a GP runs out of cash.

In the light of these reassurances, implementation went rapidly ahead. Health authorities had to define the 'natural groupings' by the end of July. By the first week in August, 480 groups had been formed, covering populations ranging from 50,000 to 220,00 people – though most are nearer the 100,000 mark. In August detailed guidance on the Groups' governing arrangements and how they should be held accountable was issued with HSC 1998/139.

The circular states that the composition of the 'boards' which will govern the Groups should ensure that:

- *family doctors and community nurses will be in the lead;*
- *active social services support in developing joint approaches to meet identified and agreed local health and social care needs;*
- *public accountability and public confidence in the governing arrangements;*
- *the board needs to be large enough to include a range of skills, knowledge and experience but not so large as to be unworkable.*

(HSC 1998/139, 13 August 1998, pp.8 & 9)

It goes on to assert that:

26. It will be essential that Primary Care Group board members, whilst reflecting their respective lay or professional perspectives, are able to take a corporate view of the tasks they agree locally to undertake. They cannot and should not be dominated by a small circle of individuals appointed to the governance arrangements or by one professional grouping. Equally, it will be important for GPs, should they choose to be in the majority on Primary Care Group boards, to demonstrate leadership by developing and maintaining a corporate approach within the board and the processes adopted that will provide advice to the board.

(HSC 1998/139, p.11)

The Groups will be accountable to health authorities, but the circular also requires them to:

- *have open and transparent processes (including open meetings) to allow stakeholders and the public the basis upon which Primary Care Groups take decisions;*
- *have regular communications with stakeholders to inform and disseminate their decisions;*
- *produce annual accountability agreements setting out their plans and reflecting on their out-turn performance. These will be public documents available through the Health Authority;*
- *have clear and open clinical governance arrangements to enable stakeholders to develop confidence in the operation of the Group.*

(HSC 1998/139, p.14)

In these and other ways it is clear that the Groups will be entering uncharted waters for nearly all concerned. The summary guidance alone lists 36 action points even though it states that it is providing advice, not a detailed blueprint. The supporting guidance gives much more 'advice' plus an indication that more is to come, including that relating to Health Improvement Programmes.

The introduction of primary care groups can be seen as a recognition that GP fundholding was one of the 'good bits' of the 1990 reforms, which ought to be generalised throughout the NHS. This appears particularly true of the total purchasing pilots which did, in principle, enjoy control over the whole of the health budget. However, as the King's Fund report, *Total Purchasing*, points out, there are in fact a large number of differences between the two forms of purchasing (see Table 1.1).

As the report goes on to note:

Locality commissioning, fundholding, total purchasing and primary care groups each represents a different way of resolving the inevitable trade-offs between the strengths and weaknesses of different scales and types of purchasing/commissioning organisation. Each is likely to be able to deliver different purchasing objectives over different service areas. For example, total purchasing can be seen as an attempt to bring together the best of the 'bottom-up', demand-led, individual patient-focused manoeuvrable, approach associated with SFH and the 'top-down', needs-based, population-orientated, strategic approach associated with HA commissioning.

(*Total Purchasing*, p.111)

The Government's White Paper does not reveal any recognition of these trade-offs. However, the staged approach set out above suggests that for all the apparent uniformity of the White Paper proposals in practice the diversity that the 1990 Act gave rise to will persist. Furthermore, the 'horses for courses' approach is reflected to a degree in the provision made for a regional or a national role for a (gradually increasing) range of services through the introduction of national service frameworks.

Table 1.1 Comparison of total purchasing pilots and primary care groups

Total Purchasing Pilot	Primary Care Group
Small (30,000-40,000 population)	Large (approximately 100,000 population)
General practitioner-led	General practitioner- and nurse-led
Volunteer practices and time-limited	Compulsory – all practices and not time-limited
Rural and suburban	All parts of England
Many simple/informal projects	More complex organisations
Few participants	Many participants
Ring-fenced TP budget and SFH budget (GMS not included)	Moving towards integrated budgets, incl. FH, TP and GMS
Some pilots still with indicative budgets and some with fully delegated budgets after two years	Moving towards delegated and independent budgets (i.e. legally the responsibility of the PCG at level 3)
Intended to be a purchasing organisation rather than concerned directly with provider role of practices	Responsibilities for commissioning services plus health improvement and primary care development
No structure of 'clinical governance' between the overarching general practitioners	Arrangements for 'clinical governance' aimed at improving quality and consistency of primary care

Source: Nick Mays *et al., Total Purchasing.* London: King's Fund, 1998, p.102

Providing

As far as hospital and community health services are concerned, the main form of provider organisation is to remain the trust. However, trusts under Labour will have rather different terms of reference from those established in the early 1990s. Then the emphasis – overstated, as it turned out – was on their independence and freedom of action. Now it is on their role as partners at the local level.

The White Paper itself announced there would be a statutory duty to work in partnership with other NHS organisations and to take part in developing Health Improvement Programmes. It also proposes that every trust will have a new duty for the quality of the care they provide and the chief executive will carry the ultimate responsibility for seeing that role is discharged: we consider this new role further in Section 1.5.

According to the White Paper:

6.5 These changes will enable NHS Trusts to retain full local responsibility for operational management so that they can make best use of resources for patient care. They will do so within a local service framework that they themselves have played a significant part in creating. They will be accountable to Health Authorities and Primary Care Groups for the services they deliver, and to the NHS Executive for their statutory duties.

(The New NHS, p.45)

Over and above these changes to the role of trusts, the White Paper also proposes a new form of trust, the primary care trust which might include community health services from existing NHS Trusts. All or part of an existing community NHS trust, after the necessary legislation is passed, may combine with a primary care trust in order to 'better integrate services and management support'.

The White Paper does not refer to the merger of NHS trusts but in September 1997 the Government indicated that it expected that there would be trust mergers with the prime aim of reducing management costs:

Contracting

Retention of the purchaser/provider split, albeit in modified form means that the apparatus of contracting has to remain. The White Paper, however, proposes that this way the apparatus itself will be much simpler. In the first place, long-term agreements will replace annual contracts (see Box). These are to ' *last for at least three years, but could extend in some circumstances for five to ten years, if that was the appropriate time horizon for implementing a programme of development and change*'. (p.71)

The White Paper stresses a number of advantages of the new form of contracting arguing that long-term agreements:

- *will focus on service delivery objectives, with primary and secondary care clinicians coming together to develop better integrated patterns of care;*
- *address health and quality objectives, as well as cost and volume, reflecting the new rounded approach to performance;*
- *increasingly focus on 'programmes of care' for the population, and pathways for patients that cross traditional organisational boundaries;*
- *recognise that NHS Trusts must share responsibility for ensuring activity does not get out of kilter with funding;*

- *provide for the benefits of greater efficiency to be shared between the commissioner, on behalf of the community, and the NHS Trust, for investment consistent with the Health Improvement Programme;*
- *contain incentives for improvement, with funding conditional in part on satisfactory progress against key targets.*

(The New NHS, p.72)

An obvious difficulty with long-term agreements is that no one, not least the NHS Executive itself, can be confident about the medium term. These concerns are downplayed in the Executive Letter accompanying the NHS Priorities and Planning Guidance 1998/99:

In practice, the overwhelming majority of spending is already committed each year. Developing longer term agreements for these services recognises this fact and should allow the dialogue between the parties to be refocused onto quality and effectiveness and the changes needed. Financial uncertainty at the margin, for example in relation to the extent of differential allocation of real growth and local cost pressures, can be dealt with through explicit terms in the agreement about risk sharing and handling change. (Appendix 1)

These comments are somewhat disingenuous, given the difficulty of forecasting demands for emergency admissions and numbers on waiting lists. The Government has, however, aimed to put public spending forecasts on a surer footing. As we note in Section 2.1, the Chancellor announced measures in June 1998 designed to create a three-year time horizon for public spending and in his speech announcing the results of the comprehensive spending review, set out a budget for the next three years. However, such a three-

Long-Term Agreements

The nature of these agreements was set out in EL(97) 39, in the following terms:

- there is a continuing relationship between commissioners and provider over a longer period and this is framed within the agreed (strategic) local context;

- the risks over the longer term are assessed and allocated to the party best able to manage each set of issues. The risk handling mechanisms should be explicitly detailed in the agreements wherever possible;

- the funding agreement is either fixed or related to a mechanism which can be referred to at agreed intervals during the contract;

- the agreement aims to secure improvements in the quality and outcome of care and the efficiency with which it is delivered, over the lifetime of the agreement. This will help promote increased ownership by clinicians.

The advantages claimed for this approach are:

- *greater involvement of clinicians* through increased opportunities to become involved in the development within agreements of clinical outcome measures, quality standards and the delivery of benefits for patients;

- *greater involvement of users and carers* for whom these are likewise the critical issues;

- *a better focus of management time and effort* on quality and effectiveness;

- *better planning for investment and change:* developing agreements into strategically focused documents should allow them to handle changes such as reconfigurations which span more than a year and deal with risk for both purchasers and providers through a time of change.

Source: EL(97)39

year horizon does not in itself dispel uncertainty. No economic forecasts can be made with complete confidence. Even if the cash figures are adhered to – and they may not be – what they will buy in terms of physical and human resources can still not be forecast with confidence. Continuing uncertainty about pay and price changes means that the amount left for real growth will remain hard to predict at local level.

Furthermore, continuation of what has already become a common practice by the present Government of targeting funds at particular problems – be these waiting lists or cancer services – will also make local long term planning difficult. By ring-fencing funding in this way, the Government creates uncertainty for individual purchasers as to whether or not they will get extra funds and at the same time reduces the flexibility they already enjoy to move funds between different uses.

In principle the new contracting arrangements allow some scope for competition between trusts, since the White Paper provides both for a continuation of extra contractual referrals – albeit in the context of a simplified administrative regime – and for primary care groups to shift contracts if performance is poor. But the clear expectation is that switching of contracts will be rare. The question therefore is: what will be the driver for change in the new arrangements? In the 1990 Act arrangement, the answer, in principle, was: competition between trusts for contracts. In the event, the main driver turned out to be the centrally imposed requirement for efficiency gains and other central initiatives, including the waiting times initiative and the requirements of the *Patient's Charter*.

The New NHS rejects both of these in favour of a range of performance measures:

> 6.16 In the new NHS, the performance of NHS Trusts will be assessed against new broad-based measures reflecting the wider goals of improving health and health care outcomes, the quality and effectiveness of service, efficiency and access. Performance will be judged by greater use of comparative information.

(*The New NHS*, p.48)

Furthermore:

> 6.20 In the new NHS, when performance is not up to scratch in NHS Trusts there will be rapid investigation and, where necessary, intervention. This will take five forms:

> • *firstly, Health Authorities will be able to call in the NHS Executive Regional Offices when it appears that an NHS Trust is failing to deliver against the Health Improvement Programme;*
> • *secondly, NHS Executive Regional offices will be able to investigate if there is a question over compliance with their statutory duties;*
> • *thirdly, the Commission for Health Improvement could be called in to investigate and report on a problem;*
> • *fourthly, Primary Care Groups will be able to signal a change to their local service agreements, where NHS Trusts are failing to deliver;*
> • *fifthly, the Secretary of State could remove the NHS Trust Board.*

(*The New NHS*, p.49)

It then goes on to suggest that 'efficiency will be enhanced through incentives at both NHS Trust and clinical team level'. What this will mean in practice remains unclear.

Structure

The new structure for the NHS is set out in Figure 1. The key changes relative to the previous situation are the reduction in the number of types of purchaser and the change in the reporting lines for trusts, which moves from region to centre.

It is a much simpler structure than the one it replaces, since the range of commissioning types and the number of commissioning organisations are reduced. That is not the same, however, as the new structure being simpler to work with since, at different points in the White Paper, closely related responsibilities, particularly for service planning, are given to different organisations.

Fig 1   Financing and accountability arrangements in the new NHS compared with the old

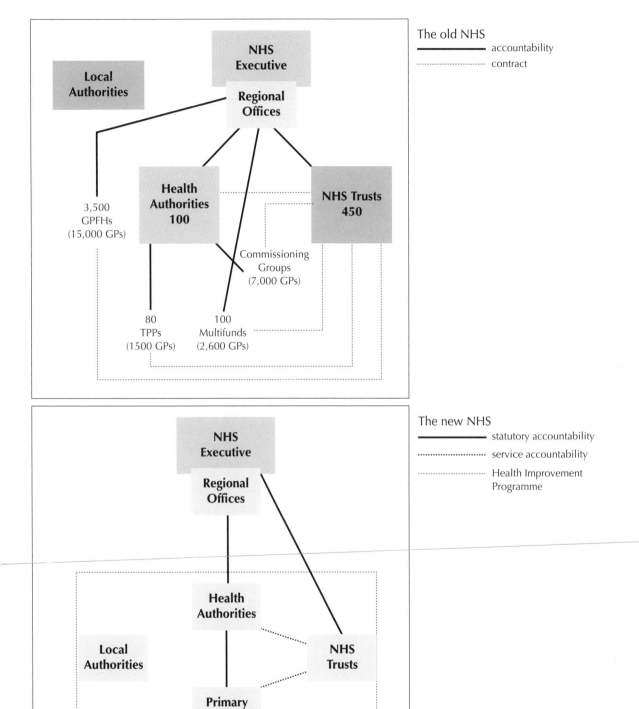

Source: *The New NHS*

As noted above, the Government intends that there should be a strong central role in determining how a range of services should be provided, in ways we discuss further in Section 1.5. The scope for local determination of how services are provided will inevitably decline.

The key element holding the structure together at local level is the health improvement programme. This is intended to cover:

- *the most important* **health needs** *of the local population, and how these are to be met by the NHS and its partner organisations through broader action on public health;*
- *the main* **health care requirements** *of local people, and how local services should be developed to meet them either directly by the NHS, or where appropriate jointly with social services;*
- *the* **range, location and investment required in local health services** *to meet the needs of local people.*

(*The New NHS*, p.26)

Despite the emphasis on 'local' in these requirements, the White Paper also makes it clear that the programmes will have to take into account national targets:

> *4.17 The Health Improvement Programme will need to include the new targets which emerge following consultation on the Green Paper* Our Healthier Nation *as well as the performance framework ... Health Authorities will need to agree and set targets for Primary Care Groups in discussion with them. In turn, Primary Care Groups will build them into their service agreements with NHS Trusts. These targets will be measurable, published and*

> *deliver year on year improvement in local health and health care services.*

(*The New NHS*, p.28)

Despite the apparently central nature of the Health Improvement Programme, no advice as to its content had emerged by August 1998.

Transition

Despite the elements of continuity, the White Paper proposals represent an enormous programme of change at local level, particularly for GPs and health authorities. The White Paper concludes by acknowledging that:

> *on some fronts there will be early progress. Others may be for the long haul. Some may take time to show visible improvements.*

(*The New NHS*, p.78)

In particular, it recognises that the structural change to purchasing will take time to bed down. Leaving aside GPs' concerns about the implications of primary care groups for their contractual status and clinical freedoms, the proposals were widely regarded as being too ambitious to push through quickly. For example, a report by Linda Marks and David J Hunter (NHS Confederation, *The Development of Primary Care Groups: policy into practice*), based on a series of seminars in early 1998 points out that the proposals draw on the diverse developments in local purchasing arrangements which the 1990 NHS and Community Care Act gave rise to but nevertheless:

> *working within localities, creating an effective governing body for primary care groups/trusts, identifying local health needs, and promoting*

public involvement will require major changes in ways of working, even for those who have been at the forefront of change. (p.1)

The report also reveals widespread lack of understanding of what the proposals meant and concerns about the practicality of making the required changes within the timetable envisaged by the Government. To a degree, the Government anticipated such fears: the White Paper sets out a range of possibilities for the form that local purchasing might take:

5.11 There will be a spectrum of opportunities available for local GPs and community nurses. Primary Care Groups will develop over time, learning from existing arrangements and their own experience. None will affect the independent contractor status of GPs. There will be four options for the form that Primary Care Groups take. They will:

1. *at minimum, support the Health Authority in commissioning care for its population, acting in an advisory capacity*
2. *take devolved responsibility for managing the budget for health care in their area, formally as part of the Health Authority*
3. *become established as free-standing bodies accountable to the Health Authority for commissioning care*
4. *become established as free-standing bodies accountable to the Health Authority for commissioning care and with added responsibility for the provision of community health services for their population.*

(*The New NHS*, p.35)

In February 1998 HSC 1998/021, *Better Health and Better Health Care*, set out a programme for implementing the White Paper proposals. This recognises that:

These policies represent a major programme of change for the NHS and its partners at local level, and nationally for the Department of Health and within it the NHS Executive. (annex 3)

The Circular follows the White Paper in setting out broad tasks against a timetable reaching to the end of 1998 and beyond as well as setting out the broad requirements for the creation of primary care groups. However, neither in the circular nor elsewhere is this undoubted fact acknowledged in terms of the claims of financial and human resources the programme of change will involve. Instead, the White Paper and other Government statements emphasise the aim of cutting down on management expenditure. We return to this issue in Part 3.

Managing the system

The New NHS makes it clear that, despite the elements of continuity, it intends to introduce a new, or third way of running the NHS based on partnership and co-operation. The White Paper contains no analysis of what these terms mean in practice nor what the obstacles to their realisation are. However, it rightly accepts the various parts of the NHS will only work effectively together if the framework within which they work is itself consistent. The White Paper states that the Department of Health:

will integrate policy on public health, social care and the NHS so that there is a clear national framework within which similar service development can take place locally. (p.55)

This is a welcome proposal. In *Health Care UK 1994/95*, we argued that consistency was a key requirement in central policy-making but had been neglected under the Conservatives. In particular, policies towards social and health care appear to have been developed in the 1990s on totally different sets of assumptions with those for health emphasising rapid turnover, and those for social care emphasising long-term continuing arrangements. We note in Section 1.2 the modest steps taken by the middle of 1998 to introduce greater consistency in policy-making across the health and social care boundary.

The White Paper proposes new central functions for the Executive and the Department of Health – scanning for emerging clinical innovation and working with the professions to strengthen self-regulation. The first of these is relatively minor, representing a timid but important step towards an explicit consideration of the world in which the NHS will have to operate in the future. The second role we look at further in Section 1.5 where we also discuss the role of the two new central bodies – the National Institute for Clinical Excellence and the Commission for Health Improvement. We have noted above the proposal for national service frameworks, which also imply an enlarged central role. Finally, the framework of performance measures, which we discuss in Part 2 of the Review, also implies a significant central monitoring and 'enforcement' role where performance is poor.

Taken together, these tasks and the new organisations represent a considerable extension of the central role. However other parts of the White Paper appear to point the other way. As noted above, one of the six principles was local responsibility – 'Local doctors and nurses ... will

be in the driving seat'. The primary care groups are one expression of this principle:

3.6 Locally there will be:

- *teams of local GPs and community nurses working together in new Primary Care Groups to shape services for patients, concentrating on the things which really count – prompt, accessible, seamless care delivered to a high standard;*
- *explicit quality standards in local service agreements between Health Authorities, Primary Care Groups and NHS Trusts, reflecting national standards and targets;*
- *a new system of clinical governance in NHS Trusts and primary care to ensure that clinical standards are met, and that processes are in place to ensure continuous improvement, backed by a new statutory duty for quality in NHS Trusts.*

(*The New NHS*, p.18)

The 1990 system promised a large degree of devolution to localities, but subsequently nullified that, at least in part, by the introduction of a large range of centrally imposed policies. *The New NHS*, in contrast, does both at the same time by announcing national initiatives while promising effective devolution, leaving it unclear what balance between centre and locality is intended.

In practice, despite the genuflections to local involvement, local choice seems likely to be over-ridden by the demands of the centre. In the recent past the expansion of the centre's role was driven, in part at least, by the previous Government's desire to show that its reforms were having an impact on the Service. The new Government has indicated that it intends to formalise its expectations of what the NHS should be able to achieve. We note in Section 2.1 new financial structures which strengthen the centre resulting from the new relationship which the Treasury is attempting to impose on each department, and look further in Section 2.3 at the implications of the new performance framework.

Thus the local doctors and nurses in the 'driving seat' may well find that the vehicle they are trying to steer already contains a large number of pre-set directions and, as they try to exploit the discretion that remains to them, find more instructions arriving from the centre which further reduce what scope for local choice they originally enjoyed. As Rudolf Klein and Alan Maynard have suggested in their comment on *The New NHS*, (*BMJ* 4 July 1998) the Government may be on the way to a political calvary or self-imposed martyrdom as it takes on a larger and more directing role. We shall see in the following sections further evidence of the ambition of the new Government which makes that risk all the greater.

1.2 Community care

Community care did not feature in Labour's election pledges apart from a commitment to appoint a Royal Commission on long-term care for elderly people and a promise to introduce an independent regulation service. The Commission was duly appointed in December 1997, with Sir Stewart Sutherland in the chair. Its terms of reference are set out in the Box.

The Commission was asked to work to a tight timetable to allow its report to be published by the end of 1998. In the Secretary of State's words:

I have asked the Royal Commission to look at short term and long term options and to come up with recommendations within 12 months.

Royal Commission on Long-Term Care: Terms of Reference

To examine the short and long term options for a sustainable system of funding of long term care for elderly people in the United Kingdom, both in their own homes and in other settings, and, within 12 months, to recommend how, and in what circumstances, the cost of such care should be apportioned between public funds and individuals, having regard to:

- the number of people likely to require various kinds of long term care both in the present and through the first half of the next century, and their likely income and capital over their life-time;
- the expectations of elderly people for dignity and security in the way in which their long term care needs are met, taking account of the need for this to be secured in the most cost-effective manner;
- the strengths and weaknesses of the current arrangements;
- fair and efficient ways for individuals to make any contribution required of them;
- constraints on public funds, and earlier work done by various bodies on this issue.

In carrying out its remit, the Royal Commission should also have regard to:

- the deliberations of the Government's comprehensive spending review, including the review of pensions;
- the implications of their recommendations for younger people who by reason of illness or disability have long term care needs.

Source: *Royal Commission on the Funding of Long Term Care for the Elderly,* Department of Health, 97/374, 4 December 1997

We do not want this to take years. Its goal will be a sustainable system of funding long-term care for elderly people, but it must also weigh the implications of its recommendations for younger age groups with long-term care needs.

(Department of Health 97/379, 4 December 1997)

On accepting his remit, Sir Stewart acknowledged that the Commission 'has a complex and demanding task ahead' and indicated that it would be looking for proposals which command consensus and respect. In the time available, both will be hard to achieve. As far as the first is concerned, research by Gillian Tindall and Harriet Clarke, reported in *Who Will Pay for Long-term Care? ESRC Briefing Note No 5*, has shown there is no consensus now among the general public:

Political thinking about the balance between the state and individuals in guaranteeing the welfare of older people has changed radically in the last twenty years. Our research suggests that the bulk of the population has not changed its thinking along the same lines, and even less its behaviour. A national debate about the level of state support for the care of older people we wish to see and the amount we are prepared to pay for it, both communally and individually, is long overdue. (p.4)

Confirming the analysis presented by Nick Morris and Tim Wilsdon in *Health Care UK 1995/96*, they found the existing private long-term care insurance schemes were not attractive, but about two-thirds of those interviewed did not care for the present arrangements either.

Figures presented to the Health Select Committee during its inquiry into long-term care suggested that the burden on the public finances of the elderly population was not likely to grow rapidly so there may be time to have the debate that Tindall and Clarke call for. However, there are pressing problems now both in the field of regulation and in the way that services for groups such as frail elderly people are designed and financed. We begin with regulation.

Regulation

By the time of writing, the Government had not published proposals for an independent regulation service. However, in May 1998, the Better Regulation Task Force, a Government-wide programme located in the Cabinet Office, published its *Review of Long Term Care*. Its recommendations for the structure of regulation are as follows:

- *the existing nursing and residential care regimes should be replaced by a single regime, capable of incorporating any regulation of domiciliary care;*
- *a national agency with wide-ranging membership should be created to advise the Department of Health on care standards. It should advise Ministers on the need for secondary legislation and on the form such regulation should take. It should also produce, or at least be responsible for proposing, approved codes of practice in consultation with stakeholders;*
- *mandatory requirements should be set nationally, with approved codes of practice provided where secondary legislation would be inappropriate or too prescriptive;*
- *consumers, providers and enforcers should be clear about the distinction between mandatory requirements and best practice or aspirational standards;*
- *any proposed changes to regulations must be supported by a cost:benefit analysis. This should take into account that*

consumers will exercise choice and providers will offer higher standards. It is these two elements – not regulation – which should determine how high aspirational standards are and how far they exceed the guaranteed standards;

- registration and inspection responsibilities should be moved away from local and health authorities; and
- local accountability, including complaints and appeals procedures, and a capacity to set local enforcement strategies should, however, be maintained, with the participation of all key interest groups. (p.13)

It also recommended that:

- the Department of Health, in consultation with its advisory body, should develop and publicise clear national assessment and eligibility criteria; and
- the Department should also develop standardised assessment methods for defining care requirements. (p.17)

In its report, Community Health Care for Elderly People (The Stationery Office, 1998), the Clinical Standards Advisory Group reported 'a widespread concern about the proliferation and lack of regulation of private agencies providing personal care' (p.33). The need to get the regulatory system right is emphasised by the growing importance of private provision of both residential and domiciliary care. The level of direct provision of home care services by local authorities, as measured in terms of contact hours, is still falling rapidly, with correspondingly high rates of growth within the voluntary and private sectors. Together the latter now account for some 44 per cent of the total: see Table 1.2.

Table 1.2 Domiciliary care: contact hours

	1992	1997
All sectors	1,687,000	2,637,800
Direct	1,647,800	1,484,900
Under contract using:		
Voluntary sector	6,800	139,900
Private sector	32,300	1,013,000

Source: DH annual return HH1

Table 1.3 Local-authority supported elderly residents

	1993	1997
Total of all supported residents	74,827	181,921
Local authority staffed	65,248	46,579
Independent residential	9,288	77,354
Independent nursing	–	56,286
Unstaffed and other	291	702

Source: Department of Health Statistics Division

The same is true of residential care: the numbers of elderly people supported by local authorities in their own, i.e. authority, homes continues to fall rapidly and the number in private establishments rise: see Table 1.3. As the figures show, the need for effective regulation and market management is growing rather than receding. Moreover, there is no sign that the Government wishes to reduce dependence on private providers: indeed, as we note below, the Audit Commission and Social Services Inspectorate reviews of local authorities suggest that some could save substantial amounts of money by making more use of private suppliers of care.

As well as appropriate regulation, however, an effective market in care services requires skilled market management by the major purchaser – the local authority. However a briefing paper from The Nuffield Institute, Purchasing Home Care:

how independent sector providers see the developing market, found that:

> The studies revealed that independent care providers felt widespread disillusionment with local authority purchasers, who were thought not to understand business pressures, and not to be aware of the differences between residential and domiciliary care. Above all, providers felt that local authorities did not understand the inherent fragilities of the domiciliary care business. (p.4)

Working together

The difficulties involved in developing proper contracting relationships between public and private sectors are, however, just one aspect of the larger issue of how services for major care groups should be financed, designed and managed. Over the years since the 1990 Act system of providing community care has been in place, the constant theme of the Health Policy Review, and the official reports and research studies it has drawn on, has been essentially the same: that the various elements which must combine to provide or ensure the provision of an effective service do not combine effectively. Drawing on research funded by the Rowntree Foundation, we have cited evidence of failures to link effectively with housing, another vast and complicated policy area with policy objectives of its own. One indication of this is the fact that the Government announced in November 1997 a separate interdepartmental review of supported housing led by the Department of Social Security, even though this clearly forms part of any consideration of long-term care.

In 1998 the Audit Commission published its review of the role of housing in community care, *Home Alone*, which confirmed the importance of housing to community care in terms of both estimated financial commitment – at least some £2bn – and its effects of individuals' ability to maintain an independent life, through the provision of aids and adaptations, such as stair lifts to their homes. However:

> Although the housing dimension of community care is significant, both in terms of the resources devoted to it and the number of people it serves, it has not been subject to the same scrutiny as that applied to health and social services authorities – in practice, if not in theory, it is the 'junior partner' in the process. (p.11)

The report concludes with a survey of what is wrong with the current policy framework at national level. In respect of finance, the report found existing financial arrangements to be complex and fragmented:

> As each new policy directive or funding mechanism is 'bolted on', the potential for confusion, incoherence and perverse incentives increases. (p.20)

Accordingly, the Commission formed the view that fundamental reform is required, involving removal of constraints on the effective use, transfer and pooling of resources across agencies in such a way that resources follow the client rather than remaining attached to particular tenures or properties. Its overall conclusion is a damning one:

> The funding regime does not promote the objectives of community care – its operation is characterised by perverse incentives, a failure to maximise value for money and inadequate targeting of resources to areas of greatest need. The policy framework has gaps which can fail the most vulnerable clients and the perspectives

of government departments have not always been well co-ordinated. (p.78)

The Commission's report concludes with a series of recommendations targeted at national level, most involving closer working links between the Department of Health and the Department of the Environment, Transport and the Regions.

The 'separateness' of housing, however undesirable it is, is in part explicable in terms of its distinct history as an area of social policy, which has not in the post-war period been the responsibility of the same central government department. However, essentially the same pattern holds true of health and social care, which have been for most of that time. Again we have cited several reports bearing on this issue over the past few years. Most recently, the links between health and other services were examined in *Community Health Care for Elderly People* by the Clinical Standards Advisory Group (The Stationery Office, 1998) which found, in terms echoing those of the Audit Commission, that:

> *The provision of community health services for elderly people is characterised by fragmentation, confusion and cost-shunting.* (p.32)

The report goes on to identify a particular weakness in the current pattern of services – lack of effective community-based rehabilitation – which stems in part at least from these weaknesses in the financial and administrative framework.

> *Despite their critical contribution to effective hospital discharge and the maintenance of people's independence, equipment services were highly inadequate, responsibility for provision is unclear, which makes problems difficult to solve by local action alone.* (p.32)

According to a King's Fund/Audit Commission briefing paper by Janice Robinson and Stuart Turnock, *Investing in Rehabilitation* (King's Fund, 1998), there is strong evidence that:

> *comprehensive assessment, followed by the implementation of individual care plans, reduces the risk of older people being re-admitted to hospitals or placed in care homes, improves their survival rates and improves physical and cognitive functioning. Such assessment ensures that treatable conditions such as depression and incontinence are recognised and dealt with and that suitable arrangements are made to enable a return to independent living.* (p.3)

Although the case for greater spending on rehabilitation is supported by most of the available evidence, that evidence is far from comprehensive. Accordingly more research is needed, but for that to be effective in changing service delivery, a change of culture in domiciliary, day and residential services is also required. To make progress, the paper concludes:

> *authorities will need a coherent joint strategy … to reshape current services and ensure improved outcomes that are sustainable in the medium and long term. These strategies will need to support developments in primary and community care settings and to target groups of people known to have restricted access to rehabilitation. They will need to be built around the knowledge base of effectiveness and good practice.* (p.3)

The case for more rehabilitation facilities received official support in an Executive Letter, *Better Services for Vulnerable People*, EL(97) 62, published in October 1997. The letter acknowledged weaknesses in existing arrangements, citing the findings of the monitoring system for continuing care arrangements. These have shown that some health and local authorities are still not able to work effectively together and that older people are increasingly not given the time or opportunity to recover from major illness in an appropriate setting.

Accordingly, the Letter reaffirms that a range of flexible and responsive health and social care services should be developed which can offer older people the opportunity to optimise their independence, particularly following an admission to hospital or a change in an individual's need, in a community setting. Although the letter acknowledges that many relevant and innovative schemes have been introduced, overall it admits that:

> the development of such community based services has suffered from the recent focus on acute care. If we are to deliver on the long term agenda, then we have to see flexible and responsive community based intensive health and social care. To achieve this all agencies may need to reconsider their current configuration of services. (p.4)

This is a prime example of the policy inconsistencies which *The New NHS* pledges that the Department of Health will aim to overcome and which the Audit Commission and the Clinical Standards Advisory Group have so clearly identified. However, the Letter does not refer to the financial framework and the perverse incentives it embodies. Instead it asks for:

- *a programme of work to achieve effective Joint Investment Plans for services to meet the continuing and community care needs of your local population;*
- *work to improve the content and process of multidisciplinary assessment of older people*

in both hospital and community health care settings;
- *the development of health and social care services for older people which focus on optimizing independence through timely recuperation and rehabilitation opportunities.* (p.1)

While this local action may be helpful, the failure to develop an adequate level of rehabilitation is a prime example of the effects of the weaknesses identified in the reports cited above. We noted in last year's Review the Audit Commission's analysis of the incentives facing local authorities which favour residential care because that can be charged for. Health authorities have no incentive to reduce use of residential care nor do the providers themselves. Over and above the immediate financial incentives, the lack of a clear focus for considering the overall pattern of provision has contributed to the gaps in basic information and understanding and to a failure to commission the type of research that would fill the gaps identified in the King's Fund overview.

The Coming of Age: improving care services for older people, a report from the Audit Commission published in 1997, confirmed the lack of a national focus:

> The most recent major national strategic document concerned solely with older people was the 1981 White Paper, Growing Older, now 16 years old. Since then, services for older people have been driven by individual policy initiatives – such as efficiency pressures on acute care, policies for community care or guidance on continuing care – that have not added up to a coherent strategy overall. Some developments have actually run counter to stated policy – for example, increased use of homes and reducing use of home care in some

authorities – and some have never been stated as policy – such as the steady reduction of long-term NHS beds. As a result, older people's needs are not being fully considered, and instead of benefiting from well co-ordinated services they have become labelled 'bed blockers'. (p.82)

What is required is a 'whole systems approach' which explicitly acknowledges all the factors and policies bearing on elderly people or any other similar group and comprises all the relevant providers. There are some signs that the Government has been trying to develop one. In the context of winter pressures (discussed further in Section 2.1), the Government has aimed to orchestrate a response across all NHS providers and social services, acknowledging that the performance of the NHS is critically dependent on social services. A survey of local authorities by the Association of Directors of Social Services found that most had been able to work effectively with health authorities and that the vast majority had received some extra funding for social services provision.

The same approach has been employed in respect of waiting lists emphasising both the need to reduce emergency admissions (thereby reducing their impact on elective care) and providing for the extra care in the community which an increase in elective activity might involve. Health Service Circular 1998/096 asked for targeted investment in community services aimed at:

- *securing any additional community health and social services needed to support the planned increases in elective activity;*
- *preventing or reducing hospital admissions (e.g. following accidents) and streamlining the admissions process;*

- *organising rapid response in the community; and*
- *supporting early discharge, intermediate care and intensive rehabilitation schemes to enable people to return to their homes and communities.* (p.4)

The future of a 'whole systems approach' will turn in part on the role of primary care groups which will make the role of GPs in effecting linkages a critical one. A study of fundholders for the NHS Confederation and the Association of County Councils, *Finding Common Cause*, published in 1997 found that:

> *It is a matter of some surprise and regret that the evidence from our study is that fundholding per se has not provided a clear route through these problems. Our conclusion therefore has to be that creating something positive and different at local level could easily take a generation, if it can be achieved at all.* (p.28)

Work carried out within the National Evaluation of Total Purchasing supports this cautious conclusion. Although some total purchasing pilots had made progress 'across the boundaries', the study by Susan Myles and colleagues (*Total Purchasing and Community and Continuing Care: lessons for future policy developments in the NHS*, King's Fund 1998) concluded that time was crucial in overcoming the inertia created by historical and cultural barriers:

> *attempting to roll this model out to practices with little or no experience in developing community and continuing care services (many of which do not enjoy good inter-agency relationships) is even less likely to be successful.* (cited in *Total Purchasing*, p.99)

We noted in Section 1.1 the warnings from both the National Evaluation and the NHS Confederation Study about the likely speed with which primary care groups would become effective. *The New NHS*, however, makes altogether nine proposals bearing on links between health and social care:

- health improvement programmes;
- a new statutory duty of partnership to 'work together for the common good';
- a duty upon local authorities to promote the economic, social and environmental well-being of their areas;
- the establishment of 'programmes of care' between clinicians and social services to promote planning and resource management across organisational boundaries;
- the pursuit of coterminosity between health and social services boundaries in relation to primary care groups;
- joint monitoring of partnerships by regional offices of the NHSE and the regional Social Services Inspectorate;
- social services membership of primary care groups;
- local authority chief executive membership of health authorities;
- the creation of health action zones based upon local partnerships.

The White Paper also refers to the potential for financial rewards to agencies which perform well. But it makes no new proposals in terms of incentives or sanctions designed to produce better continuing relationships such that would remove the perverse incentives identified above. In other words, the really hard bit, getting the national framework right, remains to be tackled. In the meantime, the Government continued to advise local agencies how to do better.

In a low key announcement in October 1997 Paul Boateng, a junior minister at the Department of Health, on the publication of *Making Partnerships Work in Community Care: a guide for practitioners in housing health and social services*, gave the following brief overview:

Community care has a chequered history. While it has brought more choice for some, others have faced frustration. Poor cooperation between local agencies has left some frail and vulnerable people without support.

More effective joint working will go a long way to solving many of these problems. Responsive local services will flourish if local agencies commit themselves to applying the advice of this practical workbook. Its recommendations will help sweep away out-dated and rigid attitudes to better community care.

(Department of Health, 97/261, 7 October 1997)

As this approach suggests, the Government has been focusing on better implementation within the existing policy framework, rather than developing a new one. In October, the Secretary of State addressed the annual social services conference on precisely this theme:

So long as there are frail old people, vulnerable children, people with physical or learning disabilities, mentally ill people and other vulnerable groups there will be a need for social care provided by professionals to augment what families provide, itself augmented by help from both professionals and volunteers organised by voluntary bodies.

(Department of Health, 97/315, 31 October 1997)

He went on to refer to the system of joint reviews by the Audit Commission and the Social Services Inspectorate:

> All authorities need to take very seriously the findings of joint review reports, not just those few where serious failures in performance are identified. In those small minority of cases, sterner measures are required both within the authority and by Ministers. It won't be a pleasant business but there really should be no complaints if the same sort of scrutiny and professional standards have been applied as were applied in earlier reports on other departments. We can't wait until some vulnerable person has suffered before something is done.

(Department of Health, 97/315, 31 October 1997)

The first indications of the 'less than pleasant business' came with a series of statements from Paul Boateng in relation to reports on individual authorities. The reports themselves are blunt: that for Barking and Dagenham (Audit Commission 1997) begins as follows:

> The Review Team concludes that overall the needs of people in Barking and Dagenham are not well met. Many people receive services but they are so thinly spread that quality is poor. Services are not sufficiently tailored to user needs and users and carers rate services more poorly than in any other authority reviewed to date. One in four users or carers rate services as 'poor' or 'very poor'.

> The Authority has failed to tackle fundamental management questions, notably the essential requirement to match its resource strategy (for example, allocation of funds) with its policies and to ensure that policy is implemented

effectively. While some progress has been made in recent years in setting policy objectives the Authority does not have clear priorities for service delivery which can be implemented and its resources are not directed or controlled to achieve such priorities. The management strategy is too detached from what is happening at operational level. (p.11)

In relation to the report on Sefton, Paul Boateng indicated that he would take what action he was currently in a position to take, but that the intention was to take stronger powers which would enable more effective intervention in the event of failure at local level:

> Sefton meanwhile are in the last chance saloon. I have some powers and unless an appropriate Action Plan is delivered within two months, and delivered on time thereafter, these powers will be used.

(Department of Health, 97/299, 23 October 1997)

However, what those powers should be was not clear at the time of writing. But evidence from the Audit Commission report *Getting the Best from Social Services*, published in July 1998 suggested that while Sefton may not be unique, it was not typical. The report aims to present lessons learned from joint reviews. Overall, it concludes that 'there is a mixed picture'. On the plus side of the balance sheet, it finds that:

- *Nearly three-quarters of users and carers rate services as excellent or good.*
- *Most councils have rigorous procedures for protecting people at risk.*
- *Links with other services are improving.*
- *Most councils fulfil their regulatory role, and some are going well beyond the minimum requirements.*

- *Most councils have maintained continuity for users and kept finances in control while taking on the new funding responsibilities for community care.*

On the negative:

- *Fewer than one-third of people know about social services before they use them.*
- *Some councils fail to keep people safe because they do not apply guidance and procedures and do not allocate staff to priorities.*
- *Many councils are not able to learn from the day-to-day experience of users and carers because they do not ask for feedback or carry out reviews.*
- *Many councils' future plans are based on shaky knowledge about needs and how well current services are working.*
- *Some councils fail to inspect properly the services they regulate and many do not enforce standards consistently in the services they run themselves.*
- *Most councils do not fully understand costs and struggle to forecast future activity and expenditure.*
- *Many councils could save substantial sums of money by using more independent providers and by tackling the costs of their own services.* (p.6)

Mental health

One of the striking omissions from the White Paper was mental health. However, in November 1997 an Independent Reference Group on mental health was established to 'advise Ministers on a range of mental health issues, including whether a sufficient range of mental health services are in place before long-stay hospitals close; reducing the stigma of mental illness; ensuring mentally ill people are cared for in safety and security in the community; and on black and ethnic minority mental health issues.'

The group's first report acknowledges a 'widespread public view that existing mental health services have failed some people with mental illness, their carers and families, and the wider community' and makes a series of recommendations, including a national framework of minimum standards for health and social care, the removal of structural and budgetary barriers to better inter-agency working and expertise requirements.

In April 1998 it was announced that mental health should be one of the first two national service frameworks to be developed, work on which will be led by Graham Thornicroft, chair also of the Reference Group. In July, before the results of that work were available, the Secretary of State announced the form the new policy should take. He described this as:

> *a third way for mental health, providing better support for patients and carers, and including:*
>
> - *a 24-hour crisis helpline;*
> - *24-hour crisis teams to respond to emergency needs;*
> - *more acute mental health beds;*
> - *more hostels and support accommodation;*
> - *home treatment teams;*
> - *improved mental health training for GPs and others in primary care;*
> - *extra counselling services in health centres;*
> - *clear and authoritative guidance from the National Institute for Clinical Excellence on the most effective drugs and therapies.*

(Department of Health 98/311, 29 July 1998)

At the same time, he announced that the 1983 Mental Health Act would be reviewed. It is to be 'a root and branch review of the legislation in the light of modern therapies and drugs'. In particular, the review was charged with examining the scope for compliance and community treatment orders which would provide the legal basis for supervised care of patients who, once discharged from hospital, decline to take the very drugs which had made their discharge appear safe.

Equity of access

The measures announced for mental health, particularly the national service framework and the central definition of a 'third way', together with the steps taken to iron out differences between areas in respect of continuing care and the recommendations of the Better Regulation Task Force, can be seen as steps towards the full nationalisation of social care provision, based on national standards, following the pattern already adopted in the education service.

The language of the 'last chance' saloon fits well with the notion of the hit squads sent in to poor performing schools. Nevertheless Ministers have shown themselves reluctant to intervene even where this would be in line with *The New NHS* emphasis on equity between different parts of the country. In the case of social services, such inequities arise from differences in the availability of services and the charges made for them. The Clinical Standards Advisory Group comments, for example, that:

> we were given many examples of elderly people who had similar assessed needs receiving different services or no services from different kinds of providers with wide variations in quality and cost. (p.32)

As for charges, in a letter (dated 20 April 1998) to Sally Greengross, Director General of Age Concern, Paul Boateng acknowledged that there was 'a strong desire to move towards greater equity and consistency' but then repeats the conventional view:

> Under the current system local authorities have discretion whether or not to make charges for non-residential adult personal social services. It is, therefore, a matter for each local authority to decide whether or not to make such charges, what level they should be and what exemptions or discounts there should be for different categories of people. The current legislation requires that any charges levied must be reasonable.

In the case of residential care however the Government has taken steps to ensure uniformity of treatment. Last year's review reported on the outcome of two significant legal judgements which bore on the precise definition of local authorities' responsibilities in respect of funding residential care. In November 1997, the Department issued circular LASSL(97)13 to elucidate the position arising from judgments on cases originating in Gloucester and Sefton.

In the Gloucester case, the central issue was whether or not local authorities could take resources into account when determining what services to offer. The circular states that the House of Lords judgement essentially restored the situation obtaining when the Chronically Sick and Disabled Persons Act 1970 was passed i.e.:

> Criteria of need are matters for the authorities to determine in the light of resources. (Circular 12/70, para 7)

The 1997 circular advises that:

> • the judgment does not give authorities a licence to take decisions on the basis of resources alone.

Authorities must still take account of all other relevant factors. Pressure on resources cannot be used as an excuse for taking arbitrary or unreasonable decisions.

In particular, it was confirmed in the course of the judicial review cases that an authority cannot arbitrarily change the services which it is arranging for a disabled person merely because its own resource position has changed. It needs to reconsider what needs it will meet (i.e. what its eligibility criteria will be), and reassess the individual against those redefined needs.

- *nor does the judgment mean that local authorities are not under any duty towards disabled people. Once a local authority has decided that it is necessary, in order to meet the needs of a disabled person, for it to arrange a service listed in Section 2, then it is under a duty to arrange it.*

In the Sefton case the issue was whether or not a person with less than £16,000 capital had an automatic right to some support from the local authorities. The Court of Appeal held that Sefton had not followed the regulations when it did not offer support in those circumstances, in effect making someone with less than that amount, but more than £3,000, pay the full cost. The circular indicated that the Government would give its backing to a Private Members Bill which would make the position absolutely clear and that, as the Community Care (Residential Accommodation) Act, became law in August 1998.

Overall

The Government has not advanced any significant proposals for national action bearing on the long-standing failures identified in successive

editions of *Health Care UK* in bringing together the various elements which make for effective care in the community. It has been, no doubt, waiting for the Royal Commission to help it consider the wide range of policies which bear on the welfare of elderly people and others in need of continuing care as well as the wider initiatives taken in respect of all public services from the Cabinet Office, such as Better Government for Older People and the successive reviews of social security, including that of housing benefit referred to above.

Whether the Commission, working to a very tight timetable will be able to accomplish what successive governments have not, remains to be seen. It seems unlikely given the magnitude and complexity of the task. In the meantime, as Janice Robinson and Richard Poxton argue in their contribution to *Implementing the White Paper* (King's Fund Policy Paper 1, 1998):

partnership is probably the best hope there is for the future planning and delivery of more integrated health and social care services – despite its inherent weaknesses. It is undoubtedly the most politically acceptable option at the present time, given the widespread reluctance to consider linking control of health and social services in unified and elected bodies. (p.64)

In other words, short of fundamental change in the roles of health and local authorities and the financial regimes within which they work, partnership may be the only game in town. But that does not mean it will work, as they go on to note:

It would nevertheless be wise not to expect too much of the partnership approach. (p.64)

Whether that will be enough for the Government remains to be seen. The Nuffield Institute report on interagency collaboration, summarised in Update Issue 6, July 1998, concludes by saying that:

> *The dominant policy framework continues to reflect the optimistic tradition which relies predominantly upon the power of exhortation rather than facilitation or requirement.* (p.6)

That may change. As part of the new arrangements following the Comprehensive Spending Review, described in Section 2.1, the Department of Health has committed itself to making progress in the better integration of health and social care within the lifetime of this Parliament. If sufficient progress is not forthcoming then we may well see the form of targeted intervention that has characterised Government policy towards waiting lists and the last chance saloon may prove to be a reality for more authorities than Sefton.

1.3 Public health

The Government came to power with a strong but non-specific commitment to shifting the balance of policy towards 'health' rather than 'health care', which was signalled by the appointment of Tessa Jowell as the first minister for public health. In a speech in September 1997 she affirmed that the Goverment's new public health strategy must be based on partnership:

> *There are three equal and complementary strands to this joint effort:*
>
> - *the Government will do those things which can only be done by Government: legislating and regulating where necessary; providing accurate, useful and timely*

> *information; ensuring that policy and action are effective and relevant;*
> - *then there is community action which will bring together people and agencies in practical, locally-focused partnerships that get things done and provide support based upon local knowledge and needs;*
> - *and finally each of us must take greater responsibility for improving our own health.*

(Department of Health 97/239, 22 Sept 1997)

Despite the early nature of the commitment it was not until February 1998 that a consultation document for England, *Our Healthier Nation: a contract for health*, was published. Again, each part of the UK has published a paper of its own (see Box). This set out two 'overriding aims':

- *to improve the health of the population as a whole by increasing the length of people's lives and the number of years people spend free from illness.*
- *to improve the health of the worst off in society and to narrow the health gap.* (p.14)

Green Papers

Department of Health, *Our Healthier Nation: a contract for health*, Cm 3852, London: The Stationery Office, 1998.

The Scottish Office Department of Health, *Working Together for a Healthier Scotland*, Cm 3584, Edinburgh: The Stationery Office, 1998.

The Welsh Office, *Better Health, Better Wales*, Cm3922, Cardiff: The Stationery Office, 1998.

DHSS Northern Ireland, *Well into 2000: a positive agenda for health and well-being*, Belfast: DHSS, 1997.

Table 1.4 Factors affecting health

Fixed	Social and economic	Environment	Lifestyle	Access to services
Genes	Poverty	Air quality	Diet	Education
Sex	Employment	Housing	Physical activity	NHS
Ageing	Social exclusion	Water quality	Smoking	Social services
		Social environment	Alcohol	Transport
			Sexual behaviour	Leisure
			Drugs	

Source: *Our Healthier Nation*, p.16

The Green Paper sets out a broad framework for the new strategy which categorises the factors bearing on health and, among those which are amenable to external influence, distinguishes four main groups: social and economic, environment, lifestyle and access to services (see Table 1.4). The NHS itself appears as only one contributor to the final group. The challenge, recognised and taken up in the Green Paper, is to orchestrate contributions to health across the full range of Government policies. Most of this section is concerned with the way in which this task has been tackled across Government as a whole.

The Green Paper argues that earlier attempts to improve health have been 'too much about blame' or have involved social engineering. It therefore tries to define, paralleling *The New NHS*, a third way, falling between 'individual victim-blaming on the one hand and nanny State engineering on the other' (para 3.3). This third way is expressed in terms of a 'contract for health', described as follows:

> *3.6 To help bring the nation together in a concerted and coordinated drive against poor health, the Government proposes **a national contract for better health.** The contract sets out our mutual responsibilities for improving health in the areas where we can make most progress towards our overall aims of reducing*

the number of early deaths, increasing the length of our healthy lives and tackling inequalities in health.

> *3.7 The national contract recognises that the Government can create the climate for our health to be improved. It pledges to deliver key economic and social policies. It places requirements on local services to make progress in improving the public's health.* (p.29)

The elements of the contract are set out in Table 1.5.

Although the logic of the comprehensive approach to improving health is compelling and, as we shall see, has led to new initiatives across a wide range of policy areas, the Green Paper acknowledges that because the scope of the strategy is so vast, there is a need for 'focus and discipline'. It therefore proposes only four priority areas:

- heart disease and stroke;
- accidents;
- cancer;
- mental health.

National targets will be set for each. Two, heart disease and mental health, have been selected for the development of national service frameworks. No target is proposed for reducing health

Table 1.5 A contract for health

Government and national players can:	Local players and communities can:	People can:
Provide national coordination and leadership.	Provide leadership for local health strategies by developing and implementing Health Improvement Programmes.	Take responsibility for their own health and make healthier choices about their lifestyle.
Ensure that policy making across Government takes full account of health and is well informed by research and the best expertise available.	Work in partnerships to improve the health of local people and tackle the root causes of ill health.	Ensure their own actions do not harm the health of others.

Take opportunities to better their lives and their families' lives, through education, training and employment. |
Work with other countries for international cooperation to improve health.	Plan and provide high quality services to everyone who needs them.	
Assess risks and communicate those risks clearly to the public.		
Ensure that the public and others have the information they need to improve their health.		
Regulate and legislate where necessary.		
Tackle the root causes of ill health.		

Source: *Our Healthier Nation,* p.30.

inequalities, but ministers have repeatedly stressed that their policies, running across the full spectrum set out in the Table are designed to do so. *Our Healthier Nation* states that:

> Within our overall programme to improve the health of the whole population a key priority will be to improve the health of those who are marginalised and worst off. We will seek to improve the absolute and relative positions of those people and areas which are hit hardest by poor health and premature death. That will narrow the gap between them and the better off. (p.12)

On the basis that 'tackling inequalities generally is the best means of tackling health inequalities in particular', it sets out a vision of health policy which takes in the wider social and economic context:

Health Action Zones

The Government is setting up Health Action Zones in England to target health inequalities. Their purpose is to bring together all those contributing to the health of the local population to develop and implement a locally agreed strategy for improving the health of local people. The first wave of around ten Health Action Zones will receive £4m in 1998/99 and £30m will be made available in 1999 to Health Authorities for joint spending with Local Authorities and other participating agencies. The intention is to set up a second wave of Health Action Zones in 1999.

Health Action Zones will bring together a partnership of health organisations, including primary care, with Local Authorities, community groups, the voluntary sector and local businesses. They will build on the success of area-based regeneration partnerships and will seek to deliver measurable and sustainable improvements in the health of the public and in the outcomes and quality of services by achieving better integrated treatment and care. They will harness the dynamism of local people and organisations by creating alliances to achieve change.

Health Action Zones are intended to release local energy and innovation, stifled by the NHS internal market and associated fragmentation and bureaucracy, to target specific health issues. Within the national framework, local partners will be encouraged to provide specific ideas and mechanisms. Organisations and groups will be expected to work in partnership with zones delivering support and 'investment' against agreed milestones. Building a sustainable capacity from local resources through working in partnership will be vital.

Health Action Zone status should provide added impetus to the task of tackling ill health and reducing inequalities in health. It will provide opportunities for the development of new partnerships to modernise and reshape services in order to improve health outcomes for the local population. The Government wants to see a range of proposals coming forward, offering the opportunity to develop custom built approaches to local problems and challenges.

Health Action Zone status will be long term, spanning a period of five to seven years, recognising the need for a strategic approach. There will need to be evidence of change taking place and of concrete gains for local people throughout that period. It will not be acceptable to plan for the large majority of the benefits to be achieved only at the end of the Health Action Zone's life with few interim benefits.

Source: Our Healthier Nation, p.43

The Government recognises that the social causes of ill health and the inequalities which stem from them must be acknowledged and acted on. Connected problems require joined-up solutions. This means tackling inequality which stems from poverty, poor housing, pollution, low educational standards, joblessness and low pay. Tackling inequalities generally is the best means of tackling health inequalities in particular. (p.12)

The new perspective is intended to inform all policy areas. Within the NHS itself, we have already noted in Section 1.1 that one of the central elements of Health Improvement Plans is the promotion of public health and the creation of effective links between the NHS and other areas of public policy at local level. The Plans are intended to cover all parts of the country. In addition, the Green Paper sets out two

Table 1.6 Areas with Health Action Zones: first and second successful bids

Wakefield	Hull and East Riding
Leeds	Merseyside
Bury and Rochdale	Walsall
North Staffordshire	Sheffield
Leicester City	Brent
Camden and Islington	Teesside
Wolverhampton	Nottingham
Cornwall	Barnsley, Doncaster and Rotherham
Bradford	The East End of London
Lambeth, Southwark and Lewisham	Luton
Manchester, Salford and Trafford	North Cumbria
Northumberland	Plymouth
Sandwell	Tyne & Wear

initiatives aimed at the areas of greatest need. The first of these, Health Action Zones, had already been announced in the previous year: its intended role is described in the Box.

The bidding process began in October 1997, and by January 41 proposals were received of which 11 were given the go-ahead in March 1998. These covered 6 million people: a further wave was announced in August 1998 – covering a further 7 million. The areas covered are set out in Table 1.6. Announcing the first tranche of successful applicants, the Secretary of State said:

To improve local health the Health Action Zones will promote local partnerships to tackle pollution, homelessness, unemployment, poverty. To improve local health services they will develop primary and community services, improve premises, promote the use of telemedicine, modernise hospital services and develop a health service moulded to the needs of local people.

(Department of Health 98/120, 31 March 1998)

As this statement indicates, the Zones are intended to have a very wide remit. Although they will address the causes of ill health generally, they will also have a substantial health service content. In contrast, the Green Paper's second initiative targeted on specific areas, Healthy Living Centres, is designed to complement mainstream health services. The Centres will:

focus on health as a positive attribute which helps people to get the most out of life, embracing both physical and mental wellbeing. They will make an important contribution to our public health strategy through improving health and tackling inequalities.

(Department of Health 97/377, 4 December 1997)

Like the Zones, Healthy Living Centres are intended to involve partnership and community participation. Unlike the Zones, they will be financed from National Lottery monies and will provide facilities *'additional to existing provision [which] will neither replace nor undermine what is currently available.'* Examples of the range of services which might be provided in this way include exercise classes to help tackle coronary heart disease, nutrition advice and health information, services which now hover on the border of mainstream NHS provision. The general principles underlying the proposals are set out in the Box overleaf.

Healthy Living Centres: guiding principles

- Placing Healthy Living Centres clearly within the context of the new public health strategy, linking them to the achievement of local health targets, and giving priority to schemes which reach those with worse health than average or who may not be accessing existing services

- Stressing the importance of community involvement, and the need for flexibility to enable schemes to be tailored to suit local circumstances

- Emphasising the opportunity to foster innovative partnerships across the voluntary, private and public sectors

- In England, ensuring that the development of Healthy Living Centres and Health Action Zones is complementary

- Ensuring that the schemes which secure Lottery funding will be sustainable after this ends

- In common with all schemes funded through the Lottery, ensuring that Healthy Living Centres are genuinely additional to services provided through core Government expenditure.

Source: Department of Health Letter, 30 Dec 1997

The broader perspective

Both Health Action Zones and Healthy Living Centres emphasise action at local level involving partnership with other statutory and non-statutory agencies. The same themes emerge from the local government White Paper, *Modern Local Government; in touch with the people*, (The Stationery Office, 1998) which proposes a new duty on councils, to promote the economic, social and environmental well-being of their areas.

The White Paper also proposes a new power for local authorities to enter into partnerships with other organisations, including NHS bodies, and provides for councils which demonstrate they are performing well to engage in new functions. In these ways local authorities as a whole are, potentially at least, to be enabled to be more effective partners or even initiators of action falling within the broad field of public health policies that the Government has opened up. Furthermore, as noted in Section 1.1, local authority chief executives are to be members of Primary Care Group boards.

Although Health Action Zones, after the second tranche is implemented, will cover over 11 million people, they are nevertheless focused on areas where the economic social and physical environment is most inimical to health. The same targeted approach is also evident at the national level in the role of the Social Exclusion Unit. Its remit is to promote effective linkage between the individual policies bearing on unemployment, lower levels of education, low incomes, poor housing, high crime rates, family breakdown and poor health. Its initial work programme has focused on truancy and school exclusion, street living and the worst estates or deprived neighbourhoods which for over 25 years have been identified as embodying the full range of economic social and physical deprivations, and the poor health associated with them.

In respect of the economic factors bearing on health – identified in the second column of Table 1.4 – the main Government responsibilities lie with the promotion of overall employment combined with effective access to jobs for all, particularly those who find it hard to participate in the labour market. The Government's New

Deal programme designed to promote economic growth, get more people into work and reduce social security spending, has been focused specifically on groups of the population such as disadvantaged young people, single parents and the long-term unemployed. Many of these are likely to suffer from a range of social and environmental disadvantages as well as low incomes, low levels of training and insecure employment.

At national level the main responsibilities for environmental factors – to be found in the third column of Table 1.4 – lie with the Department of the Environment Transport and the Regions. We noted in Section 1.2 that Department's critical role in respect of community care and the welfare of frail elderly people and other vulnerable groups. Through its responsibilities for transport and the environment, it has potentially a similarly central role in respect both of the third column in Table 1.4 and the last.

The Department's White Paper, *Developing an Integrated Transport Policy*, published in 1998 centres on an old theme – getting a better balance between private and public transport and a proper integration of transport and land use policies – but unlike earlier White Papers, it specifically identifies the links between those goals and other Government policies, including health. It describes (p.24) the New Deal for transport as comprising:

- reductions in air pollution;
- encouragement of healthier lifestyles by reducing reliance on care;
- reductions in noise and vibration;
- improvements to transport safety.

To take one example resulting from the specific identification of the links with health, the White Paper states that the Government will improve choice and reliability of journeys by promoting cycling, thereby encouraging both exercise on the one hand – healthier lifestyle – and a reduction in air pollution – healthier environment – on the other.

These linkages to health are reasonably direct. The White Paper also identifies the contribution that transport may make to the economic regeneration which is essential to ensuring the well-being of disadvantaged communities and, through that route, to health:

> Better transport is an essential building block of the New Deal for Communities which will extend economic opportunity, tackle social exclusion and improve neighbourhood management and quality of life in some of the most rundown neighbourhoods in the country. (p.17)

As these examples show, the Government has succeeded in demonstrating on the surface at least a commitment to improving health in the very broad policy area covered by the transport White Paper. But here as in other policy fields, the foundation for such action, i.e. an understanding of the links between action and health, is weak as the example of air pollution shows.

In 1998 the Committee on the Medical Effects of Air Pollutants issued a report, *The Quantification of the Effects of Air Pollution in the United Kingdom* (Department of Health, The Stationery Office), which attempted to estimate the number of people whose health is affected by exposure to air pollution. That proved difficult but it tentatively put forward the estimates set out in Tables 1.7 and 1.8.

Table 1.7 Numbers of deaths and hospital admissions for respiratory diseases affected per year by PM10* and sulphur dioxide in urban areas of Great Britain

Pollutant	Health outcomes	GB urban
PM10	Deaths brought forward (all cause)	8,100
	Hospital admissions (respiratory) brought forward and additional	10,500
SO2	Deaths brought forward (all cause)	3,500
	Hospital admissions (respiratory) brought forward and additional	3,500

* PM10: particulate matter generally less than 10 ug in diameter

Estimated total deaths occurring in urban areas of GB per year = c430,000.
Estimated total admissions to hospital for respiratory diseases occurring in urban areas of GB per year = c530,000.

Source: *The Quantification of the Effects of Air Pollution on Health in the United Kingdom,* para 1.12

Table 1.8 Numbers of deaths and hospital admissions for respiratory diseases affected per year by ozone in both urban and rural areas of Great Britain during summer only

Pollutant	Health outcomes	GB, threshold = 50 ppb	GB, threshold = 0 ppb
Ozone	Deaths brought forward: all causes	700	12,500
	Hospital admissions (respiratory) brought forward and additional	500	9,900

Source: *The Quantification of the Effects of Air Pollution on Health in the United Kingdom,* para 1.12

The Committee emphasises how tentative its estimates are. It refers, for example, to the lack of UK studies on the effects of carbon monoxide, which meant it could not estimate its impact at all. Where it did produce estimates, such as those listed in Tables 1.7 and 1.8, it comments that the relatively straightforward process it has tried to implement them is *'fraught with difficulties with many levels of uncertainty'*. Not surprisingly the report goes on to emphasise that the results 'make a compelling case for more research', a point we return to below.

A third department with responsibilities which bear on health, mainly in relation to the fourth column of Table 1.4 on page 34, is the Ministry of Agriculture, Fisheries and Food. Previous reviews have reported on some of the most serious incidents where food policies have had severe consequences for health. The most obvious and potentially disastrous is of course BSE. Although BSE has now receded from the headlines, that is not to say it no longer gives grounds for concern. In July 1998, the Government decided that all blood donations would be subject to filter treatment to reduce the risk of the disease being passed on through blood transfusions. The cost was put at £100m.

As far as identified cases are concerned, the latest figures are consistent with the disease having been contained. The numbers identified have not risen dramatically – the 1997 total of deaths was the same as 1996 – but the possibility that numbers will rise further in future cannot yet be ruled out since the incubation period may be very long.

Although BSE has been enormously expensive and had the potential to be by far the worst food-induced health risk arising from the food chain ever experienced, it is only one of several incidents in recent years which have raised questions about the risks arising from food. Last year's review referred to the *E-coli* outbreak in Scotland: in August 1997 Tessa Jowell announced that £19m was to be made available to tighten up hygiene standards in butchers' shops, following recommendations made in the Pennington report. That incident, allied with earlier concerns arising from BSE and salmonella, helped to make the case for more effective control of the food chain from production through to distribution. In the words of the House of Commons Agriculture Committee (*Food Safety*, The Stationery Office 1998):

> *3. In the last decade the safety of food has never been far from the forefront of political and public consciousness. Yet the combined efforts of central and local government, and all those involved throughout the food chain, have failed to reduce the incidence of food poisoning or to increase public confidence in the safety of food. Fresh legislative controls, primarily through the Food Safety Act 1990, and the promulgation of best food hygiene practice throughout the food production and processing industries, appear to have done little to stem the rise in notified food poisoning cases in England and Wales between 1987 and 1997, from 58.3 cases per 100,000 population to a provisional figure of 179.6 cases. The total rates of Salmonella food poisoning in humans have remained fairly stable since the late 1980s, but this conceals a worrying increase in outbreaks associated with strains of Salmonella typhimurium DT104 showing resistance to antibiotics. At the same time, two other pathogenic micro-organisms are causing increasing numbers of food poisoning cases: Campylobacter and the rarer, but more serious verocytotoxin-producing Escherichia coli O157. Potentially most alarming of all is*

> *the probable link between bovine spongiform encephalopathy (BSE) and the new variant Creutzfeldt-Jakob Disease (nv CJD). Against this background of major food safety problems are ranged a wide variety of other concerns about potential and actual risks. Some of these concerns, for example about levels of pesticides in food, are durable; others are more ephemeral, connected often with particular food products or substances contained in food. One of many examples would be the concerns over patulin in apple juice which arose in 1993.* (p.v)

As the report goes on to point out, current policy-making is marked by divided responsibilities and conflicts of interest, particularly within the Ministry of Agriculture itself. The central charge against the Ministry in respect of BSE is that its policies did not give sufficient weight to health but were instead dominated by producer interests. Whether that is a valid criticism will no doubt emerge from the public inquiry into BSE which commenced in January 1998. To avoid the risk of such conflict arising in the future the Government believes that new institutional arrangements are required.

Labour was committed before it came to office to the establishment of a Food Standards Agency. An interim proposal by Professor Philip James was published in April 1997. Subsequently, the Government published a White Paper (*A Force for Change: The Foods Standards Agency*, Cm 3830) in January 1998, which set out the principles, listed in the Box, which should underpin its operation.

The consultation ensuing after publication of the White Paper revealed that there was widespread support for the notion of an independent agency.

Food Standards Agency: basic principles

1. The essential aim of the Agency is the protection of public health in relation to food.

2. The Agency's assessments of food standards and safety will be unbiased and based on the best available scientific advice, provided by experts invited in their own right to give independent advice.

3. The Agency will make decisions and take action on the basis that:
    *   the Agency's decisions and actions should be proportionate to the risk; pay due regard to costs as well as benefits to those affected by them; and avoid over regulation.

4. The Agency should act independently of specific sectoral interests. The Agency will strive to ensure that the general public have adequate, clearly presented information in order to allow them to make informed choices. In doing this, the Agency will aim to avoid raising unjustified alarm.

5. The Agency's decision making processes will be open, transparent and consultative, in order that interested parties, including representatives of the public:
    *   have an opportunity to make their views known;
    *   can see the basis on which decisions have been taken;
    *   are able to reach an informed judgement about the quality of the Agency's processes and decisions.

6. Before taking action, the Agency will consult widely, including representatives of those who would be affected, unless the need for urgent action to protect public health makes this impossible.

7. In its decisions and actions, the Agency will aim to achieve clarity and consistency of approach.

8. The Agency's decisions and actions will take full account of the obligations of the UK under domestic and international law.

9. The Agency will aim for efficiency and economy in delivering an effective operation.

Source: *A Force for Change*, p.5

The Agriculture Committee concluded in the report already cited that:

> *an adequately resourced and structured Agency will make a significant impact on the safety of food in this country, and in public perceptions about the safety of food. The single greatest advance in food safety policy will be the Agency's ability to oversee the entire length of the food chain, fully integrating veterinary and public health concerns in a way which has not proved possible under the existing institutional arrangements.* (p.xliii)

It goes on to point out:

> *However, any over-optimistic expectations that the Agency will achieve success immediately are bound to be disappointed. Food safety crises will still occur, and the Agency will not be able to pursue its activities untroubled by political debate and criticism. Provided that the Agency recognizes this, bases its decisions on clear and scientifically-founded evidence, and fosters public confidence and participation in its operations without alienating food producers and processors, it should be able to cope with these demands and place food safety and standards policy on a surer basis for the next century.* (p.xliii)

In other words, progress will be slow. Once confidence has been destroyed, it will take a long time to rebuild. Furthermore, because of very considerable gaps in knowledge as to why food poisoning occurs and what elements in food constitute a risk, the right way forward will, in many areas, be hard to find.

Personal behaviour

As noted at the start of this section, the notional contract set out in the Green Paper 'requires' that personal behaviour is appropriate to promoting good health. At one level this a matter of taking sensible precautions in everyday living. At this mundane and local level the familiar risks of injury and illness in normal domestic surroundings still continue to cause concern. In April 1997 the Department of Trade and Industry set out proposals for better design, aimed at reducing the 2.7m accidents in the home. In June 1997 it launched a campaign to reduce the estimated 500,000 injuries in the garden (including 50 fatal ones) and in November it issued research into packaging in the hope that it would reduce the total of 70,000 people a year who go to A&E as a result of packaging accidents. In February 1998 it issued two million safety leaflets backed by TV adverts and magazine articles, focusing on burns and scalds to the under-5s. In April 1998, it issued a leaflet stressing the dangers of DIY – in this case some 180,000 A&E visits and 70 deaths. In July 1998, it warned parents about the risks to children from garden accidents – eight deaths and 125,000 requiring hospital treatment (for the population as a whole the figures are respectively 50 and 500,000).

As these figures indicate, people continue to take risks with themselves and their children which could be easily avoided if, in the words of the Green Paper, 'they take responsibility for their own health and make healthier choices about their lifestyle'. The same is true of other forms of behaviour. Previous reviews have cited evidence that trends in personal behaviour, in some age groups, were moving in the 'wrong' direction. These trends were further confirmed by surveys published this year.

The 1996 Health Survey for England, published in January 1998, recorded some gains such as fall in average blood pressure between 1991 and 1996 but it also found that the proportion of young males who smoked had risen between 1991 and 1996. *Smoking Behaviour and Attitudes*, a report by the Office for National Statistics published in September 1997, found that the proportion of the population who had been given advice on smoking was high and rising in all social groups. But of those who had received it, about half had not found it helpful. In *Effectiveness Matters* (March 1998), the NHS Centre for Reviews and Dissemination concluded that NHS-based interventions designed to help people give up smoking are effective. Unfortunately, only a minority of smokers are influenced by the advice they receive.

In 1998 the Scientific Committee on Tobacco and Health published its report on the impact of smoking. The findings set out in the Box confirm the significance of tobacco as a health risk. The Committee, going beyond its strictly scientific remit, urged that, 'The enormous damage to health and the large number of deaths caused by smoking should no longer be accepted'. It went on to argue that the Government should require of the tobacco industry:

- *reasonable standards in the assessment of evidence relating to the health effects of what it sells;*

- *acceptance that smoking is a major cause of premature death;*

- *normal standards of disclosure of the nature and magnitude of the hazards of smoking to their customers.*

The Government had already accepted that action was required, in particular that tobacco

Report of the Scientific Committee on Tobacco and Health: Summary of conclusions and recommendations

The scale of the smoking problem: conclusions

Smoking is a major cause of illness and death from chronic respiratory diseases, cardiovascular disease, and cancers of the lung and other sites.

Smoking is the most important cause of premature death in developed countries. It accounts for one fifth of deaths in the UK: some 120,000 deaths a year.

The avoidance of smoking would eliminate one third of the cancer deaths in Britain and one sixth of the deaths from other causes.

Smoking prevalence in young people rose between 1988 and 1997 and the downward trend in adult smoking, noted in the UK since 1972, was reversed in 1996.

A person who smokes cigarettes regularly doubles his or her risk of dying before the age of 65.

Addiction to nicotine sustains cigarette smoking and is responsible for the remarkable intractability of smoking behaviour.

Smoking in pregnancy causes adverse outcomes, notably an increased risk of miscarriage, reduced birth weight and perinatal death. If parents continue to smoke after pregnancy there is an increased rate of sudden infant death syndrome.

Cigarette smoking is an important contributor to health inequalities, being more common amongst the disadvantaged than the affluent members of society.

Environmental tobacco smoke: conclusions

Exposure to environmental tobacco smoke is a cause of lung cancer and, in those with long-term exposure, the increased risk is in the order of 20–30 per cent.

Exposure to environmental tobacco smoke is a cause of ischaemic heart disease and, if current published estimates of magnitude of relative risk are validated, such exposure represents a substantial public health hazard.

Smoking in the presence of infants and children is a cause of serious respiratory illness and asthmatic attacks.

Sudden infant death syndrome, the main cause of post-natal death in the first year of life, is associated with exposure to environmental tobacco smoke. The association is judged to be one of cause and effect.

Middle ear disease in children is linked with parental smoking and this association is likely to be causal.

Source: Report of the Scientific Committee on Tobacco and Health, Summary

advertising and sponsorship should be stopped. In May 1998 the Minister was able to welcome a decision by the European Parliament to ban tobacco advertising, albeit with exceptions, such as at the point of sale. It remains to be seen, however, whether the Government will take more rigorous measures still to discourage individuals from smoking by, for example, fiscal measures and more general prohibitions of smoking in public places and to reduce further the capacity of the industry to promote its produce. Although a White Paper has been promised for some time, it had not appeared at the time of writing.

We noted in last year's Review that the incidence of obesity was increasing. The *Systematic Review of*

Interventions to reduce obesity

- Health care professionals may have negative attitudes towards overweight patients and have difficulty dealing with obesity.

- Strategies which involve a combination of diet, exercise and/or behavioural change, appear to be more beneficial for weight loss than a change in diet alone.

- Family therapy programmes can be effective in preventing the progression of obesity in already obese children.

- Strategies need to be developed for identifying those at most risk of becoming obese and for monitoring obesity treatments.

- Since weight regain is common amongst those who do lose weight, effective strategies for maintaining weight loss should be integral to weight reduction programmes.

- All sorts of claims are being made for commercial diet and weight loss regimes, many of which have never been scientifically evaluated.

Source: NHS Centre for Reviews & Dissemination Press Release, 24 October 1997

Interventions in the Treatment and Prevention of Obesity (University of York, 1997) from The NHS Centre for Reviews and Dissemination found that, despite its recognition as a significant threat to health, there were very few well-conducted studies and, in respect of some possible interventions, no studies at all. A summary of its conclusions is in the Box.

In the case of smoking, a case can be made out for strong central intervention in the choices people make based on the costs to society at large, particularly children. A further case, made by the Scientific Committee, is that as nicotine is addictive, many individuals are not in a position to make a rational choice. Nanny State can therefore intervene, despite the notional contract set out in the Green Paper. Furthermore, the main objects of that intervention, the tobacco industry and its products, are readily identifiable. The same is not true of obesity, which may be effortlessly achieved through a wide range of products which are not generally addictive and most of which are not injurious to health.

Moreover, the resultant risks are largely borne by the individuals themselves. The evidence is that many ignore them: if people continue to do so and in ever larger numbers, and thereby threaten the attainment of the Government's targets for heart disease, what then?

Screening

The final column of Table 1.4 on page 34 acknowledges that the NHS itself does have a part to play in promoting the health of the nation. Previous reviews have recorded how successive reports have identified weaknesses in the implementation of existing programmes of prevention. Three further reports appeared, two on events in particular trusts, Kent and Canterbury and the Royal Devon and Exeter, and a more wide-ranging inquiry by the National Audit Office, *The Performance of the NHS Cervical Screening Programme in England* (The Stationery Office 1998), into the national cervical screening programme.

The National Audit Office concluded that the programme was now much better managed than it had been found to be in earlier reports. However, it found a number of areas where further improvement was required. Its conclusions run as follows:

28. Although the NHS Cervical Screening Programme has achieved a great deal since our last report, scope remains for improving the service women experience through more comprehensive provision of better information, and through improvements in smear taking. The performance of laboratories and colposcopy clinics falls short of the quality guidelines in many respects, although we recognise that those guidelines were set relatively recently and work to implement them is underway.

29. Smear taking, screening and colposcopy are undertaken by trained individuals, but these activities inescapably involve judgements. We accept that in a large programme like the cervical screening programme, there will be, from time to time, errors of judgement. It is vital that steps continue to be taken to minimise these errors, particularly where they are systematic. But above all, quality assurance must be improved so that any remaining errors are detected at the earliest time. (p.9)

The report into events in Exeter (*Breast Cancer Services in Exeter and Quality Assurance for Breast Screening*, by Sir Kenneth Calman and Dame Deirdre Hine, Nov 1997) was stimulated by the concerns of clinicians in the Royal Devon and Exeter Trust about a number of breast cancers missed by two consultant radiologists. The report established that the quality of the screening was below what could be reasonably expected. However, the poor performance was due to a much wider set of factors, surrounding the programme as a whole. The same was true at Kent and Canterbury, where large numbers of tests had been incorrectly read. A central finding of both reports was that management arrangements in the trusts concerned and at other levels of the NHS, were at fault. In both cases, weaknesses in the units running the service were widely known, but no effective action was taken. The Exeter report found, for example, that, '*there is no one who is clearly identified as being responsible for ensuring adverse reports by a quality assurance team are acted upon.*' (p.11)

It goes on: '*There is in England a highly-defined quality assurance service ... and yet it is unable to take effective action.*'(p.13)

The report of events at Kent and Canterbury (*Review of Cervical Screening Services at Kent and Canterbury Hospitals Trust*, South Thames Region 1997) also concluded that reporting lines were inadequate. It recommended that:

1. *National consideration should be given as to whether the existing accountability of senior NHS trust managers is sufficiently clear and properly exercised.*

2. *Management of the NHS Cervical Screening Programme should be strengthened by incorporating responsibility for issuing guidance, quality assurance and performance management of local implementation into the regular accountability structure of the NHS Executive through its regional offices to health authorities and trusts. The NHS Executive should be advised on policy by the Advisory Committee on Cervical Screening and on performance by the national coordinating office of the NHS Cervical Screening Programme.*

3. *The role of the national coordinating office in developing national standards and guidelines, in providing support and advice to local screening programmes, and in publishing information for the public, should be clarified in relation to the accountability structures of the NHS Executive.* (p.39)

The NHS Executive responded to these findings with a stream of further advice. In November EL(97) 67, *Cancer Screening: Quality Assurance & Management*, required trusts and health authorities to review their management arrangements and quality standards for cancer screening programmes.

This was followed up by EL(97)83, which required all laboratories participating in cervical screening to obtain accreditation by Clinical Pathology Accreditation (UK) Ltd or an equivalent body and to investigate thoroughly where results fall outside the current standard ranges of 1.2–2.0 per cent detection of high-grade abnormalities. These formed part of an action plan announced by the Chief Medical Officer, which in addition to the accreditation requirement indicated that:

- *Where necessary, staff from laboratories which do not meet key quality indicators should participate in refresher training. Reasons for any failure to meet the indicators will be investigated by Regional Directors of Public Health.*

- *Serious consideration will be given to the future of laboratories which are too small to maintain and improve key quality standards and skills.*

- *Progress on these points will be monitored by a high-level Action Team, comprising representatives from the Women's Nationwide Cancer Control Campaign,*

key professional bodies, and the National Co-ordinating Office of the Cervical Screening Programme.

(Department of Health 97/405, 17 Dec 1997)

Further problems were found in a survey by the Royal College of Radiologists which identified staff shortages and difficulties in recruitment. A survey carried out in the first half of 1998 found that out of 74 units, more than half had current funding problems and just over 40 per cent had vacancies. The vast majority reported the pressure of work was high: a quarter of the units had been or were involved in litigation. Overall, the picture presented was a service under stress and running up against limits to its capacity to deliver. To some extent, that may be due to other Government policies. The Exeter report noted that the Calman-Hine proposals for cancer treatment services had had the effect of diverting resources away from screening.

We noted last year the establishment of a National Screening Committee. In April, the Committee published its first annual report. More than most such reports, it is methodological in content. The report sets out a Framework for Screening and a Handbook to guide the development of a specific screening programme. It also contains an inventory, compiled for the first time, of screening programmes currently in place, those where there is an explicit policy not to offer them and those under current review (See Table 1.9 overleaf).

Overall

When *The Health of the Nation* initiative was announced in 1991 it was widely acclaimed because of its emphasis on health rather than health care but also criticised for its neglect of

Table 1.9 An inventory of screening programmes

Screening programmes	UK policy
Programmes where current guidance exists:	
Breast cancer	All women aged 50–64 invited once every 3 years, women over 65 on request
Cervical cancer	All women aged 20-64 invited once every 5 years; every 3 years in Scotland
Phenylketonuria	All neonates
Congenital hypothyroidism	All neonates
Physical examination	All neonates
Child health screening	GMS regulations
Cardiovascular risk factor screening	GMS regulations: newly registered patients and patients not seen within 3 years
Elderly – general assessment	GMS Regulations: patients aged 75 years and over assessed every 12 months
Bladder cancer	Occupational exposure
HIV antibody	PL/CO(92)5: all women receiving antenatal care MEL(1993)154
Explicit policy not to offer:	
Prostate cancer	Executive Letter (97)12 which appears as Neuroblastoma Appendix B & MEL(1997)38
Under current review or planned for review when evidence is available:	
Aortic aneurysm	
Chlamydia trachomatis	Awaiting outcomes from other
Colorectal cancer	research programmes
Hepatitis B in pregnancy	
Cystic fibrosis	Awaiting outcomes from systematic
Down's syndrome	reviews; the expected timescales
Fragile X syndrome	range from the present time until 2001
Haemoglobinopathies	
Inborn errors of metabolism	
Ovarian cancer	

Source: *First Report of the National Screening Committee*, April 1998, p.33

health inequalities. The Labour Government has re-emphasised the first message and, with its willingness to tackle inequalities and its emphasis on the broader environmental factors which have an impact on health – particularly income and work – made, in principle at least, a major step forward.

That said, the new policies face tremendous difficulties in terms of implementation, evaluation and underlying philosophy. The initiatives set out above are designed to look across the full spectrum of policies and factors bearing on the health of individuals with a special emphasis on breaking down barriers between organisations and their areas of responsibility. But however desirable the 'joined-up policy-making' supported in *Our Healthier Nation* may be, it is hard to achieve in practice.

The Government has made many of the 'right noises'. *Our Healthier Nation* reports that the Government has set up a committee of ministers from 12 departments to 'drive the policy across Government'. Furthermore, the Comprehensive Spending Review recognises that 'dividing up responsibility for overlapping policy areas between several departments can make Government intervention less effective.' It therefore proposes a number of cross-department budgets as well as 'invest to save' budgets to help projects which bring together more than one public service. None of the examples fall into the health field with the exception of budget pooling in relation to health and social services but the potential for such pooling in the public health field has been created.

These proposals are innovatory but there is a long history of failure of attempts to bring together successfully different government departments at national level and different agencies locally which these new ideas may not be sufficient to overcome. Although past failures can be attributed to individual parts of the government machine at national and local level looking after its 'own' interests, they are also attributable to the genuine difficulties involved in linking effectively across organisations with different aims and different cultures, as the history of health and social care so amply demonstrates. These difficulties are all the greater where the message to co-operate is mixed with targets for specific services of the kind that the Government is aiming to introduce for the NHS and other services.

Second, there are major technical difficulties involved in evaluating policy impacts – for example, in isolating the impact of specific interventions against an ever-changing background, or of detecting changes over a very long period of time. Recognising this, the Government has commissioned a programme of technical work. *Our Healthier Nation* acknowledges that:

> *Ministers and civil servants alone do not have the expertise and knowledge to make our strategy a success.* Our Healthier Nation *will need a great deal of expert advice to ensure that it makes maximum impact with the resources available. For example, the Government will need technical advice on monitoring progress and measuring improvements in health and the Chief Medical Officer's* Our Healthier Nation *group will bring together experts to assist in monitoring the national targets and to provide other expert advice. Government will also need advice on how best to involve the range of non-Government bodies who can play a part; and it will need support in making the*

most of the contribution of the NHS and Local Authorities. (p.33)

In respect of health inequalities, Sir Donald Acheson was commissioned in July 1997:

- *To moderate a Department of Health review of the latest available information on inequalities of health, using data from the Office for National Statistics, the Department of Health and elsewhere. The data reviewed would summarise the evidence of inequalities of health and expectation of life in England and identify trends.*
- *In the light of that evidence, to conduct – within the broad framework of the Government's overall financial strategy – an independent review to identify priority areas for future policy development, which scientific and expert evidence indicates, are likely to offer opportunities for Government to develop beneficial cost effective and affordable interventions to reduce health inequalities.*

(Department of Health, 97/157, 7 July 1997)

In May 1998 a programme of research was announced, to be commissioned by the Department of Health, complementing programmes run by the MRC and the ESRC.

In February 1998, the Chief Medical Officer Sir Kenneth Calman circulated a consultation document, *Chief Medical Officer's Project to Strengthen the Public Health Function in England.* This identified five themes where change was needed:

- a wider understanding of health
- better co-ordination

- an increase in capacity and capabilities
- sustained development
- effective joint working

and went on to identify a number of specific areas where improvements were required:

- *involvement of citizens in understanding public health issues, health risk, and what action can be taken is currently inadequate;*
- *the present resource of specialist public health expertise is already very stretched and there is a need for more dedicated staff from a number of disciplines to deliver the current agenda;*
- *capacity for public health doctors, nurses and other professionals to work both within the NHS on health care development and on the wider public health issues needs strengthening;*
- *joint work between health and local authorities to drive strategic change; there is some very good practice, but it is not found everywhere;*
- *the recognition of different contributions to public health e.g. the preventative work of GPs and dentists with individual patients, the wider community development work of other members of the primary care team, the role of public health doctors and of other professionals and of environmental health officers in local government;*
- *the fragmentation and relative under-development of public health research.* (p.5)

In respect of each of these a large number of short- and long-term actions are identified, at local, regional and national levels.

There can be little doubt that understanding of health inequalities needs to be improved and that the public health function should be strengthened. But they represent only a small fraction of the new knowledge and skills that are needed properly to implement the vast agenda that the Government has created. We noted above the fragility of the calculation of the impact of air pollution. The report itself comments on its own calculations as follows:

> Calculating such a range [of health impacts] implies an understanding of the level of uncertainty involved in the calculations. In the case of air pollution we have only a weak grasp of this. (p.55)

The same is true of many of the areas underlying the government plans for food safety. The Government response to the Agriculture Committee report, *Food Safety*, acknowledged the need for a number of new programmes of research – including, for example, attempts to explain why the incidence of food poisoning varies widely between different parts of the country as well as to gain greater understanding of the underlying science, such as the way particular pathogens work.

Third, the field of possible influences on the UK's health gets ever wider. Some come from the physical environment, others from developments in the world economy, others from political change. The risks of global warming seem to rise, though the health implications remain to be identified. In September 1997, Sir Robert May, the Government's Chief Scientific Adviser, officially confirmed on the basis of the work done by the United Nations Intergovernmental Panel on Climate Change (DTI Press Release 97/621) that global temperatures are expected to rise but that the health implications had yet to be unravelled.

In the economic field, growing internationalisation of the world economy and its increasing interdependence mean that the scope for any one nation to control its own economic destiny is reduced. The impact of financial collapse in the Far East will be greatest on its workforce, but there will be repercussions in the UK in terms of job losses and pressures on pay, particularly on those with the lowest incomes. While the Government has responded to the latter by accepting the recommendations of the Low Pay Commission for a national minimum wage, it can do much less for job security. As for political change, the risks of cross-border epidemics, e.g. syphilis and influenza, appear to be growing in part because of a deterioration in health conditions in the former Soviet Bloc. A contingency plan for the latter eventuality was published in March 1997.

Finally, there are also philosophical issues focused on choice, acceptance of risk and information. The tensions between different philosophical bases for public health policies was illustrated by, on the one hand, the banning of beef on the bone by Jack Cunningham when he was Agriculture Minister, and the acceptance, on the other, of much higher levels of risk from everyday activities such as gardening enjoyed by a large proportion of the population. This tension must be resolved if the notion of a contract is to have any meaning and 'the third way' is to be more than a rhetorical device.

1.4 Serving the consumer

The Labour Manifesto promised a review of the Patient's Charter as a whole, leading to the production of a new one and, in relation to waiting lists for elective care, to cut numbers waiting by increasing activity by 100,000. We look further at this latter commitment and its consequences in Section 2.1.

Before turning to the new Charter, some aspects of the existing Charter also needed attention. In July 1997 the Secretary of State announced that the standard for immediate assessment in A&E departments would be replaced by October as it had become clear that the original formulation had encouraged so-called 'hello' nurses, whose services allowed trusts to meet the standard but which offered no genuine improvement to patients. Executive Letter (97)60 issued that month announced a new standard, as follows:

> If you go to an Accident and Emergency Department needing immediate treatment you will be cared for at once. Otherwise you will be assessed by a doctor or trained nurse within 15 minutes of arrival.

> Following assessment you will be given a priority category which will be communicated to you. This priority will determine the urgency with which you will be treated.

The Government inherited a commitment to remove mixed-sex accommodation by:

- ensuring that appropriate organisational arrangements are in place to secure good standards of privacy and dignity for hospital patients;
- fully achieving the Patient's Charter standard for segregated washing and toilet facilities across the NHS; and
- providing safe facilities for patients in hospital who are mentally ill, while safeguarding their privacy and dignity.

(Department of Health 98/060, 18 Feb 1998)

Health authorities had been asked to meet targets for the elimination of mixed-sex accommodation in all three areas. The results, reported in August 1997, revealed that a number could not meet the targets by April 1999. The Chief Executive of the NHS, Alan Langlands, therefore asked regional offices to see what could be done in these cases. However, the Government subsequently acknowledged in February 1998, in the light of the response to Sir Alan's request, that it would still take years before all health authorities could meet their targets in full – even by 2002 there would still be a small number who had not.

In October 1997 Greg Dyke, Chairman and Chief Executive of Pearson TV, was appointed to lead the Patient's Charter Advisory Group. The Group's remit was to develop a new charter which, according to the Secretary of State:

> will concentrate on measuring success across a broad front. It will focus on the things that really matter to people. There will be clearly measurable standards of care and the kind of accessible information which people need to make informed choices about their health. The rights of patients to high quality, effective treatment will be enhanced. However, these rights will be balanced with their responsibilities to the Health Service – for example, to keep appointments and to treat NHS staff with respect.

(Department of Health 97/264, 8 October 1997)

To support the Advisory Group's work, the King's Fund was commissioned to assess professional and other views on how it had worked in practice. The summary findings of this work relating to the general merits of the existing Charter are set out in the Box.

The report goes on to consider what changes patients and professionals wanted to see.

Patient's Charter Pros and Cons

Advantages of the existing Charter(s):

- has raised staff awareness of patients' needs, issues and rights
- helped set [some] standards and identified priorities for action
- set comparable standards for reviews of performance
- helped to move NHS culture towards a 'user perspective'

Disadvantages of the existing Charter(s):

- lack of clarity about its aim – this engendered wide scepticism
- not enough user or staff involvement in creating the document
- too much emphasis on quantitative standards
- ignores clinical standards and outcomes
- some standards irrelevant to patients' real needs, especially those of vulnerable people
- hard to monitor – data costly to collect and sometimes fudged and/or ignored
- hospital services dominate at expense of primary care
- low patient awareness of Charter
- patients' expectations unrealistically raised
- too little stress on patients' responsibilities

Source: C Farrell, R Levenson and D Snape, *The Patient's Charter: past and future,* London: King's Fund, 1998

Patients' own priorities were found to be:

- *equality in access to and quality of services*
- *comprehensible information*
- *positive interaction with NHS staff*
- *a good standard of clinical treatment*
- *improved access to the NHS*
- *assurance of privacy and confidentiality*
- *more choice.* (p.104)

Staff on the other hand emphasised:

- *clinical quality*
- *service responsiveness*
- *provision of information to patients*
- *neglected groups*
- *respect and dignity*
- *patients' responsibilities.* (p.108)

Although some items appear on both lists, patients placed more emphasis on choice, and access while professionals more on user responsibilities. The report goes on to argue that a new NHS charter should be both more precise and more comprehensive, by including:

- *an unambiguous statement about its aims and values*
- *principles of openness, accountability and equity*
- *a much stronger focus on primary and community care and a wider and clearer statement of patients' rights of access to services*
- *wider standards which focus on quality of service:*

  - *for clinical need, effectiveness, and outcomes*
  - *for equity and access to services/treatment*
  - *for the quality of the patient experience*
  - *for better communication and information in a usable form*

- *emphasise not only patients' rights but also their responsibilities and foster ways of encouraging such behaviour*
- *better publicity for the Charter*
- *regular reviews of the content and impact of the Charter.* (p.ix–x)

The results of the Advisory Group's work were not available by the time this Review was written nor of the work started in summer 1998 on the Charter for Long-Term Care. There were nevertheless a number of other developments during the year bearing on the interests of NHS users.

In June 1998 *Service First*, a wider initiative targeted at all public services, was announced by David Clark, then Chancellor of the Duchy of Lancaster but sacked in the July reshuffle. The initiative consists of a number of elements, including *Better Quality Services*, a guidance manual for service managers, the establishment of regional Quality Networks, the initiative *Better Government for Older People* (see Section 1.2) and publication of *People and Public Services*, a review of research into people's expectations and experiences of public services.

Service First is designed to ensure that public services as a whole:

- *work in partnership with one another and take a more co-ordinated approach;*
- *are responsive to the needs of users and involve frontline staff in the development of services;*
- *make services more accessible through for example extended opening hours, use of plain language and new technology;*
- *shift the emphasis from 'value for money' to 'more effective use of resources';*
- *treat everyone fairly in line with the Government's commitment to a more just society.*

Mr Clark also announced that a 'people's panel' would be set up, consisting of 5,000 people nationwide, who would be consulted about how public services are delivered and how delivery

> ## National Performance Assessment Framework: Patient/carer experience
>
> The framework will include user/carer perceptions of the delivery of services such as:
>
> - responsiveness to individual needs and preferences;
> - the skill, care and continuity of service provision;
> - patient involvement, good information and choice;
> - waiting times and accessibility;
> - the physical environment; the organisation and courtesy of administrative arrangements.
>
> **Source:** *The New NHS: Modern, Dependable: a national framework for assessing performance*

could be improved from the viewpoint of the user. Subsequently, the Cabinet Office published a guide to preparing national charters, *How to Draw up a National Charter*, aimed at all those responsible for the delivery of public services.

In respect specifically of the NHS, a number of innovations were announced in line with this general policy. *The New NHS* states that: 'The Government will take special steps to ensure the experience of users and carers is central to the work of the NHS'. One such step is the introduction of a new annual survey designed to record what patients feel about the care the NHS offers. This is to be carried out annually, at health authority level, and the results will be published both locally and nationally.

As the White Paper accurately claims: '*For the first time in the history of the NHS there will be systematic evidence to enable the health service to measure itself against the aspirations and experience of its users*'.

Another step is the inclusion in the national performance assessment framework of a set of measures – see Box – intended to cover the experience of patients and carers.

The White Paper asserts that *'The needs of patients will be central to the new system'* (p.5), and then adds that: *'Local doctors and nurses, who best understand patients' needs, will shape local services'* (p.5). However, the *Supporting Guidance for Developing Primary Care Groups*, recognising that the professional does not always know best even when that professional is locally based, states that the PCGs will *'have a key role in communicating with local people and ensuring public involvement in decision making about local health services'*. (p.24)

The Guidance argues that greater involvement will:

- *contribute to greater openness and accountability in the NHS;*
- *develop a greater local understanding of the issues involved in major local service changes;*
- *help to strengthen public confidence in the way major changes in local health services are planned;*
- *develop a greater sense of local ownership and commitment to health services;*
- *lead to better quality and more responsive services through listening to and understanding the needs and wishes of health service users and involving them in service planning, development and monitoring;*
- *enable local people to have access to better information about health and health services which can lead to more appropriate use of services.*

(Supporting Guidance to HSC 1998/139, p.24)

How these objectives are to be promoted is left to the PCGs to determine. However, they are asked to:

- *put in place plans for the early, systematic and continuous involvement of users and the public;*
- *be able to demonstrate how in carrying out their role they have involved users and the public;*
- *provide feedback to users and the public on the outcome of their involvement.* (p.25)

The publication of Patient's Charter league tables was originally intended to allow patients to decide which hospital to go to. In Labour's new NHS, this option is less likely to be open to them since choice does not feature prominently in the Government's proposals for the new NHS. Nevertheless, the Government indicated in July 1997 that the standard of information contained in the existing hospital league tables would be improved so as to emphasise quality rather than quantity. Fifteen new indicators were proposed which had been derived in conjunction with the Joint Consultants Committee of the BMA (see Box overleaf).

As noted in earlier editions of *Health Care UK*, the Scots have been publishing such indicators for several years. An unpublished survey carried out by Stephen Kendrick and colleagues of Incomes and Statistics Directorate in Scotland of the way that clinical indicators had actually been used in Scotland suggested they had not had a dramatic impact either on professionals, or, via the media, on public opinion as indeed the manner of their publication encouraged. If the indicators eventually used in the national performance framework are given greater publicity that may change and whether or not users can make effective use of them may become apparent. In the past, the

Proposed Clinical Indicators

- Deaths in hospital within 30 days of surgery following emergency and non-emergency admissions

- Emergency re-admissions to hospital within 28 days of previous discharge

- Wound infection in hospital following a surgical procedure undertaken after emergency and non-emergency admissions

- Discharge home within 56 days of emergency admission from home with a stroke

- Surgery for recurrence of hernia following previous surgery

- Deaths in hospital within 30 days of emergency admission with heart attack

- Damage to organs in hospital following a surgical procedure undertaken after emergency and non-emergency admission

- Blood clots in lungs in hospital following a surgical procedure undertaken after emergency and non-emergency admission

- Heart complications in hospital following a surgical procedure undertaken after emergency and non-emergency admission

- Central nervous system complications following a surgical procedure undertaken after emergency and non-emergency admission

- Adverse events related to the use of medicines in-hospital following emergency and non-emergency admission

- Re-operation after previous surgery on the prostate gland

- Discharge home within 56 days of emergency and non-emergency admission with a fracture of neck of femur (thigh bone)

- Deaths in hospital within 30 days of emergency and non-emergency admission following fracture of neck of femur (thigh bone)

- Frequency of procedure of curettage (scraping) of the uterus (D&C) among women under 40 years of age

Source: Clinical Indicators for the NHS: a consultation document, NHS Executive, 1997

failure to publish indicators has been defended on the ground that people would not know how to interpret them, a defence which has considerable validity unless satisfactory ways are found of allowing for the impact of differences in the nature of the workload handled by different hospitals. But, as noted in Section 2.3 of the Review, even had the Government not already been determined to publish clinical indicators, the Bristol case discussed elsewhere in this volume, emphatically changed the terms of that discussion.

Whether users can make effective use of clinical indicators at hospital or trust level may remain an open question for some time. But, as the findings of the King's Fund work for the Patient's Charter review cited above confirm, users are keen to have better information about the decisions which affect them directly. In the past, professional bodies have been slow to respond, but two recent publications marked a significant change in professional attitudes. The General Medical Council issued a revised version of *Duties of a Doctor*, and the Senate for Surgery of Great Britain and Ireland issued *The Surgeon's Duty of Care* – both of which accepted the case for patients having more information about the risks of treatment. As the following extract from the latter indicates, the professions have moved noticeably in the direction of making informed choice a reality. The Senate accepts that surgeons should:

> *Inform competent adult patients aged 16 and above of the nature of their condition, along with the type, purpose, prognosis, common side effects and significant risks of any proposed surgical treatments. Where appropriate, alternative treatment options (including non-surgical) should also be explained, together with the consequences of no treatment.*

> *This information should be provided in the detail required by a reasonable person in the circumstances of the patient to make a relevant and informed judgement. The first language and ability to understand English should be taken into account in the provision of information for patients.* (p.6)

Desirable though this may be, there is only limited experience of what is involved. Previous Reviews have noted the King's Fund programme on informed choice which has focused on a number of specific conditions. More generally, a recent survey from the NHS Centre for Reviews and Dissemination (Developing Information Materials to Present the Findings of Technology Assessments to Consumers, The Experience of the NHS Centre for Reviews and Dissemination, V A Entwistle *et al.*, *International Journal of Technology Assessment in Health Care* 14:1, Cambridge University Press, 1988) concluded that:

> *The development of research based information materials to support patient involvement in decision making is resource-intensive and requires a range of skills and expertise.* (p.66)

As these findings indicate, implementing the user perspective requires substantial investment. We have noted before the Patient Partnership programme – one sign on the part of the previous Government that they were prepared to make such an investment, albeit a small one. Progress here has been slow. Lady Jay, in a speech in May 1997 and again in October 1997, affirmed the new Government's support for this approach, but made no specific commitments to develop it. However, in November 1997, the Centre for Health Information Quality was established as part of the Patient Partnership Strategy. Its aims are set out in the Box overleaf.

Centre for Health Information Quality

The Centre aims to raise the quality of information made available to patients and their carers, by empowering those responsible for its creation, including the NHS, patient representatives and self help organisations.

This will be achieved by raising awareness of key issues in the development of information, including:

- **Communications:** including legibility and readability
- **Evidence Base:** including source material, current knowledge and the acknowledgement of areas of uncertainty
- **Consumer Involvement:** including the stage at which patients, and their carers are involved in the development of materials, and their level of involvement.

Source: http://www.centreforhiq.demon.co.uk/aims.htm

In July 1998 a new R&D programme was announced, *Health in Partnership*, which is designed to increase understanding of lay involvement in health care decision-making and thereby looks set to take up the challenge posed by the findings of the York review.

Its specific aims are:

- to compare and evaluate different models of involvement of patients and carers in the process of decision-making about their treatment, care and support;
- to explore ways of involving patients, carers and the public in planning and setting priorities in health care, comparing the impacts, benefits and drawbacks of different methods;
- identify the implications of this for the development, education, training and support of staff in health and related services.

Complaints

In previous Reviews we have noted the introduction of a new complaints procedure. In January 1998 the first detailed official information, *Handling Complaints: monitoring the NHS complaints procedure*, was published. The main findings were that there were 38 written complaints per 10,000 acute care episodes, six for each 10,000 in A&E, one complaint for each GP and one each three general dental practitioners. Two-thirds of complaints were resolved locally within four weeks. In 1,612 cases independent reviews were requested of which just under a quarter were referred. In the case of family health services, a much higher number of complaints requested an independent review of which about one in five were referred to an independent panel.

The National Consumer Council also published a report, *NHS Complaints Procedures: the first year* in September 1997 which covered the first year of the new system. The local resolution stage appeared to be working well but the report found distrust of the independence of the review process and obstacles to access as well as a number of procedural failings – for example, failure to share information about the two 'sides' views. Overall, the report led to the view that more resources were needed to make the procedure work and a change of attitude was required on the part of staff towards complaints and complainants. Further evidence that it is the second stage, independent review, which appears to be giving rise to most dissatisfaction comes from the Health Service Commissioner. Of the 400 complaints to the Health Service Commissioner on the procedure, 353 were about refusal to set up independent panels.

Medical Defence Union: A Review of General Practice Complaints

The Medical Defence Union undertook a study of 2,159 complaints notified by GP members during the first 21 months of the procedure from April 1996 to December 1997. The results suggest that most complaints are dealt with satisfactorily 'in-house', with the vast majority of complaints resolved at local level. However, numbers grew rapidly over this short period.

Highlights

- 92 per cent of the complaints over the 21-month period were resolved at local level.

- There was a substantial increase in the number of complaints notified to the MDU by GP members between 1996 and 1997.

- Failure or delay in diagnosis remains the main reason for the complaints against GP members, accounting for 27 per cent in this study compared with 25 per cent in a 1995 MDU study of the old complaints procedure.

- 13 per cent of complaints were related to the attitude of staff and doctors, compared with 10 per cent in the 1995 study. 20 per cent were notified after a bereavement.

Source: *The Journal of the MDU,* Vol 14, Issue 2, June 1998, p.11

In his 1996/97 report, the Health Service Commissioner focused on a number of incidents where complaints were handled badly – these are discussed further in Section 2.3. In his subsequent annual report, the Commissioner recorded that he had issued a memorandum analysing 117 cases relating to the role of convenors. The report also makes clear that the new procedures are still not working properly in a variety of other respects.

That may be ascribed to teething problems. More seriously, the Commissioner's report indicates that not only has the total number of complaints been rising but also the proportion upheld. The results of a survey by the Medical Defence Union showing a rapid increase in complaints are given in the Box.

An analysis in the Commissioner's report found considerable geographical variations in the number of complaints per head. A breakdown of the figures indicated that the rate of complaint varied considerably from one part of the country to another although all regions show an increase. When asked about the possible factors underlying

NHS complaints: geographical breakdown, 1997–98 (1996–97)

Region of origin	Population (000s) per complaint
North Thames	14 (15)
South Thames	16 (18)
North West	24 (26)
South and West	24 (29)
West Midlands	25 (37)
Trent	27 (33)
Northern and Yorkshire	28 (33)
Anglia and Oxford	29 (31)
Cases with no NHS region	–
Total for England	**21 (25)**
Scotland	34 (30)
Wales	20 (26)
Overall Totals	**21** (26)

Source: Health Service Commissioner for England, Scotland and Wales, *Annual Report 1997–98*

this variation by the Public Administration Committee, the NHS Chief Executive was unable to offer any explanation: however, as Jack Kneeshaw records elsewhere in this volume, public opinion surveys have found a similar pattern, with Londoners being the most likely to complain and Scots least likely.

In 1998, the Select Committee on Public Administration reviewed the Commissioner's 1996/97 report (*Report of the Health Service Commissioner for 1996–97*, Select Committee on Public Administration, Second Report, House of Commons, 1998) and in the light of earlier investigations came to the view that, despite the new procedure for handling complaints, little had fundamentally changed:

> *This Committee's predecessors have made recommendations relating to the management of the NHS almost every year since 1976. Nevertheless, year after year, the results of investigations by the Ombudsman reveal the same failings. Our predecessors wrote in 1996 that despite the circulation of the Ombudsman's reports within the NHS, 'in certain areas such as complaints handling, records management and dealing with bereavement there is as yet no obvious improvement'. What we say in this Report shows that all this is still true.* (p.xxxviii)

The reason, they concluded, was that basic procedures as well as leadership at senior management level were poor:

> *The evidence we have heard, concerning a number of cases investigated by the Health Service Ombudsman, has included all too many examples of poor care and poor management, inadequate administrative procedures and, perhaps most depressingly, simple failure to make a decent and timely*

> *apology for these breakdowns in the basic standards of the NHS. We have been greatly concerned by the quality of leadership and management in some NHS authorities and Trusts, particularly in those 'recidivist' Trusts which have been the subject of repeat reports by the Ombudsman.* (p.v)

In extremis, patients sue, but here too they have been faced with a system which responds poorly to their needs. Last year we noted Lord Woolf's recommendations for major reform of the way that claims of clinical negligence were handled by the courts following his findings that existing arrangements were highly unsatisfactory. Further evidence for this view came from *Affording Civil Justice*, a study for the Law Society (J Shapland *et al.*, Research and Policy Planning Unit, Research Study No. 29, London: The Law Society, 1998). This found that although a significant number of medical negligence cases drop out after initial medical reports are received and before a case formally begins – between 25 and 80 per cent of cases – if they did proceed beyond this stage they tended to be strongly defended by the trusts concerned and hence became very expensive to all concerned. Furthermore, a greater proportion went to trial than any other form of personal injury (5 to 35 per cent with a median of 8–10 per cent).

In 1997 the Lord Chancellor's Department published a consultation paper on proposed new procedures for handling clinical negligence, following up his report, which made a number of procedural recommendations designed to make the process easier and more effective. Another response to Lord Woolf's findings was the establishment of the Clinical Disputes Forum, designed to bring together all the interest groups, ranging from lawyers, the NHS Litigation Authority, the Defence Unions to the Legal Aid Board.

Table 1.10 Cost of clinical negligence claims 1996/97

Account entries for clinical negligence	£m
Charge to income and expenditure account	
Health authorities	88
NHS trusts	73
NHS Litigation Authority	74
Total	**235**
Provision at 31 March 1997 (amounts charged to income and expenditure accounts, either in 1996/97 or earlier years)	
Health authorities	232(a)
NHS trusts	129
NHS Litigation Authority	69
Total	**430**
Contingent liability at 31 March 1997 (amounts not charged to income and expenditure accounts)	
Health authorities	271(b)
NHS trusts	191(c)
NHS Litigation Authority	92
National Blood Authority	3
Total	**557**
Adjustment to NHS Litigation Authority contingent liability	66(d)
Adjusted Total	**623**

Notes:
(a) includes all provisions other than those in respect of pensions: mostly clinical negligence but an element of the figure relates to employer negligence.
(b) includes clinical and employer negligence.
(c) includes all contingencies (mostly clinical negligence).
(d) £92m adjusted to £158m to reflect the Authority's share of total claims rather than the most likely payment.

Source: *Summarised Accounts for NHS England for 1996/97*, The Stationery Office, 1998

This has developed a protocol for clinical disputes resolution, which was also out to consultation, the prime aim of which is to bring the parties together before formal legal action begins and hence reduce the likelihood of it being necessary.

As Lord Woolf made clear in his report, the system of civil justice as a whole was inefficient, and dealing with claims for clinical negligence particularly so. But despite the difficulties facing potential litigants, the cost of successful claims has continued to rise. The Comptroller and Auditor General devoted a section to the issue in his report on the 1995/96 accounts and those of the following year. In the first, he estimated that liabilities of trusts might be in the range £200–500m and that they were likely to rise. His report on the 1996/97 accounts confirmed the seriousness of the situation. The figures shown in the accounts are set out in Table 1.10.

The report goes on to point out that the cost to the Department is likely to be of the order of a further £900m plus a further £1bn for incidents not yet reported. Not surprisingly, in April 1998 the Secretary of State issued a letter to all interested parties entitled *Lawyers out of Hospital, Doctors out of Court*, seeking 'ideas and suggestions' on three main areas:

- *what can we do to reduce the occurrence of events which give, or might give, rise to claims?*
- *what can we do to keep patients' expectations of the NHS reasonable?*
- *how can we improve further the way in which the NHS deals with clinical negligence claims when they do arise?*

(Department of Health 98/162, 29 April 1998)

In his review of civil justice and legal aid as a whole, Sir Peter Middleton proposed a no fault scheme which would have meant that patients would be compensated if they suffered harm, no matter what the reason. This would have removed the need to prove negligence which, according to Andrew Philips, whose analysis we cited last year, would have considerable advantages for both patients and professionals.

The notion of a no-fault scheme has had considerable support over the years. The BMA reiterated its support for this idea in a statement made in March 1998:

> The BMA has long advocated establishing a 'no fault' compensation scheme which would allow patients who have suffered a medical mishap to be compensated without the need to prove fault in court. However the BMA also believes that any such scheme, and any reform to the system of legal aid, should not prevent plaintiffs from taking their case to court to seek justice, if that is the route they wish to choose.

(*Legal Aid*, British Medical Association, Press Release, 4 March 1998)

The Secretary of State, however, rejected this approach:

> I am clear that, as in any other sphere, the NHS should only be expected to pay compensation where it can be shown that it has liability. My key objective is to ensure that the NHS spends as much of its money as it possibly can on direct patient care, and I cannot condone the use of that money to make payments where there is no legal obligation in respect of the injury being alleged. (98/162)

This rebuff begs the question of whether there *should* be such an obligation.

NHS Direct

First wave pilot areas:

Milton Keynes
Preston
Northumbria

Second wave pilot areas:

West Country
Manchester
Essex
West Yorkshire
Hull and East Yorkshire
Hampshire
Nottinghamshire
North West Lancashire
Birmingham and the Black Country
South London
Newcastle and the North East
West London
Buckinghamshire
Northamptonshire and Oxford

Source: Department of Health 98/322, 4 August 1998

Responsive services

The New NHS announced that there would be pilots of a new form of service, NHS Direct, a 24-hour advice line to provide easier and faster advice and information. The first round of pilots began in Preston, Milton Keynes and Northumbria in March 1998, and a second was announced in July 1998 to cover ten million people. The areas covered by the first and second wave are set out in the Box.

Subsequently, the Comprehensive Spending Review confirmed the White Paper's intention that they would be extended nationwide.

Although the details given as to the impact of the first-wave pilots were very limited – 80 callers put through to the ambulance service, some of whom would otherwise not have contacted it, and 1,500 given advice and reassurance and that enabled them to look after themselves – the Government hailed it as an immediate success, which justified the subsequent rapid expansion. Indeed, according to a statement issued in May 1998, lives had been saved.

The origins of NHS Direct can be found in the telephone access offered in some A&E departments. Although the means of access may be novel, it remains a professionally delivered service. Information technology can be used to change the nature of the relationship between professional and user entirely.

In October 1997 the first computerised self-treatment for psychiatric patients was announced. More conventionally in June 1998 the NHS Home Healthcare Guide was launched; this contains 'handy tips' for anyone with a minor illness or facing a sudden health problem at home. Over 2m were distributed but it remains to be seen whether this too will save lives.

Overall

We concluded last year's Review by suggesting that a fundamental change is slowing coming about between the NHS and its users. Further evidence of that is in the changes bearing on consent, in the proposed new survey of users and careers, in the release of clinical information and the changes in professional codes of behaviour, in the new R&D programme, the introduction of NHS Direct and the new Patient's Charter, when that materialises.

While these developments appear to have genuine promise, a pessimist might wonder what the implications for the user will be of the changes set out in Section 1.1, the central direction of priorities for purchasers and the growing central management of providers. This point is particularly apposite to the Government's policy on waiting lists. This commitment, which we consider further in Section 2.1, was not based on any serious analysis of what concerned users most – numbers waiting or time spent waiting – yet, it is being pursued relentlessly to the possible detriment of other objectives. Similarly, the King's Fund evidence cited above indicates that people want more choice – of consultants, GPs, types of treatment and other matters – but the proposals reviewed in Section 1.1 appear to be moving the other way.

We noted at the end of that section that Labour's new NHS appeared to be offering more scope to both the centre and the locality: equally, it appears to be offering more to the professionals and more to the users. As the King's Fund study demonstrates, professionals and users naturally enough do see things differently even though there are significant areas where their views are similar. What is hard to predict is how the various elements making for change in the NHS will interact and how the balance between user and provider will alter overall.

1.5 Clinical knowledge

The Conservative Government introduced a series of new policies bearing on the creation and application of clinical knowledge, including: the creation of a centrally guided R&D programme, the introduction of clinical audit and the general drive for clinically effective, or evidence-based, practice. The Labour Government has taken these a step further by placing greater emphasis on the effective application of clinical knowledge and backing this up with a system of clinical governance. While bearing ultimately on all the elements introduced earlier, it goes beyond them by bringing the quality of clinical care into a framework for accountability similar to that already introduced for finance. We consider first the proposals for each element of the new approach and then how they are to be brought together in the new process of clinical governance.

The New NHS sets out five routes to spread good practice and promote clinical and cost-effectiveness:

- by ensuring through the **Research and Development Programme** *the provision and dissemination of high quality scientific evidence on the cost-effectiveness and quality of care*
- by developing a programme of new **evidence-based National Service Frameworks** *setting out the patterns and levels of service which should be provided for patients with certain conditions*
- by establishing a new **National Institute of Clinical Excellence** *which will promote clinical and cost-effectiveness by producing clinical guidelines and audits, for dissemination throughout the NHS*
- by establishing a new **Commission for Health Improvement** *to support and oversee the quality of clinical governance and of clinical services*
- by working with the professions to strengthen the existing systems of **professional self-regulation.** (p.56)

Research & development

The Government inherited a set of arrangements for commissioning research within and for the NHS, which was designed to allow a central

direction of priorities to be imposed. One feature of the pattern of research spending which had grown up in the NHS in the absence of an effective central policy was that it was carried out within and largely served the needs of hospital care. In November 1997 the report of the National Working Group on Primary Care (*R&D in Primary Care*, NHS Executive 1997) was published and it was announced at the same time that the annual budget for research into primary care would be increased to £50m in steps of some £4–5m a year – a proposal already foreshadowed in announcements by the previous Government. The report argues that there is a substantial 'evidence gap' which the new programme should aim to fill:

2.3.2 The Working Group [believe] that there is a substantial 'evidence gap' which is limiting the provision of the highest quality care in relation to four areas of clinical activity in primary care:

- *the recognition and clinical management of the early presentation of disease;*
- *the clinical management of established disease treated predominantly in primary care;*
- *the clinical management of chronic disease (which again takes place predominantly in primary care);*
- *the assessment and clinical management of disease risk.*

These areas require research in a number of overlapping fields of scientific enquiry including the epidemiology and natural history of disease, screening, help-seeking behaviour, risk perception and management, preventive medicine, clinical examination and clinical investigation. (p.10)

The current level of resources devoted to primary care research was put at £31m or about 7 per cent of total spending. The report concludes that small shifts in the balance of R&D funding will have a major impact on primary care precisely because of the current low level of research effort in this area.

> *There is a serious mismatch between the financial and clinical importance to the NHS of decisions made in primary care and the available evidence and research capacity in this sector. The correct balance is unknown and we need to move in a measured way. We must not expand faster than is consistent with the achievement of high quality R&D, and we must take regular stock of return on investment. However, the need to begin to shift the balance is clear. (p.14)*

As noted last year, a start had been made to implementing the Culyer proposals for research financed and carried out within the NHS itself. However desirable change in the allocation of that finance might be, it risked destabilising the finances of those trusts heavily dependent on research funding. As the Committee noted:

> *The increase in NHS R&D annual expenditure on primary care from £25m to £50m will reduce NHS R&D expenditure on secondary care by about 5%. As most other research funding agencies spend less on primary care R&D than the NHS, increasing the proportion of resources devoted to primary care is unlikely to make a major impact on the resources available to hospital and laboratory based specialities. However, as many hospital research costs are fixed in the short term, sudden shifts in funding may be destabilising and where this is the case they should be avoided. (p.14)*

In December 1997, the first results of the new system of financing R&D in the NHS became apparent in changes in the allocation of those funds between trusts: about 60 no longer receive support and a similar number gained it. According to the letter from John Swales announcing the allocations:

> *R&D spending in the NHS is more visible and accountable. It is better able to respond to the needs of the NHS and external funders in line with the Strategic Framework for the Use of the R&D Levy, and its management has improved at all levels. I have been impressed by the progress described in many of the bids.*

> *This new funding system is a cornerstone of the R&D levy, but there are also significant funds being provided by the NHS R&D Programme budget. Allocations in this round have taken account of other funding available and we shall look to regional offices to advise on resources which might be available to support the development of new R&D capacity in NHS providers.*

> (Letter from Professor John Swales, Director of Research and Development to NHS Providers bidding for R&D Support Funding, dated 18 December 1997)

The shifts announced in this letter are, of course, only part of a much wider process, begun with the publication of *Research for All*, of making an effective link between the research that the NHS pays for and the needs of the Service. It will be many years before the benefits of the shifts in monies and the more explicit management and accountability arrangements emerge through the publication of the results of more relevant research than would otherwise have been undertaken. The extract from the White Paper suggests that this is one of the 'good bits' the new Government is happy to build on.

The New NHS indicates that the Government is content with the general policy but puts forward a small number of additions to it.

> *The NHS R&D programme already supports a major programme of research assessing the clinical and cost-effectiveness of health technologies. A new programme of work on service delivery and organisation will look at how care is organised. It will provide research-based evidence about how services can be improved to increase the quality of patient care. In addition, the NHS Executive will take a systematic approach to scanning the horizon for emerging clinical innovations. This will help to set research priorities, to provide information for planning services, and to identify the need for clinical and service guidelines which the new National Institute may be commissioned to develop. (p.57)*

Of particular note is the planned programme on service delivery and organisation, which reflects the recognition that the existing programme is geared too closely either to specific clinical interventions or to other narrowly defined topics. The result has been that the R&D programme has so far had very little to contribute to many of the issues facing the Service, such as arising from the pressures for change within the hospital service and, as we shall see next, the requirements of service planning.

Spending on R&D

Data collected by the Office for National Statistics and published in *Science, Engineering and Technology Statistics* allow spending on NHS R&D as well as the Department of Health and the Medical Research Council to be put in a national context (see Tables 1.11 (a) & (b)).

Table 1.11(a) Net Government expenditure on health R&D (1996/97), £m

MRC	277.7
DH	62.5
NHS	407.6
Total	**747.80**

Table 1.11(b) Government funding of net R&D by objectives (1996/97)

Agriculture, forestry & fishing	4.5
Industrial development	2.5
Energy	0.7
Infrastructure	1.7
Environmental protection	2.2
Health	14.5
Social development & services	2.1
Earth and atmosphere	1.7
Advancement of knowledge	29.7
Civil space	2.8
Defence	37.2
Not elsewhere classified	0.4
%	**100.0**
Total £m	**5,759.3**

Source: Science, Engineering and Technology Statistics 1998, Cm 4006, p.25

Table 1.12 Intramural expenditure on R&D performed in UK businesses (1996), £m

Broad product groups

Manufacturing: Total	6,943
Chemicals	626
Pharmaceuticals	1,852
Mechanical engineering	605
Electrical machinery	1,265
Transport equipment	997
Aerospace	812
Other manufacturing	896
Services	2,358
Total	**9,301**

Source: Science, Engineering and Technology Statistics 1998, Cm 4006, p.35

Table 1.13 R&D scoreboard: top UK companies ranked by R&D spend (1998)

	Rank	Current R&D spend £m	R&D spend as % of sales
Glaxo Wellcome	1	1,148	14.4
SmithKline Beecham	2	841	10.8
Zeneca	3	653	12.6
Unilever	4	546	1.8
General Electric	5	458	7.0
Shell	6	403	0.5
Ford Motor	7	338	4.9
Pfizer	8	313	99.1
British Aerospace	9	301	3.5
BT	10	291	1.9

Source: *Science, Engineering and Technology Statistics* 1998, Cm 4006, p.39

If we look at the private sector (Table 1.12), we find that the health-related expenditure is by far the largest industrial programme, and that predominance has been growing, either looked at by sector or by firm.

Even if spending by the Medical Research Council is added to the other publicly financed programme, the total is less than the in-house spend of one company, Glaxo Wellcome (see Table 1.13). The figures themselves do not prove there is an imbalance, but as David Melzer (Health policy and the scientific literature: what kinds of evidence should we expect to find? *Evidence-Based Health Policy and Management*, March 1998) has remarked:

> While 27 adequate trials are available to judge the effects of a single new drug for schizophrenia, Cochrane reviewers were able to find only four each on short vs. long admission

or community teams for people with severe mental illness. Indeed, in both of these latter reviews, drawing conclusions on core issues such as impact on clinical state, social functioning or carers was not possible …

> Detailed development studies of the many interventions, staff skills and organizational arrangements needed to support effective community care are sparse. In addition, development questions continually change: policy-makers must now ask what types of arrangements best fit the latest legislation and the new electronic technologies for communication and computerized case-notes, for example. These development questions are clearly at least as complex as finding the right chemical for the next new drug, yet the institutional support for exploring them has been largely absent.

Although attempts have been and continue to be made to demonstrate the benefits from research, none can be as convincing as the contribution of a successful drug to a company's bottom line and share price. As long as this is true, and there is no alternative in sight, the NHS R&D programme will continue to be the poor relation.

National Service Frameworks

The concept of a national framework is described in *The New NHS* as follows:

> 7.8 The Government will work with the professions and representatives of users and carers to establish clearer, evidence-based **National Service Frameworks** for major care areas and disease groups. That way patients will get greater consistency in the availability and quality of services, right across the NHS. The Government will use them as a way of being clear with patients about what they can expect from the health service.

7.9 The new approach to developing cancer services in the Calman-Hine Report, and recent action to ensure all centres providing children's intensive care meet agreed national standards, point the direction. In each case, the best evidence of clinical and cost-effectiveness is taken together with the views of users to establish principles for the pattern and level of services required. These then establish a clear set of priorities against which local action can be framed. The NHS Executive, working with the professions and others, will develop a similar approach to other services where national consistency is desirable. There will be an annual programme for the development of such frameworks starting in 1998. (p.57)

In April 1998, the Government announced that the next two national frameworks would be for mental health and coronary heart disease and set out a timetable designed to produce these frameworks by Spring 1999. The process by which each is reached is described in Health Service Circular 98/144 (16 April 1998) as follows:

9. Each National Service Framework will be developed with the assistance of an expert reference group which will bring together health professionals, service users and carers, health service managers, partner agencies, and other advocates. The reference groups will adopt an inclusive process to engage the full range of views. The Department of Health will support the reference groups and manage the overall process.

10. To set national standards and define service models, each National Service Framework will include an assessment of the health and social care needs to be addressed; the evidence on effective and efficient interventions and organisational arrangements; the present position and the issues to be tackled; resource implications; and the timescale for change.

National Service Frameworks

These will comprise the following elements:

- a definition of the scope of the Framework;
- the evidence base:
  - needs assessment
  - present performance
  - evidence of clinical and cost-effectiveness
  - significant gaps and pressures
- national standards, timescales for delivery;
- key interventions and associated costs;
- commissioned work to support implementation:
  - appropriate R&D, including through the NHS R&D programme (including Health Technology Assessments (HTAs))
  - appraisal
  - benchmarks
  - outcome indicators
- supporting programmes:
  - workforce planning
  - education and training
  - personal and organisational development (OD)
  - information development
- a performance management framework

Source: *A First Class Service,* Department of Health, 1998, p.27

The proposal for National Frameworks is targeted at a serious weakness present in the NHS since its foundation – the lack of capacity to design systematically how services should be provided. In *Health Care UK 1996/97* we used extracts from the Health Advisory Service relating to care for people suffering from brain injury to illustrate the lack of design facilities for particular care groups. The previous Government had acknowledged this failure in respect of cancer care by first appointing an expert group chaired by Sir Kenneth Calman and Dame Deirdre Hine and then accepting its findings for implementation. However, despite what the White Paper says, the Calman-Hine report can only be regarded as a precursor, rather than a model, since, as a 1997 King's Fund study, *The Workforce and Training Implications of the Calman/Hine Cancer Report*, showed, many of the elements of service planning were not covered, particularly the staffing and training implications.

Furthermore, the evidence base for their recommendations was far from complete, underlining the need for the new programme in service delivery and organisation. The proposals for the new Frameworks recognise this. *A First Class Service* sets out the elements of each framework (see Box).

This wide specification of the task, including the need to commission more research, represents an acknowledgement of the weaknesses of the earlier work which drew strong conclusions even while recognising that the knowledge base for its report was incomplete.

Already, however, another service framework, for paediatric intensive care, was being implemented. That had been brought into being in 1996 in response to the evident failure of the existing pattern of services, revealed in a report from the North West Regional Office in relation to Robert Geldard, a boy who eventually died in a Leeds hospital after failing to find admission to hospitals much closer to his home in Stockport. A subsequent report from the NHS Executive, *Paediatric Intensive Care: a framework for the future*, recommended increasing the number of beds and improving transport facilities. With the introduction of the explicit concept of a national service framework, a reporting and progress-

chasing process has been established for these proposals involving a range of requirements for regional offices, health authorities and hospitals to meet, including a five-year workforce plan.

The failure to identify a process for defining the right way (or ways) to provide individual services

The Future of Hospital Services: the Royal College of Surgeons' view

Emergency surgical services should be organised and financed for a population of 450-500,000 to enable:

- A consultant based emergency service

- 24-hour 7-day availability of operating and imaging facilities dedicated to emergencies

- Cost-effective use of expensive modern high technology equipment

- Optimum experience for surgical trainees in the care of emergencies within current legislation

- Integrated emergency ambulance services

- Admission of emergency patients to a unit with the skills and resources required.

This requires:

- Major expansion in the number of consultants

- Recognition by the public and politicians that it is not possible for each small local hospital to provide a satisfactory service for surgical emergencies.

Source: Royal College of Surgeons, *The Provision of Emergency Surgical Services,* June 1997, p.1

based on care groups is part of the wider issue of hospital configuration. During virtually all the previous Government's time in office this issue was ignored: it was also ignored in *The New NHS*. However, a number of reports have been published by the BMA, the royal colleges, the Standing Medical Advisory Group and the Scottish Office, which combine to suggest that major changes in configuration are required if quality of care is to be maintained or improved.

The pressures for change are particularly strong in respect of emergency surgery where increasing specialisation, on the one hand, and the perceived benefits of scale in terms of workload and of a 24-hour cover, on the other, inevitably lead to larger units (see Box).

Subsequently, the BMA, the Royal College of Physicians of London and the Royal College of Surgeons of England set up a joint working party, which reported in July 1998. The report, *Provision of Acute General Hospital Services*, restated the arguments for further hospital reconfiguration.

13.1 Comprehensive medical and surgical care of the highest quality requires the concentration of resources and skills into larger organisational units.

13.2 Smaller acute hospitals serving populations of 150,000 or less should not continue as independent clinical units. Where isolated, they would need to develop protocols for admission or transfer to neighbouring larger hospitals to ensure that patients receive care not compromised by lack of skills or resources.

13.3 It is no longer necessary or acceptable for consultants and their teams to feel obliged to undertake operations or care outside their field of expertise. (p.17)

This analysis has profound implications for hospital care in many parts of the country but, confirming Melzer's point, the R&D programme has virtually nothing to contribute to evaluating it. The typical project it supports is too narrowly focused to make a significant contribution to the wider debate about the future pattern of hospital provision. As a result, and as the report from the royal colleges acknowledges, it is not possible to demonstrate the nature and scale of the benefits that would ensue were hospitals restructured on the lines they suggest.

The National Institute of Clinical Excellence

The White Paper states that:

A new National Institute for Clinical Excellence will be established to give new coherence and prominence to information about clinical and cost-effectiveness. It will produce and disseminate:

- *clinical guidelines based on relevant evidence of clinical and cost-effectiveness*
- *associated clinical audit methodologies and information on good practice in clinical audit*
- *in doing so it will bring together work currently undertaken by the many professional organisations in receipt of Department of Health funding for this purpose.*

It will work to a programme agreed with and funded from current resources by the Department of Health. (p.58)

NICE, as the Institute has already come to be called, has a largely technical remit which as the extract indicates, tidies up and consolidates a large amount of existing activity.

The need for a tidying-up operation arises because, as *A First Class Service* argues, the present situation is confusing:

> There is currently no coherent approach to the appraisal of research evidence and the subsequent production of guidance for clinical practice. Guidance is issued by numerous bodies, at national, regional and local levels, each of which have different ways of appraising the evidence and developing recommendations. The status and implications of the products are not always clear, nor what actions are expected to follow as a result of them. (p.16)

NICE therefore will produce guidelines which can be applied nationally:

> 2.13 Guidance from NICE will include guidelines for the management of certain diseases or conditions and guidance on the appropriate use of particular interventions. Wherever appropriate, NICE guidance will cover all aspects of the management of a condition – from self care through to primary care, secondary care and more specialist services. (p.17)

The key innovation involved in NICE's role is described as follows:

> For the first time in the history of the NHS the Government, working with clinical bodies, will systematically appraise medical interventions before these are introduced into the NHS. Clear, authoritative, guidance on clinical and cost-effectiveness will be offered to front line clinicians. NICE will offer doctors, nurses and midwives more support than they have had before in making the complex decisions about individual patient care often required in modern health care. That support will enhance the ability of individual clinicians to make such

decisions. It will also inform the decisions of those commissioning care. (p.22)

The intention is to set it up as a special health authority accountable to the Secretary of State with its own Board and Partners' Council. At the time of writing, precise proposals had not emerged.

The Commission for Health Improvement

The Commission, widely known as CHIMP, is to be established as an independent statutory body directly accountable to the Secretary of State. Its role is described in *A First Class Service* as follows:

> To ensure the drive for excellence is instilled throughout the NHS, the Government will create a new Commission for Health Improvement. It will complement the introduction of clinical governance arrangements. Past performance on quality has been variable and the health service has sometimes been slow to detect and act decisively on serious lapses in quality. As a statutory body, at arm's length from Government, the new Commission will offer an independent guarantee that local systems to monitor, assure and improve clinical quality are in place. It will support local development and 'spot-check' the new arrangements. It will also have the capacity to offer targeted support on request to local organisations facing specific clinical problems. (p.58)

Unlike NICE, CHIMP has a monitoring role, the force of which turns on the enforcement mechanisms to be used to follow up the identification of poor performance. The Commission is not intended to replace existing NHS performance and management procedures but to reinforce them. Its role is to:

- *provide national leadership to develop and disseminate clinical governance principles;*
- *independently scrutinise local clinical governance arrangements to support, promote and deliver high quality services, through a rolling programme of local reviews of service providers;*
- *undertake a programme of service reviews to monitor national implementation of National Service Frameworks, and review progress locally on implementation of these frameworks and NICE guidance;*
- *help the NHS identify and tackle serious or persistent clinical problems. The Commission will have the capacity for rapid investigation and intervention to help put these right;*
- *over time, increasingly take on responsibility for overseeing and assisting with external incident inquiries. (p.52)*

It is also envisaged that the Commission will have a trouble-shooting role:

> *There may be cases where there is an unacceptable delay in putting serious problems right, or a persistent failure to act. In such cases, the Secretary of State for Health (or Health Authorities for Primary Care Trusts) will be able to ask the Commission to investigate the problem and make recommendations for rapid action. This will usually happen only where there are very serious concerns about the quality of clinical services. NHS organisations will be required to release information that will assist the Commission in its investigation. (p.58)*

Through these activities, CHIMP should emerge as a clinically focused external auditor of the NHS, building on and extending the roles of the existing auditors, particularly the Clinical Standards Advisory Group and the Audit Commission.

Professional self-regulation

Athough the proposals in the White Paper can be seen as a challenge to the professions, the White Paper itself emphasises their continuing role:

> *But the Government will continue to look to individual health professionals to be responsible for the quality of their own clinical practice. Professional self-regulation must remain an essential element in the delivery of quality patient services. It is crucial that the professional standards developed nationally continue to be responsive to changing service needs and to legitimate public expectations. The Government will continue to work with the professions, the regulatory bodies, the NHS and patient representative groups to strengthen the existing systems of professional self-regulation by ensuring that they are open, responsive and publicly accountable. (p.59)*

A *First Class Service* effectively challenges the professions to put their house in order:

> *Recent events have dented public confidence in the quality of clinical care provided by the NHS. The challenge for the professions is to demonstrate that professional self-regulation can continue to enjoy public confidence. If this confidence is to be restored, our systems of professional self-regulation must be modernised and strengthened to ensure that they are:*
>
> - *open to public scrutiny;*
> - *responsive to changing clinical practice and service needs;*
> - *publicly accountable for professional standards set nationally, and the action taken to maintain these standards. (p.47)*

As Rudolf Klein notes elsewhere in this volume, the medical profession has, in the Bristol case, accepted the need to demonstrate such accountability. The planned publication of clinical performance indicators is a step in that direction: so too are the plans, announced in June 1998 (98/225), to require all relevant clinicians to participate in the hitherto voluntary audits, the National Confidential Enquiry into Perioperative Deaths, the Confidential Enquiry into Stillbirths and Deaths in Infancy, the Confidential Enquiry into Maternal Deaths and the Confidential Enquiry into Suicide and Homicide by People with Mental Illness.

Clinical governance

Perhaps the main innovation, however, lies in what has come to be termed 'clinical governance'. The White Paper points in different directions, but the overall message is clear: the Government is seeking to ensure that the measures set out above are reflected in the day-to-day working of the Service:

> *Professional and statutory bodies have a vital role in setting and promoting standards, but shifting the focus towards quality will also require practitioners to accept responsibility for developing and maintaining standards within their local NHS organisations. For this reason the Government will require every NHS Trust to embrace the concept of 'clinical governance' so that quality is at the core, both of their responsibilities as organisations and of each of their staff as individual professionals.* (p.47)

To ensure that clinical governance is in fact embraced at this level, NHS and primary care trusts will be given a statutory duty in respect of the quality of services they provide. Furthermore they will be required to ensure that proper processes are in place for assuring quality inside their trusts, that one person, accountable to the chief executive and board is nominated to develop clinical governance and that annual progress reports are published.

The Guidance issued on the development of Primary Care Groups complements these proposals. It states that:

> *Each Primary Care Group should appoint a senior doctor or nurse to take responsibility at board level to ensure that a proper process for clinical governance is in place. That person will therefore take responsibility for formulation of an agreed action plan. Each practice within the Primary Care Group will also wish to ensure that one person is remitted to take forward the plan. Individual practices may wish to, and the Primary Care Group will, show what action has followed Clinical Governance principles through an Annual Accountability Agreement.* (p.30)

Taken together these proposals signal the Government's intention to tackle clinical issues head on and to move much further and faster than the previous Government in holding clinicians responsible for the use of the resources at their disposal.

Overall

The measures set out here can be seen as the logical culmination of what now appears to be timid steps taken by the previous Government to make clinical audit a routine process as part of the 1990 reforms. The notion that care should wherever possible be evidence-based and that processes should be in place to ensure that it is delivered to an appropriate standard of quality now appear scarcely worth debating. For all that, while the direction may be clear, the agenda remains large.

At all levels, however, there are obstacles to rapid progress. At national level, the definition, introduction and interpretation of indicators of clinical performance represents a considerable technical task. Equally, the development of National Service Frameworks. As the announcement of the first two proposed frameworks indicates, the knowledge gaps despite the R&D programme remain. That programme continues to be dominated by areas of research and styles of investigation which do not meet the requirements of such frameworks, or, as we have noted, others such as hospital configuration. The new programme is a step in the right direction, but it may prove difficult to execute it promptly given the scarcity of relevant skills and the risks of destabilising existing institutions.

At local level, an interim report from the King's Fund programme PACE (*Turning Evidence into Everyday Practice*, M Dunning *et al.*, King's Fund, London, 1998) confirmed the findings reported last year that progress will be slow. The report focuses on a series of distinct clinical areas and looks at the process of effecting change within each. While the report shows that change can be achieved, the process is far from straightforward. There are a large number of general barriers to change, which require a sustained effort to overcome:

- lack of perception of relevance;
- lack of resources;
- short-term outlook;
- conflicting priorities;
- the difficulty in measuring outcomes;
- lack of necessary skills;
- no history of multi-disciplinary working;
- limitations of the research evidence on effectiveness;

- perverse incentives;
- intensity of contribution required.

Experience with clinical audit echoes these findings. We have cited in previous Reviews evidence from academic studies and also from the National Audit Office about the impact of clinical audit. A recent study (*The Clinical Audit Programme in England: achievements and challenges*, R C Fraser and R Baker, Audit Trends, Vol 5, December 1997) concludes that:

> *Mistakes have undoubtedly been made, and with the benefit of hindsight, it is clear now that early expectations were over-optimistic. It was not appreciated sufficiently that it takes time to 'change the culture' especially against a backdrop of so many other changes within the NHS. Nevertheless, the quality drive within the NHS is now established and is, in our view, irreversible. The main practical problem remains a perceived, and often real, lack of time to become involved in audit. Since initiatives will increasingly have to be 'resource neutral', this calls for clear leadership and more focused involvement in audit than has hitherto been the case.* (p.134)

The measures set out above are perhaps the most important, as far as the NHS is concerned, of all the Government's proposals, in that for the first time, the question of clinical performance has been put at the centre stage. But while that may be its rightful position in a 'modern' health service, there are many obstacles lying in the way of rapid progress. The rhetoric of *The New NHS* and *A First Class Service* ignores what Steve Gillam termed, in his review of the clinical governance proposals (*Implementing the White Paper: pitfalls and opportunities*, edited by Rudolf Klein, King's Fund 1998) 'the dearth of evidence to underpin the settings of standards in many areas of *clinical endeavour'* and ignores the complexity of the notion of quality at which its proposals aim. Furthermore, it is not based on any understanding – because no such understanding exists – of the links between the structural issues surrounding hospital configuration, the size and role of community trusts, and other 'macro' features of the NHS such as the structure of clinical specialisation and the definition of professional roles, and the practice of the individual clinician. That agenda still remains to be systematically tackled.

Part 2 Commentary

As in previous years, the second part of the Policy Review assesses developments within three broad headings: Efficiency and Finance, Equity, and Accountability.

2.1 Efficiency and finance

In July 1997, the new Government announced that it would conduct a comprehensive spending review of all public spending programmes. Although in principle the review was 'zero-based', in fact, it was founded on some fixed points. Before the results were announced a year later, the Government made it clear that it intended to maintain the financial basis of the NHS as it was.

The New NHS bluntly asserts that:

> *The NHS funded through general taxation is the fairest and most efficient way of providing health care for the population at large. Systems in other countries cost more, are less fair, and deliver little overall extra benefit. The cost-effectiveness of the NHS helps to reduce the tax burden to well below the European Union average, encouraging investment and strengthening incentives to work and save.*

> *The alternatives – rationing or a 'charge-based' system – would dissipate these advantages.* (p.9)

Despite this commitment to a publicly funded health service, the Government came to power having stated it would maintain public spending within the limits set by the previous Government's expenditure plans, which would have implied virtually no increase in real-terms spending on the NHS. It appeared at the time of the election that the spending figures were incompatible with the Government's stated objectives for the NHS.

In the event, although the overall commitment was retained, gradually extra funds were found, beginning with an extra £269m in England for use in the winter of 1997/98. In July 1997 the Chancellor announced that the NHS in England would enjoy an increase of £1bn in 1998/99 and that was increased by some £417m in the March 1998 Budget. These increases were still modest by historic standards. Anything more substantial, for health as for other programmes, had to wait on the results of the comprehensive review of all spending programmes. The terms of reference for the health programme are set out in the Box.

By the time the March 1998 Budget announcement was made, the public finances looked much healthier than they had been when the Government came to power and hence there appeared to be scope for a more rapid increase in spending on the NHS. However, in June 1998, the Chancellor issued a consultation document, *Fiscal Policy: current and capital spending*, which argued that the conduct of fiscal policy had in the past been 'imprudent and not in the national interest'. In particular:

- decisions did not accurately reflect how future generations would have to pay for current public spending;
- the arrangements were widely seen as biased against capital spending, and tended to encourage cutbacks in capital rather than current spending;
- structural deficits were not identified sufficiently quickly to be tackled without significant costs.

In respect specifically of the NHS, the document makes two significant points:

- that practices in the past had led to investment cutbacks and a backlog in maintenance;
- that within the proposed fiscal framework the case for the private finance initiative rests purely in value-for-money terms, not in terms of a temporary reduction in public sector borrowing.

We return to both these points later in this section.

The implication of this new policy for public spending as a whole was that there would be no immediate bonanza. Instead, any surplus of revenues over spending would be used to reduce the level of Government indebtedness relative to gross domestic product. In fact, the public finances are still not strong enough to allow debt repayments and no sooner had the Chancellor made his announcement than doubts about the performance of the economy began to grow.

Terms of Reference for Comprehensive Spending Review in the Department of Health

Review NHS objectives and the services that are provided, so that the Government's objectives for health services continue to be met.

Review the funding of the NHS.

Assess how the components of the health programme contribute to the Government's wider objectives.

Examine the contribution of the Health Service to the economy as a whole.

Examine how best to improve equity of access to health care.

Examine how to modernise the Health Service, including the future roles of primary care, community and acute secondary services and social services.

Carry out a rigorous scrutiny of the scope for increasing value for money through better economy, efficiency and effectiveness, including through better use of assets and public/private partnerships.

Examine each element of spending on non-front-line budgets, including management costs.

Review social services objectives, effectiveness and value for money in the light of the Government's overall objectives.

How much the NHS would get as a result of the comprehensive spending review became apparent in July. By the time the Chancellor made his statement in July 1998, there was widespread anticipation that the NHS would, despite the cautious fiscal policy announced a month earlier, get a substantial increase. In the event, the Chancellor surprised everyone by announcing an increase of £21bn over the coming three years for the NHS in the UK as a whole.

Unfortunately, appearances were deceptive; the figure of £21bn – of which £18bn was for England – was reached by summing the increases in cash terms over three years over the estimated figure for 1998/99, a unique and confusing method of presentation. Nevertheless the plans announced for the years 1999–2001 represented a much larger increase, 4.7 per cent in real terms (i.e. adjusted for the general level of inflation), than in the Government's first two years in office and more than the Conservatives in their last term: see Table 2.1.

The forecast growth in capital spending is particularly marked, but such a rapid increase is in line with the analysis in the Treasury paper that NHS capital expenditure had suffered in the past from the pressure on the current account. As the paper also proposed that in future there should be a strict division between capital and revenue spending, the prospect for a substantial growth in capital spending appears a real one, provided that the contribution of privately financed schemes grows as fast as the figures assume. The previous Government had been overconfident of how much capital spending could be financed in this way, but, as we report below, the new Government has taken effective steps to remove the barriers to the introduction of private finance into NHS hospital building.

Soon after the Chancellor's announcement, the Treasury Select Committee issued a report, *The New Fiscal Framework: the Comprehensive Spending Review* (The Stationery Office, 1998), which was critical of the Chancellor's assumptions.

Table 2.1 NHS current spending: England (£m)

	1996/97	*1997/98*	*1998/99*	*1999/00*	*2000/01*	*2001/02*
Total (£m)	33,023	34,681	36,507	39,581	42,415	45,179
Annual increase (%)	–	2.3	2.3	5.7	4.5	3.9

Source: Health Service Circular 98/131

Table 2.2 NHS capital spending: England (£m)

	1996/97	*1997/98*	*1998/99*	*1999/00*	*2000/01*	*2001/02*
Total (£m)	1,341	1,107	1,854	2,272	2,722	2,910
Annual increase (%)	–	–21.1	67.4	19.4	16.9	4.3
Private Finance (£m est.)	65	55	310	610	740	690

Source: Health Service Circular 98/131

In particular the report argued that he had not demonstrated that the plans could be sustained if growth in the economy as a whole did not match up to what was forecast. Furthermore, it found the evidence given by the Chancellor and by the Chief Secretary on the way that budgets would be adjusted, if inflation was higher than forecast, to be in conflict. The former appeared to be ruling out any cash increases, while the latter appeared to acknowledge, as did the Comprehensive Spending Review itself, that there would be, if inflation turned out to have been significantly underestimated.

The implication for health authorities and trusts is that there is a possibility the purchasing power of the funds they are allocated will not be as large as the Chancellor suggested. Furthermore, they may find themselves having to award higher-than-average pay increases in order to retain and attract the staff they will need.

As we see below, the Government had already recognised a need to increase the clinical workforce. Two days after the Chancellor's statement, the Secretary of State announced how the extra money allocated to the health budget was to be used. The statement was very broadbrush: 7,000 more doctors, 15,000 more nurses, 3m more patients treated, 1,000 GP surgeries to be improved, 30 more new hospitals. He followed this by announcing that there would be an extra 1,000 medical students every year up to 2005, in addition to the extra 7,000 doctors.

What is striking about this list is its lack of structure, or indeed justification or explanation. On this basis it would seem that the Comprehensive Spending Review has produced nothing substantive as to how savings might be made other than through the established formula

of reducing management costs and nothing as to where extra money could be used to best effect.

Moreover, the crudity of this announcement seemed at odds with another of the Chancellor's innovations. In making his announcement the Chancellor indicated that the Treasury would be looking, in respect of each spending programme, for 'service agreements' – quasi contracts between Treasury as financier and Departments as spending agencies. The Comprehensive Spending Review, the results of which were announced for health and other programmes in *Modern Public Services for Britain: investing in reform* (Cm 4011, The Stationery Office, 1998), indicates that:

> *Progress will be monitored by a process of continuous scrutiny and audit, overseen by a Cabinet Committee.* (p.35)

Modern Public Services goes on:

> *The Government is determined to improve the effectiveness of public services. As part of the new public service agreements, each Government department will be set new quality standards:*
>
> - *key targets have been set for each department spelling out what will be delivered by the end of the Parliament;*
> - *Departmental Investment Strategies will ensure that capital investment will be carried out efficiently and deliver the maximum economic and social benefits; and*
> - *the Output and Performance Analysis produced by each department to prepare for Resource Accounting and Budgeting will help to demonstrate the extent to which objectives are being achieved, the quantity and quality of outputs delivered and the efficiency of resource use.* (p.36)

In line with this approach, the Review announced a £5bn modernisation fund as part of the additional £18bn for health. Details of how the fund would be deployed were not announced at the time. However, *Modern Public Services* indicates that the Department had agreed a series of targets to be met by the end of the Parliament in return for the extra spending. These were:

- to reduce NHS waiting lists to 100,000 below the level the Government inherited;
- to begin to reduce avoidable illness, disease and injury, which will result in time in lower death rates from heart disease and stroke, cancer and suicide, and a reduction in health inequalities;
- to improve co-operation between the NHS, social services and other services, which will strengthen the focus on patients' needs, and help to reduce the rate of growth in emergency admissions to an average of 3 per cent a year over the next five years for people over 75;
- for children in care, improve the educational achievement, increasing from 25 per cent to at least 50 per cent the proportion of children leaving care at 16 or later with GCSE or GNVQ qualifications.

What is not made clear is how the Cabinet oversight is to be exercised and how sanctions would be imposed on a poorly performing department. If waiting lists refused to come down would that be a signal for cuts in the NHS budget?

Financial strains

The announcement in July 1998 of extra money for the NHS for the coming three years was welcome news for an NHS which had felt under extreme financial pressure towards the end of the Conservatives' period of office. In July 1997, the National Audit Office published its report on the NHS accounts for 1995/96, which drew attention to widespread financial difficulties in that year. In the following year the pattern was repeated (see Table 2.3).

The NHS (England) Summarised Accounts 1996/97 list health authorities and trusts with cumulative deficits greater than 5 per cent of income (see Table 2.4).

Table 2.3 Financial performance of NHS trusts, 1996–97

Duties achieved	Number of trusts achieving duty	% of trusts achieving duty	% failing due to technicalities or immateriality	% failing for non-technical reasons
All 3 duties	155	36.1	28.7	n/a
Required return	208	48.5	20.5	31.0
Break-even on income and expenditure	292	68.1	11.4	20.5
EFL	412	96.0	2.3	1.7

Source: The Government's Expenditure Plans 1998–1999, Department of Health, Cm 3912, April 1998, p.61

Table 2.4 Health authorities with cumulative deficits greater than 5 per cent of income as at 31 March 1997

Health authority	Accumulated deficit as a percentage of total income in 1996/97	Accumulated deficit as at 31 March 1997 (£m)
West Surrey	10.7	40.5
Wakefield	8.5	17.8
Enfield and Haringey	7.9	25.5
Redbridge and Waltham Forest	7.3	21.8
North and East Devon	7.3	21.4
East Kent	6.6	24.9
North Essex	6.5	31.5
Barking and Havering	5.9	14.2
Ealing, Hammersmith and Hounslow	5.7	26.8
Newcastle and North Tyneside	5.2	16.7
West Hertfordshire	5.1	15.9
Kingston and Richmond	5.1	10.5

Source: Health authority accounts 1996/97

The Comptroller and Auditor General notes in his commentary on the accounts that the duty on trusts to break even can be met by doing so over a three-year period (in exceptional circumstances longer) and that, where accumulated deficits are due to non-recurring factors, they may not have to be recovered. Even so the number of trusts facing what the Executive considered to be *serious* financial difficulties at the end of 1996/97 had risen to 54, but the total trust deficit, after technical adjustment, had fallen over the previous year. Tables 2.4 and 2.5 report the deficit for the trusts and health authorities in the most serious trouble.

Service strains

In the winter of 1996/97, as we noted last year, a larger than usual number of elective operations had to be cancelled to maintain emergency services. In order to avoid a repeat of these events the Secretary of State set out in October 1997 a strategy for winter pressures which provided for:

- *increasing staffing levels at times of peak pressure and extra opening hours to cope with medical emergencies during the winter months*
- *more rehabilitation and recuperation services, home care, and extra places in care homes, to reduce delays in discharging patients from hospital*
- *more specialist nursing and therapy – particularly for older people – in their own homes and in care homes to reduce the need for people to be admitted to hospital in the first place.*

(Department of Health 97/290, 21 October 1997)

The announcement also referred to a Department of Health Executive letter, *Better Services for Vulnerable People*, issued on better care for elderly people to health and social services. As noted in Section 1.3, the Letter emphasises three priorities:

Table 2.5 NHS trusts with cumulative deficits greater than 5 per cent of total income as at 31 March 1997

NHS trust	Accumulated deficit as percentage of total income in 1996/97 (%)	Accumulated deficit as at 31 March 1997 (£m)
Liverpool Women's Hospital	13.2	3.8
Royal United Hospital, Bath	10.3	7.5
South Warwickshire General Hospitals	9.5	4.3
Greenwich Healthcare	8.6	8.2
United Leeds Teaching Hospitals	8.3	17.0
Anglian Harbours	8.1	2.5
Scarborough and NE Yorkshire	8.0	5.1
Humberside Ambulance	8.0	1.1
Dorset Community	8.0	2.6
Sheffield Children's Hospital	7.7	2.2
Swindon and Marlborough	7.2	5.0
South Manchester University Hospital	6.8	10.6
Horizon	6.6	2.2
Pinderfields Hospitals	6.6	4.5
Wellhouse	6.5	5.4
Airedale	6.4	4.3
Trecare	6.4	0.8
Forest Healthcare	5.7	7.0
The Royal West Sussex	5.7	2.6
East Anglian Ambulance	5.7	1.5
Royal National Orthopaedic	5.5	2.0
West Dorset General Hospitals	5.3	2.6
Poole Hospitals	5.1	3.4

Source: Trust accounts 1996/97

- *effective Joint Investment Plans for services to meet the continuing and community care needs of local populations*
- *improved multidisciplinary assessments of older people in both hospital and community health care settings*
- *development of recuperation and rehabilitation services for older people by health and social services.*

(EL97 (62))

As noted already in Section 1.2, these measures were designed to promote a 'whole systems'

approach across the health and social services divide. In the event, winter 1997/98 was mild and that, combined with the measures the Government took to promote more effective local planning – not only within health but within social services as well – led to a much easier winter for the hospital service than in previous years. The number of cancelled operations fell by 12 per cent in the period January to March 1998 relative to the same period in the previous year.

As far as elective care was concerned, however, the pressure on the Service grew. As noted in Section 1.4, the Government had made a

Measures to improve the health care system

Family Doctor and Other Primary Care Services

- Initiatives aimed at reducing the need for hospital admission in the first place and enabling appropriate self-care by providing care closer to home
- Improved primary care management of patients on waiting lists
- Help prevent unnecessary re-admissions

Community Services

- Supporting the planned increase in elective hospital activity by securing additional community health and social services
- Preventing or reducing hospital admissions and streamlining the admissions process
- Organising rapid response care teams in the community
- Enabling people to return to their homes and communities by supporting early discharge from hospital with intermediate care and intensive rehabilitation schemes.

Source: Department of Health, Press Release 98/190, 18 May 1998

manifesto commitment to reducing numbers waiting for elective care by treating 100,000 more patients. Unfortunately, numbers waiting rose throughout 1997 and continued to rise in 1998 up to the end of April.

As with the extra finance for dealing with 'winter pressures', the Government made money available in March specifically for the reduction of waiting lists for elective care. A first tranche of some £288m was allocated in April for treating more patients. A further £32m was held back as a performance fund to reward health authorities meeting their target for cutting their lists. In May 1998, a further £65m was allocated to primary community mental health and social services, in ways which were aimed at reducing pressure on hospital facilities, in another attempt to promote a whole systems view (see Box).

These measures were backed by an unprecedented statement from the Secretary of State that implied

he would sack trust non-executives where targets – to be determined for each trust – were not delivered. To ram the message home, all trust and health authority chief executives and chairs were summoned to Richmond House to hear the message in person. To support their efforts, in November 1997, Stephen Day was appointed leader of a national waiting list action team, and in April 1998, Peter Homa, Chief Executive of Leicester Royal Infirmary, was appointed 'list buster' with a specific remit to spread good practice but with no executive authority.

In May 1998 the Secretary of State set out regional targets for waiting-list reductions, giving regional offices the task of converting these to trust level targets. Referring to the £32m, the Secretary of State indicated it would be used as a 'carrot and stick'. The 'carrot' is in the form of extra money for health authorities on targets for cutting their lists by the agreed amounts – they could receive a further 10 per cent of their initial

Table 2.6 Targets for waiting list reductions

Region	Target reduction compared with: March 1997	March 1998	Region	Target reduction compared with: March 1997	March 1998
Northern and Yorkshire	-2.0%	-9.4%	South & West	-0.7%	-10.4%
Trent	-6.0%	-11.7%	West Midlands	0.0%	-18.3%
Anglia and Oxford	0.0%	-12.9%	North West	-4.3%	-10.3%
North Thames	-2.6%	-17.6%	England	-2.1%	-13.1%
South Thames	-0.1%	-14.6%			

Source: Department of Health 92/200

allocation. The 'stick' is to be used where targets are not being met. In this case extra money will be used for remedial action, which might include sending in managers and clinicians who have proved themselves successful in getting lists down.

By the end of March 1998 no patients in England had waited more than 18 months for treatment (not allowing for waiting to be seen at outpatient clinics) and just before the NHS 50th anniversary conference, the Secretary of State revealed that for the first time since Labour came to power, numbers on the list had fallen, albeit by a small amount. The figures released at the end of August, covering the three months May, June and July, showed the numbers on the list had fallen by 45,000 and activity had risen over the corresponding three months of last year by 83,000 cases.

But while this announcement seemed to suggest that the Government's policies were proving successful, were they in fact aiming at the right target? The Government's policy of targeting the numbers waiting was criticised by outsider commentators, including the King's Fund and the medical profession. All were agreed that waiting times were important together with the observance of clinical priorities. Unfortunately,

the Government reaffirmed its commitment to numbers both in the Comprehensive Spending Review and in the Prime Minister's speech to the NHS 50th anniversary conference. As Jack Kneeshaw shows elsewhere in this volume, the Prime Minister was right in that speech to argue that people were fed up with waiting. However, the public does appear to be able to distinguish waiting from list numbers: in effect therefore the Government is pursuing a target of interest to no one but itself.

Experience in other countries, and indeed experience with a similar initiative under the previous Government (which came to be called, however, the 'waiting times initiative'), suggests that list numbers can be made to fall by targeted action, but they tend to rise once the targeted effort is relaxed. And they do so even if a higher level of elective work is sustained.

If the Government does pursue a reduction backed by the sanctions it seems prepared to impose, it may be that list numbers will continue to fall. The Service will adapt by, for example, introducing delays before patients are added to the list as well as carrying out more operations. If, however, numbers remain stubbornly high, the risk is that the Government will introduce even more draconian measures, the costs of which, in financial terms and in terms of the distortions to clinical priorities which might result and diversion of effort from other objectives, may be very high.

Supplementary finance

Despite its commitment to a tax-funded service, the Government took the opportunity to benefit from the National Lottery to the tune of £300m to finance healthy living centres. The scheme will be run by the New Opportunities Fund provided for in the Lottery Reform Bill. The aim of the centres is described in Section 1.3.

In December 1997 the Secretary of State announced that serious attempts would be made to ensure that the provision of the 1988 Road Traffic Act, which allows the NHS to charge for treatment of accident victims, would be exploited.

Capital finance

The figures set out above in Table 2.3 indicate that the Government plans to increase both the absolute level of spending on health capital and the proportion of capital spent financed directly from private sources. However, by the time Labour came to power, no substantial scheme had been financed in this way. The Conservative Government had tried but failed to finance a major hospital scheme through the Private Finance Initiative, despite last-minute attempts to do so before the Election.

The key stumbling block was the finance community's continuing concern that contracts with trusts were not secure. The National Health Service (Private Finance) Act 1997 received the Royal Assent in July. This effectively removed the

fears of the financiers that the security of lending would depend on the financial state of the specific trust and opened the way for the schemes already in the pipeline to move ahead.

Financial arrangements for the first major scheme, at Dartford and Gravesham were announced later that month. In the same month, the Government announced that 14 hospital schemes would go ahead at a total cost of £1.3bn. A further scheme was added in September in Greenwich and then a further 11 schemes were announced in April 1998, four of them in London, following the recommendation of the Turnberg review. The announcement notes that:

> *these schemes will be given intensive support with a view to advertising for private sector partners during the coming year.*

(Department of Health 98/134, 7 April 1998)

We noted last year the process by which hospital schemes were being developed in a haphazard manner. All these schemes had, however, been subject to a prioritisation process, via the NHS Capital Prioritisation Advisory Group established in December 1997 to meet that objection. In London the Turnberg review played that role. However, both groups could only deal with the schemes put forward to them to consider: they could not set the terms on which schemes should be prepared and hence to impose their priorities on the process of capital planning as a whole.

When making his announcement in July 1997 (Department of Health, 97/127), the Minister Alan Milburn said that there would be action on three fronts to improve the Private Finance Initiative:

Capital Prioritisation Advisory Group: terms of reference

- To select those schemes with a capital cost of £25m or more which should be recommended to ministers for development.

- To agree a methodology for selection that ensures that only schemes satisfying the demands of Health Service need are recommended.

- To agree the criteria against which Health Service need will be assessed by the regional offices.

- To ensure that schemes are only recommended for development if they are affordable nationally without adverse cost to other priorities and/or there is sufficient market capacity.

Source: Department of Health, 97/380

- secure the market, by getting some schemes through all the stages required to allow building to commence;
- improve the process through standardised documents and procedures, and by providing better support to NHS trusts;
- develop the product – a more fundamental review looking into value for money, innovation, affordability and non-acute fields, such as primary care and mental health.

Given the policy, all three are clearly desirable. It is generally recognised among those involved in the first round of schemes that the process was wasteful because, for example, the same contractual problems were addressed in several different sets of negotiations.

But while measures to standardise and streamline procedures should reduce the costs of negotiating a schemes they do little to justify the policy itself. As noted above, the Treasury Statement on private finance indicated that its prime test was value for money, not the temporary reduction of the public sector borrowing requirement. At the time of the announcements mentioned above, no such evidence had been presented.

However, in evidence to the Health Committee, the Department provided figures designed to show the scale of the benefits achieved by the first few hospital schemes. The figures reveal that the direct financial benefits are modest (see Table 2.7).

At the request of the Committee, the Department provided further information about the composition of these figures. In the case of Carlisle, for example, the public sector comparator turns out to be substantially cheaper before risk is allowed for. Once this is included, the balance tips the other way. The same is true of other schemes. The submission does not explain how the risk premium in the public sector is calculated but it would seem from the overall

Table 2.7 Public and private capital costs

	Public cost £m	Private cost £m
S Bucks	169	162
Norwich	1,681	1,642
Carlisle	174	173
Dartford and Gravesham	943	928
Calderdale	1,235	1,223
Bishop Auckland	60	58

Source: House of Commons Health Committee. *Public Expenditure on Health & Social Services.* The Stationery Office, 1997.

figures that the main innovation effected by the Private Finance Initiative is the treatment of public sector risk. Without that, there would be no case for financing hospitals in this way. That judgement ignores the other benefits claimed for the private finance initiative such as innovation in design and lower running costs but there is no substantial evidence for either.

As noted above, the Chancellor's statement on fiscal policy says clearly that the merits of using private finance are to be judged solely by whether it offers value for money for the NHS, not because it reduces the public sector borrowing requirement. It becomes all the more imperative therefore that evidence for its effectiveness in these terms is made available.

Management costs

In opposition Labour pledged to cut back bureaucracy: in May 1997 measures were announced designed to produce an immediate saving of £100m. In December 1997, a further cut of £80m was announced comprising:

Department of Health running costs	£7m
Health authority management costs	£12m
Trust management costs	£36m
GP fundholder management allowances	£25m

(Department of Health, 97/414, 22 December 1997)

The New NHS pledged that £1bn would be saved over the life of the Parliament – another figure like the £21bn cited above, which comprises a cumulation of gains over three years. Even so, it represents a sizeable slice out of the existing spending levels.

The main source of that saving is intended to be a reduction in transaction costs, i.e. the administrative costs incurred between trusts and fundholders and the reduction resulting from the proposal to make contracts (service agreements) last for three years, rather than one. From the trust viewpoint, there should be scope for reducing the administrative and billing costs associated with dealing with a large number of fundholding practices where fundholding has been the norm.

However, the scope for management cost reductions in the commissioning process is less clear. The White Paper recognises that primary care groups will need management support. An allowance of some £3 per head is to be included in an aggregate figure set for health authorities and primary care groups combined. This figure is less than the costs incurred by the total purchasing pilots started under the Conservatives despite the substantial increase in responsibilities that the switch from total purchasing pilots to primary care groups entails.

Overall, trust and health authority management costs were planned to fall in 1997/98 by 4 per cent in real terms from the 1996/97 total of £1.68bn according to *Health Authority Costs and Management Costs in NHS Trusts: financial year 1996/97 and planned costs for 1997/98* (NHS Executive, 1997). The Comprehensive Spending Review confirmed the Government's intention to take £1bn out of management costs over three years. As noted already, this policy sits oddly with the vastly enlarged agenda which management within the NHS will have to deal with.

Fraud

As part of its efforts to make every pound spent on the NHS pay in terms of patient care, the

Government launched a campaign against fraud, particularly within community-based services. In June 1997 the results of an efficiency scrutiny into prescription fraud were published *NHS Prescription Fraud* (Department of Health, 1997). This concluded that evasion of patient charges, e.g. through false claims for exemption or identity, theft or alteration of valid forms, might cost between £70 and £100m: fraud by contractors was estimated to be much less than this but the data were much less reliable. The report concluded that some of these sums could be saved and made a large number of recommendations to that effect.

This was the first of a series of announcements bearing on fraudulent use of NHS funds. In September 1997 action was announced to combat fraud in dental services, including false claims by patients for exemption and frauds by dentists.

In December 1997 the NHS Executive set out an action plan for dealing with prescription fraud, which took up the 100 recommendations made by the scrutiny. The Letter asks health authorities:

- *to review the resources they commit to anti-fraud activity;*
- *to note new arrangements which will help Health Authorities to meet the costs of anti-fraud work and will enable some of the resulting savings to be retained for the benefit of local health care;*
- *to nominate a senior manager, accountable to the Director of Finance, to take responsibility for the Health Authority's anti-fraud work in the FHS;*
- *to draw up plans to implement those recommendations of the recent scrutiny on prescription fraud which fall to Health*

Authorities; and to note that further action will be required in due course on optical and dental fraud.

(EL(97)74, 30 December 1997)

At the same time, the Health Minister indicated that a new criminal offence would be created to deal with patient evasion of charges.

In April 1998, HSC 1998/076 *Combating Fraud in the Family Health Services* was issued setting out more detailed guidance to health authorities. While much of this represents a reiteration of earlier advice and requirements, the Circular also suggests that:

28. As part of their management responsibility for family health services, Health Authorities should, as far as possible, promote wider preventive and deterrent measures. These will supplement measures taken at a national level. In particular, Health Authorities should consider how they may be able to:

- *help deter fraud through running – and publicising – local probity checks;*
- *promote high standards in systems for prescribing and dispensing (e.g. repeat prescribing, signing of patient declarations, management of dispensing GP practices) such as may reduce the scope for fraud;*
- *help ensure that practitioners are aware of, and understand, rules on claiming payments.*

(Health Service Circular HSC 1998/076)

In May 1998 James Gee (formerly with Lambeth Council where he set up a corporate anti-fraud team) was appointed as 'fraud supremo'. A fraud hotline was established (Freefone 0800 068 6161) and two fraud Web sites, one for the general public and one for NHS staff. In recognition of the priority given to the work, Mr Gee will have direct access to ministers.

In July 1998 a major increase in the fraud staff attached to the prescription-pricing authority was announced as well as a 'Pharmacy Reward Scheme', designed to encourage pharmacists to examine the forms presented to them for evidence of counterfeiting or tampering.

The aim of these efforts to eradicate fraud are of course as welcome as 'cuts in bureaucracy'. However, as health authorities' staff numbers continue to fall, the real (i.e. opportunity) cost of the measures announced against fraud, measured in terms of the other objectives that will be less vigorously pursued, will rise. The nature of that trade-off, as with management costs, has yet to be acknowledged.

Efficiency

The New NHS makes a virtue of the Government's decision to abandon the purchaser efficiency index which, as the White Paper correctly says, created incentives for individual trusts which were not in line with the overall interests of the NHS. In its place it proposed a 'more rounded' set of indicators. The consultation paper, *The New NHS: Modern, Dependable: a national framework*, set out the Government's first thoughts on what they should comprise.

As noted already, the Government has rightly judged that the efficiency index produced perverse incentives and that the NHS should be judged by a wider set of indicators. One of the six areas is efficiency, for which the consultation

document proposes a number of familiar measures: unit costs; labour productivity index; capital productivity; costed HRGs.

The White Paper itself had indicated that:

> The new approach will include demanding targets on unit cost and productivity throughout the NHS. The Government will develop a programme which requires NHS Trusts to publish and benchmark their costs on a consistent basis. This will provide a national schedule of 'reference costs' which will itemise the cost of individual treatments across the NHS. Costs for major areas of hospital activity will be available in time to inform long-term agreements for 1999–2000. (p.73)

In June 1998, a consultation document, *Reference Costs*, was issued which set out the NHS Executive's proposals to publish three different information sets:

- a National Schedule of Reference Costs;
- a National Reference Cost Index;
- individual trusts' costs for health resource groups.

Taken together, they should allow judgements to be made by purchasers on the efficiency of each trust and for the trusts themselves to see how their performance compares with others. These benefits, however, will not be achieved quickly. The consultation document acknowledges that a number of technical issues have to be solved before the new arrangements can be properly implemented, and does not itself specify a timetable for implementation.

Since the early 1980s data have been available for a wide range of performance indicators relating to costs and activity. The significant change heralded by these proposals is the attempt to produce uniformity of measurement at a fairly detailed level, i.e. HRGs as opposed to broad specialities, and to use the information along with the other elements of the performance framework to assess performance at local level.

How that assessment process should work remains to be seen but, however desirable it may be to gain the rounded picture, using it is far from easy. Experience in Scotland with clinical performance data suggests that impact has been modest perhaps because the data have been left to speak for themselves and not supported by an active central role. If, however, the indicators are used within a 'punitive' context as the White Paper allows for, then the risks of the data themselves being distorted or other aspects of performance which they do not cover suffering as a result of managers placing too much emphasis on the measurable, become significant.

In June 1997, an NHS Efficiency Task Force was established as a permanent strategic think-tank, charged with examining the systems and processes of the NHS for potential savings and sharing best practice within the Service. In October 1997 the Health Minister announced that the Task Force had identified two areas where savings could be made – insurance and recruitment. The sums involved, like those identified by previous scrutinies, such as that into general practice, are modest. In August 1998, it was announced that about £45m would be saved by the introduction of a risk pooling scheme for all trusts, as opposed to the use of commercial insurance. The Comprehensive Spending Review, however, claimed that £1bn or about 3 per cent a year will be saved through value-for-money improvements

but did not make clear how these sums were to be extracted. It will take a lot of £45ms to achieve it and the means of finding many such gains are far from obvious.

Pay and human resources

In May 1997, in a speech to the Royal College of Nursing, the Secretary of State indicated that there would be national pay awards for staff on national contracts and that the pay review body would be asked to make a national recommendation for 1998/99. The Pay Review Bodies reported in January 1998, recommending increases for doctors, dentists and nurses higher than the rate of inflation. These awards were staged, with 2 per cent being awarded as from 1 April and the rest from 1 December:

- *Doctors and dentists to get a 4.2 per cent increase – 2 per cent from 1 April, rising to 4.2 per cent from 1 December.*
- *A 5.2 per cent increase in the intended average net income for general practitioners – 2 per cent from 1 April, rising to 5.2 per cent from 1 December.*
- *The pay element of general dental practitioners' fees to increase by 4.2 per cent – 2 per cent from 1 April, rising to 4.2 per cent from 1 December.*
- *Pay scales for nurses, midwives, health visitors, and the professions allied to medicine to increase by 3.8 per cent – 2 per cent from 1 April, rising to 3.8 per cent from 1 December.*

(Department of Health, 98/042, 29 January 1998)

Both Review Bodies, however, were under strong pressure from the Government to keep its awards down. The report of the Review Body on Doctors' and Dentists' Remuneration records a meeting with the Chancellor as follows:

1.13 The Chairmen of the Pay Review Bodies were invited to a meeting with the Chancellor of the Exchequer on 25 November 1997. The Chancellor stressed that he had no wish to impinge on the independence of their position in making recommendations to the Government. But he was mindful of the tight timetable to which they were working and he wanted to alert them at the earliest opportunity to the supplementary evidence they would be receiving later in the day.

1.14 The Chancellor emphasised the British economy's traditional proneness to inflationary pressures but observed that the decision in May to grant independence to the Bank of England in setting the level of interest rates now ensured that the Government's inflation target would be met. This meant there was a choice for the country: paying ourselves more now and risking higher interest rates later on, or exercising pay responsibility now with the benefit of securing more jobs in the future. A responsible approach by all those involved in pay bargaining, combined with success of the Government's labour market reforms, would allow the economy to grow faster than would otherwise be possible. (p.9)

It then goes on to remind its readers of the nature of its remit:

1.27 The machinery of a Pay Review Body to recommend on doctors' and dentists' remuneration was originally mooted by a Royal Commission[1] back in 1960. One of the Commission's aims was to give the professions assurance that their standards of living would not be depressed by arbitrary Government action. The Commission's report made the important observation that it might sometimes

be considered expedient to avoid increased expenditure on the remuneration of people paid from public funds and that it might be tempting to describe this as an economic necessity or in the national interest. The report acknowledged that while clearly the Government of the day must govern, doctors and dentists must have confidence that their remuneration would be settled on a just basis. We make two important observations: first, we believe that the impartiality of the Review Body system will be undermined if the bodies themselves are not perceived to be independent by all the main parties; and second, in reaching our own conclusions we aim to be fair to both tax payer and members of our remit group alike. For that reason we take note of the evidence on affordability as presented to us by the Government and by the NHS Confederation but at the same time we weigh affordability against other considerations such as recruitment and retention; nature and volume of workloads; morale; job security; our findings on pay comparability, pensions and other benefits; and economic indicators such as price inflation and the level of pay settlements in the wider economy. To that end we have carefully noted the respective parties' evidence but our approach remains unchanged.

(Cm 3835, p.11)

---

[1] Royal Commission on Doctors' and Dentists' Remuneration 1957–1960 Report

Both Chancellor and Review Body were only repeating the arguments which have raged since its establishment. There is an inherent and continuing tension between the national interest, whether that is defined in terms of inflation, spending or taxation targets and the interests of the workforce. Where the two sides of the argument can in principle agree is that NHS staff should be paid at least enough to ensure that the Service can meet whatever demands are placed upon it.

But while that may seem obvious enough, in practice even this can become contentious. Evidence from the Royal College of Nursing argues (as it did in the previous year) that shortages were widespread. However, it acknowledges the 'absence of a ... robust official source of useful information', another long-standing complaint, exacerbated by recent reductions in the amount of centrally collected data. The official evidence, however, referred to measures to be adopted at local level to aid recruitment and retention implying that any shortages could be dealt with in this way.

The BMA also disagreed with the Health Department's assessment of the state of the medical labour market. In particular, it pointed to a growing number of GPs leaving the profession, particularly those over 45 (see Table 2.8).

Furthermore, the commitment inherited from the previous Government to bring the hours of junior hospital doctors down was reaffirmed in June 1998 by the announcement that the regional taskforces will continue their work. Eighty-three per cent of posts were judged to be by then acceptably defined.

In announcing his intention to scrap local pay in May 1997, the Secretary of State nevertheless referred to the Government's commitment to retaining 'appropriate local flexibility'. *The New NHS* repeated this:

> *NHS Trusts will retain their role as local employers within the NHS. In a national health service, the current mix of national and local contracts is divisive and costly. The Government's objective for the longer term is therefore to see staff receive national pay, if this can be matched by meaningful local flexibility, since current national terms of service for a multitude of staff groups are regarded as inequitable and inflexible. Exploratory discussions on these issues are already under way with staff organisations and NHS employers. (p.50)*

The very tentative nature of the wording indicates that the Government had not, by the time of the White Paper, found a clear way ahead. The paper circulated to interested parties in the autumn (*Possible Changes to the NHS Pay System, Letter from NHS Executive to Staff Organisations, NHS Chief Executives/HR Directors,* dated 24 September 1997) was confined to raising questions round a series of generalities (see Box).

The Pay Review Body for Nursing Staff, Midwives and Professions Allied to Medicine (*Review Body for Nursing Staff, Midwives, Health Visitors and Professions Allied to Medicine,* Fifteenth Report, Cm 3832, January 1998) welcomed the

Table 2.8 Doctors leaving general practice

Age of leavers	October 1991/92	October 1994/95	Increase (%)
Under 39	363	396	9
45–59	429	541	26

Source: BMA Memorandum of Evidence to the Review Body on Doctors' and Dentists' Remuneration

Values, objectives and context for the NHS pay system

What should the underlying values and objectives of the NHS pay system be? The objectives below represent a broad statement for your consideration but we would be happy to explore the way they are interpreted or go beyond this list.

Objectives for the NHS pay system

- Should help deliver NHS strategic objectives
- Should ensure affordability
- Should give local flexibility where it matters and national consistency where it matters
- Should be felt by staff to be fair
- Should deliver results without disproportionate effort, confrontation or delay.

How can the NHS pay system support the delivery of high quality, cost-effective patient care?

What should the relationship be between the pay system and professional boundaries?

Government's intention to find a new pay system but it was very sceptical of its capacity to do so quickly:

> Much as we welcome the Government's initiative to develop proposals for a revised approach to NHS pay, there seems little hope of early widespread agreement on the detailed arrangements. The evidence we have received suggests that while consideration of separate strands of work is under way to inform future NHS pay options, the strategic framework in which to consider these options is not yet clear. In particular we consider that an overall strategy is needed to handle the tension between limited resources; growing demand for health care, fuelled by higher patient expectations and advancing technology; and the need properly to

remunerate and motivate the nursing staff providing the patient care. In the absence of such a strategy at this stage, and given the scale of the task, we are not convinced that significant progress on a revised approach to NHS pay is likely to be made before we next meet to consider our recommendations for 1999–2000. (p.4)

By the time of writing, no new proposals had emerged. However, *Modern Public Services for Britain* states that:

> Departmental Ministers will have to be satisfied that any increases will be consistent with achieving their service targets. This will also apply to pay settlements for the pay review body groups. The terms of reference of these bodies will be revised to make clear the need to consider:
>
> - recruitment, retention and motivation of the groups concerned;
> - the requirements on departments to meet their output targets for the delivery of services;
> - requirements on departments to stay within their three-year expenditure limits; and
> - the Government's inflation target which will require responsibility in pay settlements across the public and private sectors. (p.37)

How these requirements are to be squared with the targets for increases in the workforce set out above remains to be seen. The obvious but difficult route is to increase productivity which in the past has been sufficient, for hospital and community health services, to counter rises in the real costs of the resources used in supplying them. They have not been sufficient to reduce them.

All parties accept that pay alone does not determine whether or not the NHS has an adequate well-motivated staff. A review paper prepared for the Nuffield Trust, *Improving the Health of the NHS Workforce*, by Sian Williams and others, found:

> The problem of high levels of ill health in all groups of NHS staff has long been recognised. Recent figures from the CBI show that NHS staff have higher sickness absence than comparable staff groups in other sectors. A recent large study shows that 27 per cent of health care staff report high levels of psychological disturbance, compared with 18 per cent of working people generally.

> Overwork is increasing both in hospital and community services. There are two elements to this overwork: the amount of work required of the individual in a given time and the excessive number of hours the individual is required to work. Shorter hospital stays mean faster throughput of patients; early discharge means sicker patients for general practitioners, practice staff and community services to care for in the community; closure of large psychiatric hospitals means more people requiring community care. Recent figures from the Department of Health show that over the last 10 years NHS activity has increased by 32 per cent while expenditure has increased by only 16 per cent. To bridge this gap there has been improved efficiency, but this has led to major pressures on staff. (p.16)

These findings suggest that recruitment and retention of NHS staff will become increasingly difficult. Furthermore, figures published in August 1998 by the UK Central Council for Nursing Midwifery and Health Visiting showed that the number of nurses completing their training had fallen by over 1,000 from the previous year and was about 6,000 less than in 1991. The figures would have shown a much larger fall had not the number of nurses from overseas risen sharply. Furthermore, the longer-term prospects do not look good. For the first time over half of those on the register are over 40. Moreover there has been a rapid growth in numbers who start their training at a later stage – they obviously will have shorter careers – and in part time work.

The Government had already acknowledged a need for more training places for nurses. In October 1997 Baroness Jay announced a series of measures designed to aid nursing recruitment and retention:

- £1.2m on high profile national press advertisement, aimed at potential new recruits, careers advisers and qualified nurses interested in returning to the NHS or retraining;
- £950,000 on complementary, low profile national publicity programme aimed at attracting and retaining qualified nurses in areas of shortage and strategic development which will include:

  – a local 'tool kit' of centrally produced material to help local managers recruit nurses, midwives and health visitors;
  – continuation of a programme targeted at young people to attract them to working in the NHS, with particular emphasis on reaching young people from black and ethnic minority backgrounds.

(Department of Health, 97/295, 30 October 1997)

As for doctors, the Standing Advisory Committee on the Medical Workforce reporting in November 1997 recommended an increase of 1,000 in the intake to UK medical schools, the second year in succession in which the Committee recommended an increase. This, like the many reports over the years which have considered the question of how many doctors should be trained, acknowledged the very large uncertainties attached to any estimate of the number required.

A central plank of the Committee's position is that the UK should aim for self-reliance, but in fact its recommendation will only achieve that, as it acknowledges, in some fairly unlikely circumstances:

> 5. We favour **self-reliance** as a long-term goal and believe that, as a minimum, the home share should be maintained at its present level of 76 per cent and preferably increased. In saying this, we strongly re-affirm the need to move towards greater reliance on UK doctors. Given the extent of the imbalances between demand and home supply, this means a substantial increase in medical school intake, as illustrated in [the] Table [below]. Indeed some scenarios of future wastage levels and demand growth would require very large increases to medical school intake to maintain home share at 76 per cent. Our recommendation on future intake is based on a balanced judgement, which should result in the maintenance of (or a slight increase in) the home share in many scenarios, while limiting the fall that would occur if growth and wastage rates turn out to be high.

INCREASE IN MEDICAL SCHOOL INTAKE

Future Doctor Wastage (% pa)	Annual growth in demand for doctors (% pa)		
	1.4%	1.7%	2.0%
3.1%	0	800	1,800
3.3%	200	1,000	over 2,000
3.5%	500	1,400	over 2,500

(*Planning the Medical Workforce*, Medical Workforce Standing Advisory Committee: Third Report, 1997, p.33)

The Committee recognised that measures needed to be taken to increase the supply of doctors and to moderate demand for medical skills:

Supply:
- measures to improve retention of home doctors;
- giving attention to how to motivate and retain those doctors who are considering leaving or retiring early;
- training more doctors.

Demand:
- slower progress on certain service and medical workforce policies;
- improved productivity;
- skill substitution;
- reconfiguring patient services;
- slower growth in levels of patient services. (p.37)

These suggestions are not new: the question is whether they will be vigorously examined. The issue of substitution, for example, was raised in a similar report 20 years ago but has never been rigorously pursued at national level since and, although in general terms the scope for using nurses and other professionals in medical roles is frequently acknowledged, the potential for new divisions of work, including entirely new mixes of skills, remains to be systematically explored.

Overall, serious questions remain about the future NHS workforce. In the short term it seems likely that the Pay Review Bodies will be faced for yet another year with evidence suggesting that pay will have to rise faster than it has done in recent years if the NHS is to get the staff it requires to meet what is still an ever-increasing demand. If so, then the apparently generous increases announced in July will appear much less so.

Offloading services

Drugs

The price of prescriptions was raised in April 1998 from £5.65 to £5.80 – the first time since 1981 that it had fallen in real terms. As far as the overall cost of drugs is concerned, the main instrument of control has been since 1957 the voluntary, i.e. non-statutory Pharmaceutical Price Regulation Scheme. The Scheme was given a qualified endorsement by the Health Committee in its 1995 report, but the Committee was particularly concerned about the Scheme's opacity. The then Government accepted that an annual report on the workings of the scheme should be produced: that principle was also accepted by the new Government. The first report appeared in May 1996 and the second (*Pharmaceutical Price Regulation Scheme*, Second Report to Parliament, Department of Health, 1997) in December 1997. According to the latter, the PPRS aims:

> to strike a balance between price levels which provide value for money for the NHS in its drug purchases, and profit levels for the pharmaceutical companies which allow them to conduct long-term programmes to develop new medicines. It recognises that the NHS has an interest in the prices it pays now for its drugs, and in the emergence of new and improved medicines – as do the patients it serves. (p.2)

The Scheme's critics have focused on the unspecific nature of the trade-off which the aims of the Scheme embody: they have also pointed to the range of alternatives available to it, ranging from a regulatory regime based on that applied to the public utilities to complete abandonment combined with increased emphasis on better purchasing of drugs within the NHS. The second report like the first sheds no light on the basic trade-off nor does it discuss any of the available policy options. It remains to be seen whether the revision of the Scheme due to replace the present arrangements in autumn 1998 does so.

The drugs bill is of course determined by many factors other than price. The second PPRS report indicates that most of the increase in the total bill between 1992–96 was accounted for by volume, i.e. increase per head, and 'product-mix effects', i.e. a shift to higher priced products. The number of items per prescription and the entry of new medicines to the market place also contributed to the increase. Overall, the share of drugs in the total NHS budget has continued to rise – by nearly two percentage points between 1992/93 and 1995/96.

Sight tests

We noted in last year's Review evidence that sight-test charges were discouraging some people from having them. The Comprehensive Spending Review announced that such charges would be discontinued for older people. The cost of this was not published at the time.

Long-term care

As noted in Section 1.2, the Government established a Royal Commission to report on the finance of long-term care: overall policy, as far as the NHS is concerned, continues as before, with localities determining their levels of provision in the light of national guidance. This still appears to be producing significant variations between different parts of the country.

Dentistry

In September 1997 an *Investing in Dentistry* scheme was announced which was designed to tackle inequities in the availability of service. In *Health Care UK 1996/97* we reported survey findings which suggested that access to NHS dentistry was poor in many parts of the country. *Investing in Dentistry* is intended both to 'fill' gaps in coverage, but also to target 'places where the standard of oral health is low'. In January 1998 further funding was announced for 1998. In addition, 25 schemes were supported within the pilot scheme arrangements of the Primary Care Act 1997. In April, Alan Milburn announced that the Government intended to publish a new strategy for NHS dentistry later in the year, designed to:

- *reduce inequalities in oral health;*
- *improve the population's access to NHS dental services;*
- *play a part in providing more integrated health services to patients;*
- *guarantee the high quality of service patients expect;*
- *allow all members of the dental team to use their full potential to improve patients' services.*

(Department of Health, 98/156, 23 April 1998)

According to an announcement by Alan Milburn in May 1998 (98/186), *Investing in Dentistry* had already produced a commitment by dentists to bring about 250,000 people into NHS dental care. The pilot schemes announced at the same time included several designed to make NHS services more widely available and accessible. On this basis it would seem that the Government is determined to ensure that what remains of the NHS dental services is available to all who wish to use it so pushing outwards again, here as with sight tests, the effective boundaries of the Service.

Overall

The Government fulfilled its central funding promise – to provide extra funding in real terms for the NHS on an annual basis. It has also set the NHS a series of demanding targets, such as those for reductions in waiting lists and increases in efficiency combined with reductions in management costs. At the same time, it has continued and developed the habit adopted by the previous Government of linking additional resources to particular activities – winter pressures, waiting lists, cancer care, 'modernisation' – which in turn require target-setting and monitoring. That implies, along with the performance assessment framework, a much more active management role than any Government has previously envisaged, a role which, by virtue of the proposals for clinical governance set out in Section 1.5 extends for the first time to clinical performance.

Taken together with the provisions in the comprehensive spending review for a notional contract with the Treasury as financier, the omens for a massive centralisation of power are strong. The large number of targeted allocations for specific services, such as breast cancer, and the Secretary of State's statement after the Comprehensive Spending Review could be seen as the first elements of a centrally planned NHS, where targets are set for all main services and the proposals for national service frameworks and the other measures described in Section 1.5 as key elements of the process.

2.2 Equity

The New NHS made it clear that equity was to form a central plank of the Government's reforms. According to the White Paper, the intention is to create

> [a] national health service ... based on need and need alone – not on your ability to pay, or on who your GP happens to be or on where you live. (p.5)

This is backed up by a full chapter called 'The national dimension' emphasising the NHS's objective of offering 'fairness and consistency to the population as a whole'.

> *The new NHS will have quality at its heart. Without it there is unfairness.* (p.17)

The aim is to more than simply retain the historic principle that the NHS should be 'free at the point of use' and ensure that resources are allocated fairly as between different parts of the country – the policies pursued by the previous Government. The aim is also to achieve a uniform (high quality) service across the country as a whole.

The measures described in Section 1.5 – national service frameworks, NICE, CHIMP – are specifically aimed at ensuring that there is only one central point of reference – a prerequisite for equity – for guidance and action on cost-effectiveness and ensuring consistent quality. Similarly, the new performance assessment framework, including a new set of indicators of activity and clinical outcome which will be uniform across the country as a whole, completes the picture of a new emphasis on fairness in the delivery of care. As the White Paper puts it:

> *The public expects a one-nation NHS, with consistent standards and services, wherever they live. The single minded focus on the old market-driven measures of performance disguised the wide variations that exist in the level and quality of services provided. The new performance framework will encourage greater benchmarking of performance in different areas, and the publication of comparative information will allow people to compare performance and share best practice.* (p.65)

At first sight, this new emphasis on similar levels of performance in different parts of the NHS makes obvious sense. Indeed, it can be regarded as an outstanding anomaly that a nationally financed service has not made systematic attempts in the past to ensure that the standard of service was not broadly similar in different parts of the country. Free access at the point of use (to the majority of services), combined with equalisation of the availability of resources relative to need, bears on access to, and purchase of, care. While in principle they create the potential for equity of access across different parts of the country, they do not in themselves guarantee that service levels and service quality will in practice be similar in all parts of the country and for all groups of the population.

Although equity and fairness are ideas which most people would sign up to, this does not imply that there is agreement or clarity about what they mean in practice. Indeed, it is this lack of precise definition which allows so much apparent agreement. But consensus begins to evaporate when the question becomes what counts as relevant to considerations of equity – equity of what? Even apparent tightening of the definition – such as 'equal access for equal need', a commonly cited version of what equity means in the NHS – does not get us far. Precisely what 'access' means (is it use of health services, or the costs of arriving at the front door, or is it just an absence of charges?) and what 'need' refers to (is it the degree of ill health, the ability to benefit from treatment, and does it include 'social needs' such as the existence of dependants?) are typically unspecified. Neither the previous Government in *A Service with Ambitions* nor the new one in *The New NHS* attempts to do so.

Financial allocations

Disregarding these difficulties, the new Government continued to press on with the humdrum task of operationalising at least one version of equity: that health authorities should be funded according to their level of 'need', understood as 'existence of ill health' as reflected in a series of statistical indicators. The importance of this form of equity was given symbolic weight by the publication of the *National Health Service (Equity of Funding) Bill*, presented to Parliament on 18 November 1997. The Bill itself was uncontroversial:

> **Section 1** *(1) There shall be established a National Health Service Funding Advisory Body whose function shall be to examine and report from time to time on the formula used by the Secretary of State for determining the distribution of National Health Service funding between health authorities …*
>
> *(5) …the advisory body shall have regard to considerations of equity and to such social, economic, geographical, environmental, medical and epistemological factors as in their opinion are relevant.*

The search for a satisfactory formula which allows for differences in needs and the costs of meeting those needs has been in progress since the Resource Allocation Working Party started work in the 1970s. Since then a series of internal working parties and external research reports have contributed to refining the formula for allocating resources with a view to improving the fairness of that allocation. What is noteworthy is that the Government felt compelled to codify this work in legislation – perhaps so that it might refer to this as evidence of its commitment to the NHS and equity within it. Whatever the reason, for the first time 'equity' will be enshrined in law as an operating principle of the NHS, whereas previously it was only implicit in the 1977 Act's requirement for all reasonable needs to be met and the requirement that people should not in general be charged.

Over the years, formulae for achieving the goal of equitable allocation of funds have regularly been modified to take better account of socio-demographic data and statistical techniques for establishing levels of need. In September 1997 a new committee of 26 academics and other specialists was announced by Alan Milburn. (There will have to be a further committee when the Equity of Funding Bill becomes law, which, it is anticipated, will have only between six and twelve members.)

The new committee's terms of reference are:

- *to advise the Secretary of State for Health on the distribution of resources across primary and secondary care, in support of the goal of equitable access to healthcare for all;*
- *to develop and apply methods which are as objective and needs-based as available data and techniques permit.*

(Department of Health 97/220, 11 Sept 1997)

As noted in last year's edition of *Health Care UK*, to take primary care into account could potentially lead to major changes in the way that funds are allocated. Despite the sustained efforts of the Medical Practices Committee, the distribution of general practitioners remains uneven although the number of areas where no restrictions to the establishment of new practices has fallen steadily over the past ten years (see Table 2.9).

Table 2.9 Number of open areas

Year	No. of areas	Year	No. of areas
1987	71	1992	47
1988	57	1993	39
1989	42	1994	30
1990	49	1995	25
1991	55	1996	22

Source: Official Evidence to Review Body on Doctors' and Dentists' Remuneration, September 1997

Changes had, however, already been made to the formula for allocations for 1998/99. The principal adjustments are set out in *HCHS Revenue Resource Allocation to Health Authorities: weighted capitation formulas. Supplement to the 1997 edition*, published by the NHS Executive in February 1998. The changes to the formula outlined in last year's Review are as follows:

- the introduction of 100 per cent weighting for 'additional need' (that is, need not already accounted for by means of adjustments for age and cost);
- the number of pay zones used to inform the 'cost' adjustment (staff market forces factor (MFF)) was reduced from 61 to 51;
- the introduction of an adjustment for emergency ambulance costs.

The first of these adjustments means that hospital and community health services are now 100 per cent adjusted for additional need rather than just the acute sector and part of community health services. The breakdown of the 100 per cent weighting for need was:

		(%)
Acute		70.25
Psychiatric:	Non-community	13.22
	Community	2.69
Community		12.23
Total		**100.00**

The Market Forces Factor compensates for the higher cost of providing services in some parts of the country than others. The change noted above represents only a marginal refinement of the much more significant changes in this element reported in last year's Review. Those changes – effective in 1997/98 – had a substantial impact on some areas, as indicated by an answer by Alan Milburn to a Parliamentary Question. For example, East Sussex, Brighton and Hove had their target allocation reduced by 5.42 per cent over the previous year (1996/97), whereas Avon gained 3.43 per cent.

The impact of these changes on allocations to health authorities for 1998/99 is summarised in Table 2.10. As with the previous year's increases, all health authorities were guaranteed a minimum increase of 1.35 per cent in real terms.

Purchasing

In July 1997 Frank Dobson confirmed that GP fundholders would no longer be able to gain preferential treatment for their patients ahead of those on health authority waiting lists. The instruction was that trusts would have to

Table 2.10 Changes in financial allocations

Highest increases	(%)	Lowest increases	(%)
Barnsley	2.65	Barnet	1.35
KCW	2.63	Bexley and Greenwich	1.35
Wigan and Bolton	2.59	Brent and Harrow	1.35
East London and the City	2.49	Camden and Islington	1.35
Walsall	2.44	Dorset	1.35
Berkshire	2.43	Ealing, Hammersmith and Hounslow	1.35
North West Lancashire	2.43	East Surrey	1.35
West Pennine	2.43	Gloucestershire	1.35
Stockport	2.41	Isle of Wight	1.35
Bedfordshire	2.40	Kingston and Richmond	1.35
		Merton, Sutton and Wandsworth	1.35
		Morecombe Bay	1.35
		North and Mid Hants	1.35
		Redbridge and Waltham Forest	1.35
		South Humber	1.35
		South Lancashire	1.35
		Suffolk	1.35
		Warwickshire	1.35
		West Herts	1.35
		West Surrey	1.35
		Wiltshire	1.35

Source: HSJ, 6 November 1997, p. 9

operate common waiting lists for non-urgent admissions and would not be able to differentiate between fundholders and non-fundholders' patients other than on 'clinical or social' grounds:

From next April, hospitals will no longer be able to set different waiting time standards between GP fundholder and Health Authority patients ...

- *health authorities must have maximum waiting time standards that are common to all their residents*
- *within this common standard the admission of a health authority's residents for non-urgent treatments must be on the basis of clinical priority, regardless of who is the patient's GP*

- *trusts cannot offer preferential admission to the patients of GP fundholders, and fundholders cannot press for faster treatment except on clinical or social grounds.*

(Department of Health 97/169, 16 July 1997)

In this way, Labour's pre-election commitment to abolish fundholding was realised – well before the new form of primary care purchasing, primary care groups, had been formulated.

The principle here is that chance, i.e. place of residence and thus type of GP, should not affect one's likelihood of treatment. Whereas most would agree with the principle, the situation is rather more complex than the Government's response to it suggests. First, those patients who gained from fundholders' waiting list contracts are only the 'visible' half of the full picture. Assuming *per capita* funding is equal, fundholders could press for faster treatment by devoting more resources with the consequence that fewer resources were likely to be available for other treatments. We cannot tell whether the health authority was providing advantages to other, less visible, groups than non-urgent elective acute care.

Second, as Nick Goodwin pointed out in his review of fundholding in *Health Care UK 1996/97*, it may be that fundholding allowed the more efficient use of resources, in which case fundholders were not necessarily diverting resources away from others, but taking advantage of an overall improvement in how those resources were used.

As it turns out, all patients will soon become the responsibility of primary care groups. This will, in one sense, be more equitable because place of residence will no longer determine the institutional design of purchasing – although, as noted in Section 1.1, in fact there will still be some differences arising from the different stages through which the groups may pass. The visible forms of inequity such as operating separate waiting lists will disappear. But it may be harder to remove the inequity resulting from the existence of different purchasing policies altogether, because primary care groups will themselves differ one from another in what they choose to purchase – indeed it would be pointless to introduce them if they did not – and may operate more or less efficiently. Whereas this may not result in overt 'two-tierism', different patients will still do more or less well depending on where they live.

Dentistry was another area where the previous Government had come under fire for differences in the availability of services, but in this instance they stemmed from a shortfall in NHS provision. Since the inception of the NHS the universal subsidy has been gradually reduced and it now stands at just 20 per cent of the cost of provision of standard reconstructive and check-up procedures. As we noted last year, dentists had been withdrawing from NHS work and were increasingly expanding their private practices. Where this meant withdrawing from NHS provision altogether, those who were entitled to 100 per cent subsidy began to find it difficult to gain access to dental care which they could afford.

As noted in Section 2.1, the Government has accepted that it must take positive steps to ensure that the NHS does offer nationwide the full range of fully and partially subsidised services: the pilots announced in May 1998 contain several designed to fill gaps in provision or to target particularly needy groups, including children.

Regardless of this initiative, what is 'equitable' for dental patients is clearly judged in different terms by both political parties, since neither has seriously challenged the fact that for most of the population dentistry is not free at the point of use. The underlying principle here is that if you can afford to, you should contribute toward a significant proportion of the cost – quite different from most other areas of NHS provision. Thus low income families who just fail to satisfy eligibility for exemption may find themselves paying amounts for treatment which would represent a significant drain on their resources, and decide to go without. It is still not clear how dental problems – which can be highly distressing and unavoidable – have come to be classed separately

Proposed measures of fair access

Surgery rates – a composite indicator of elective surgery rates, consisting of age and sex standardised:

- CABG and PTCA rates;
- hip replacement rates (for those aged 65 and over);
- knee replacement rates (for those aged 65 and over);
- cataract replacement rates.

Conceptions below age 16 (rate, girls aged 13–15).
People registered with an NHS dentist – percentage of population registered.
Early detection of cancer – a composite indicator, consisting of:

- percentage of target population screened for breast cancer;
- percentage of target population screened for cervical cancer.

District nurse contacts – a composite indicator looking at access to community services, consisting of:

- district nurse contacts for those aged 75 and over;
- district nurse contacts over 30 mins for those aged 75 and over;
- assisted district nurse contacts for those aged 75 and over.

Source: *The New NHS: Modern, Dependable: A National Framework for Assessing Performance*, Consultation Document, pp.22–6

in this way, an issue which Bill New discusses elsewhere in this volume. (See pages 178–97).

For those services which remain in the mainstream NHS, the equity issues turn on whether they are actually provided at similar levels in different parts of the country and whether all those who might benefit from them actually gain access to them. The National Performance Assessment Framework sets out a small number of indicators which bear on this definition of equity (see Box).

The proposed introduction of indicators along these lines reflects the persistence of variations in treatment rates which cannot be explained by variation in case-mix or other measures of need. The main explanatory factor for differences of this

kind is differences in clinical judgement. How these work in practice emerged clearly from a 1998 report by the National Audit Office, *Cataract Surgery in Scotland*, which found substantial variations in treatment rates among GP practices in 21 out of 57 local government districts. These varied from over 3,500 cataracts treated per 100,000 over 65s in one GP practice, to under 500 per 100,000 for the same sector of the population in another. It is likely that social deprivation and other socio-economic factors will explain some of this variation, but it is too large for there not to be other elements. The National Audit Office suggested three additional factors:

- whether GPs actively search for cataract or respond to patient demand;

- how active local opticians are in identifying cataracts;
- the threshold for visual acuity at which GPs normally refer.

The last point illustrates how implicit rationing and the limiting of demand takes place in the NHS in ways which bear just as unevenly on patients with the same need for treatment as fundholding was claimed to do. Visual acuity is measured from 6/6, which is good vision, to 6/60 which is virtual blindness. Although some GPs referred at surgeons' recommended rates of between 6/9 to 6/18, others were referring only at 6/36 or worse. Clearly, different GPs perceived what was a reasonable claim on the NHS rather differently, perhaps reflecting factors such as the length of waiting lists in their area.

The findings of this study have considerable bearing on the relevance of the Government's policy on waiting lists to its attempt to make the NHS more equitable, indicating as they do that the need for action to ensure equity lies outside the hospital's sphere of responsibility. Furthermore, it also shows how demand for health care is able effortlessly to rise in line with resources: those GPs with low referral rates could easily increase these referrals to match supply if they believed there was a greater chance of treatment, or simply if their threshold for referral changed for some other reason. The 'bottomless pit' of ill-health may not be infinite, but it is large enough for demand to increase immediately when allowed to do so by the NHS's gatekeepers.

Health inequalities

The principal benchmark on which they will be judged, if ministerial statements are anything to go by, will be whether inequalities in health status continue to grow between social classes. As noted in Section 1.3, the Government has introduced a range of measures targeted at reducing such health inequalities. The new arrangements for determining how resources are allocated within the NHS will undoubtedly mean that the scope for placing more explicit weight on general indicators of physical, economic and social deprivation will be fully explored. But even if resource allocation reflects differences in these factors, that will not itself guarantee that health resources are used in ways which reduce inequalities.

One reason they may not, is that the access particular groups enjoy in practice may not be in line with their measured needs. The Government has recognised this in the form of a number of targeted initiatives. People with learning difficulties were provided with new advice and guidance on their rights and responsibilities to NHS care: *Our Health Services*. The document emphasised the need for the NHS to play a key role in partnership with other agencies focusing on the individual needs of users and carers. The concern was that although those with learning difficulties used health care services at the same rate as the population as a whole, they on average had greater needs and so should be making greater use.

In February 1998 Public Health Minister Tessa Jowell announced eight schemes aimed at improving the health of minority ethnic groups, and at improving how the NHS responds to their needs. The perception was that people from black and minority ethnic groups find it difficult to gain access to NHS services when compared with the general population. This perception is partly backed up by research evidence. Chris Smaje and Julian Le Grand reported in a study of ethnic minority use of the NHS that, although use of GP services by minority ethnic groups is in general as high or higher than the white population, this use reflected higher patterns of need and, furthermore, use of outpatient services is lower than need might suggest by comparison with the white population (*Soc Sci Med 45(3)*, pp.485–96).

Our Healthier Nation committed the Government to a reduction in health inequalities, i.e. differences in health status. Like equity itself, this is an objective most would support but its precise interpretation is also problematic. Taken to extremes, it might mean denying those with relatively good health, but still with need, *any* health care. Less extremely it would mean interpreting a gain in health status across all social groups which left inequalities unchanged as being undesirable or a decline in the health status of those currently enjoying high levels of health as being desirable, provided that those of other groups did not decline as well. Neither are judgements it would be easy to justify.

Clearly the most desirable change would be one where all groups gained, but those currently enjoying the poorest health gained most. Whether that is achievable remains to be seen but the Government can at least claim that by targeting substantial resources on the least advantaged, in the ways described in Section 1.3, it is maximising the chances of that outcome. But it will be hard to achieve. Frances Drever and Margaret Whitehead, in the concluding chapter of *Health Inequalities* (The Office for National Statistics, 1998) summarise the evidence they and their colleagues have reviewed as follows:

> *Although there is some variation in the absolute rates calculated from these different sources, the socio-economic patterns of health are remarkably consistent. All the sources show a marked socio-economic gradient in mortality and morbidity persisting into the 1990s.* (p.224)

They go on to report that while mortality has declined for all social classes, rates have deteriorated for some subgroups or stood still and hence the gaps between social groups have widened. The pattern found among the mortality data is also found in other measures such as self-reported chronic sickness and disability. The task therefore is a challenging one requiring as it does, at least for some groups, a reversal of existing trends.

Finally, we look at how the NHS measures up *now*. Two academic studies have recently looked at this question. The starting point for both was some conceptual clarification along the lines discussed above. In addition to problems of deciding what the appropriate distribution of health *outcome* should be, there is a further complication: one can either examine the equity of *access* (are the costs, including non-financial costs, of attending at the NHS equal for equal need?), or the equity of *treatment* (is the quantity of resources consumed equal for equal need?). The difference between the two is that the latter conception is affected by people's preferences – whereas the costs of attending may be the same, some people in equal need may decide not to make use of the services that are available.

This makes the task of determining what is or is not equitable a complicated one because it is easy to import a paternalistic desire to 'encourage' people to consume health care when they do not necessarily desire it. On the other hand, hidden cultural differences may be preventing some health consumption, for example, out of fear or uncertainty. Disentangling variations in utilisation from those of access costs is extremely complex, and even where it is possible, utilisation measures are themselves crude and may disguise substantial variations in the quality of care. There are also difficulties of measurement: 'need' and 'equal need' are not objective states, and yet some judgement must be made before inequalities can be agreed to exist.

Maria Goddard and Peter Smith of the University of York (*Equity of Access to Health Care*, 1998) note that the difficulty of disentangling access and treatment meant that most of the studies they reviewed concentrated on inequalities in treatment, as this was easier to measure. The following conclusions of their review were not able to remove the possibility that variations in preferences were at least partly the cause of variable treatment rates:

- minority ethnic groups experience inequity after controlling for need and deprivation factors, both *increasing* utilisation (e.g. schizophrenia among Afro-Caribbeans) and *reducing* it for GP consultations and outpatient attendances for Chinese, African and Pakistani populations;
- some evidence that socio-economic status ('class') may result in lower access at specialty level, and in investigation and treatment rates for some elective surgery and coronary heart disease procedures;
- elderly people appear to experience inequity in relation to particular treatments such as CHD and screening;
- women also have fewer investigations and surgical interventions for CHD after controlling for need;
- those living further away from care services

experience lower utilisation rates after controlling for other factors (a supply-side 'cost' element).

The authors are cautious in drawing too many firm conclusions from these findings, however:

In general we have found the policy implications of the above inequities to be far from clear cut and to require further research … Broadly speaking, policy makers may have more direct control over supply factors and less over demand factors. (p.10)

A 1998 pamphlet from Age Concern (*Equal Access to Cardiac Rehabilitation*) presents evidence on the provision of cardiac rehabilitation which strongly suggests that there is systematic bias against older people, a bias which extends to research as well. Most studies of the effectiveness of cardiac rehabilitation exclude older people even though they are by far the largest need group. What evidence exists – only three studies are cited – suggests that older people can benefit from such services.

The report goes on to examine the reasons given by programme co-ordinators for operating an age cut-off: insufficient resources and failure to comply. As the report points out, the first is not a reason for introducing an age criterion and it argues neither is the second, even if there was evidence to support it. But if there were such evidence and hence as a result, treating older people was more expensive, would that be a relevant criterion? Or if they did not benefit so much, i.e. if a lower proportion exhibited a benefit?

The same point arises in a rather more uncomfortable guise in relation to ethnicity and class: if people in some ethnic or social groups are, for whatever reasons, in general less able to enjoy health gains from otherwise similar interventions, should clinicians maximise the good that can be done by 'discriminating' against them? It may be that some of the measured inequities arise from the aggregate of individual decisions about which potential patients are likely to gain most from treatment, not necessarily from any bias or social discrimination. In the case of elderly people, for example, some of the evidence suggests that many clinicians believe that their ability to benefit is generally less than younger people. The empirical studies of inequity should not lead us to assume that correcting them is unambiguous or morally straightforward. The old conflict between maximisation and distribution of benefits remains.

The second study also leaves such issues unresolved. Carol Propper (*Equity in the Finance and Delivery of Health Care in the UK,* Nuffield Institute, 1998) separated her review into finance and delivery. On the finance side she concluded that the NHS is one of the most equitable health care systems. However, on the delivery side:

> the picture is more mixed. Detailed studies of particular interventions and populations appear to indicate that the NHS is not achieving its goal of equal treatment for equal need. But studies using nationally representative data from household surveys contradict these findings. (p.42)

So, as with the previous review, age, sex, class and ethnic origin are all suspected of resulting in unequal use in relation to need. But the 'broad brush' household surveys indicate a mild 'pro-poor' distribution of health services even after controlling for need, although less so than for some other European countries. There are severe methodological difficulties in understanding these contradictions, and the author concludes that:

> the evidence is still mixed. While inequalities in receipt of NHS health care clearly still exist, the extent to which these inequalities are a result of systematic differential treatment of individuals in the same need is a good deal less clear. What seems likely is that inequalities exist in the treatment of certain conditions and not for others. (p.36)

In other words, all the difficulties of interpretation noted above remain.

Perhaps it is the conflict between attempting to achieve maximum health gain, by utilising a cost-effectiveness framework for allocating resources between patients, and the desire of the NHS and the country as a whole to achieve equity between social groups, where the intractable nature of the equity debate lies. These issues are brought into sharper relief when we consider equity in the context of rationing and priority-setting, and try to puzzle out why these two debates operate so separately.

Rationing and priority-setting

We consider rationing under the heading of 'equity' in this review because we consider it to be inevitable: it is simply impossible for the NHS, or any other health care system, regardless of the level of expenditure, to provide the last drop of potential benefit for all those in need. Thus the critical question is how to decide who is going to be denied what. Should resources go to drugs for chronic conditions to extend life, or to treatments which improve quality of life such as hip replacements? What should determine who is admitted next from waiting lists? These are fundamentally questions of fairness, and thus of equity.

But the new Labour Government, like the previous Tory one, continues to shy away from using the term. Other terms are preferred, such as 'priority-setting' and the 'fair allocation of resources'. 'Rationing', perhaps, contains too many connotations of 'cuts', of services being less than acceptable, or certainly of a move to lower quality than in the past.

What this semantic sleight-of-hand leaves obscured, however, is what precisely priority-setting consists of or why it is necessary, if rationing is not. Whatever one's view of the usefulness of one word over another, it is hard to deny that the NHS will always have to deny beneficial things to people. This hard fact is left implicit, leaving a continuing confused debate about precisely how the NHS should manage its limited resources and the implications of doing so. It also leaves the public increasingly concerned, as media examples of rationing continue to appear and are inevitably characterised as a 'failure' of the system. This confrontational state of affairs – media reveal 'rationing', Government denies it – may have contributed to continuing ebbing of public confidence in Government as evidenced by British Social Attitude Surveys. In the most recent, *British Social Attitudes, the 14th Report*, the proportion of people who believe that British Governments of any party place the needs of the nation above party 'just about always' or 'most of the time' has fallen to an all-time low of 22 per cent in 1996.

Denial or dilution of benefit is, in fact, simply the practical manifestation in specific terms of the need to set priorities at higher levels of the system, either by health authorities or by the resource allocation formula. Regardless of Government rebuttal, examples continued to appear during the year.

The case of the drug Beta Interferon, and of other new drugs for chronic and incurable conditions, provided the most dramatic example of inequitable rationing. Decisions about whether to fund such drugs, or provide 'new' money so that resources do not have to be redistributed from other departments, are typically made independently by health authorities. The result can be that patients who are otherwise in identical need may find that receipt of the drug depends on where they live. One health authority, North Derbyshire, took the view that Beta Interferon did not provide enough benefit for the cost and were taken to court by Kenneth Fisher, a patient with multiple sclerosis who was refused drug treatment. In this case, because of the unusual existence of guidelines on the provision of the drug, which the health authority had failed to take account of, in July 1997 the court found in favour of the plaintiff.

This case illustrates a number of issues in rationing and equity. The first is that the decisions of health authorities are highly visible, whereas the 'normal' rationing decision with regard to cases such as this would be hidden under the cloak of clinical decisions about which patients should get the drug. Those that were 'refused' in this system would be personally told that there was little prospect of benefit, or some other form of words. The second issue is that the court only found for the plaintiff because of the existence of guidelines which were ignored. Normally guidelines do not exist, prescribing or otherwise is in the hands of the clinician, and therefore considered outside the courts' jurisdiction. It is this *absence* of central guidance in almost all cases of new technologies that causes the visible extreme geographical variation in availability – and thus the failure of equitable availability.

However, hidden inequity is almost certainly also in existence. Finally, the case highlighted the fact that much of the rationing debate occurs over highly marginal improvements to health, such as ameliorating the symptoms of multiple sclerosis, and not over life and death issues.

Another area where rationing is commonplace is the management of waiting lists. The main concern of waiting-list policy during the year was the election promise that lists would be shorter. Not discussed so candidly by the Government was whether lists are managed fairly as between different parts of the country and according to reasonable criteria, and whether there is consistency from one list to another. It is almost certain that there is not, if only because of the absence of any central policy.

However, local initiatives continue to sprout up whereby trusts attempt to formalise admission from lists by means of points systems. The latest such example (*Independent on Sunday*, 21 June 1998) was reported in a Channel 4 programme, *The Goldring Audit*, on 28 June. Patients who might need an angiogram are given one if they score 40 points or more, based on criteria such as severity of symptom, results of exercise test, whether there has been a previous heart attack, currently on medication, has diabetes or cannot work because of the symptoms. It does not apply to urgent cases with unstable angina. Such schemes clearly make rationing more visible, but they also provoke debate about which criteria are appropriate. Here, whether one is prevented from working – a social criterion – is included. In a similar New Zealand system, other social criteria have been included, such as the existence of dependants and ability to work. A survey commissioned by the National Infertility Awareness Campaign (*The Independent*, 22 June, p.7) found that social criteria are used commonly in choosing patients for infertility treatment.

The puzzle remains as to why the equity and rationing debates continue to take place separately, both in the policy world as well as in Government – where at least it is understandable from a political perspective. It is possible that those who wish to promote equity in the access or use of the NHS do not have the inevitability of limiting beneficial interventions in mind when conducting their studies. Instead, the concern is simply with everyone gaining the same level of (access to) service – implicitly assumed to be of acceptable quality – for everyone relative to need. As we have seen, the nature of need is assumed to be simply existence of ill health. But unlike the rationing debate in relation to criteria for waiting lists, noted above, what precise constituents of need are appropriate and how to weigh them are left unanalysed.

The difference is one between vertical and horizontal equity. The 'empirical' analysts consider that horizontal equity is at stake – people with the same need should be treated the same. Although also important in the rationing debate, it is vertical equity where the hard choices lie – which differences between people are relevant. In this debate it is acknowledged that assessing what counts as being in similar 'need' is a highly complex question. The result is a curious divergence in the moral direction of the two camps, with the former pressing for resources to be devoted to where there is simply an existence of ill health and the latter increasingly to where they can achieve the greatest cost-effectiveness. This is more than just an academic point when 'inequities' are claimed in the treatment of elderly people, for example, which may be defended by others as morally justifiable. Resources tend to be directed to 'elderly' areas in RAWP terms, a policy accepted by most commentators. Conversely, some health economists defend the fact that comparatively less is offered to elderly people in particular service areas, such as renal replacement therapy. The need for both these camps to work more closely together will become increasingly urgent if and when a government finally becomes willing to pick up the rationing baton. This may happen sooner rather than later once NICE starts its work.

2.3 Accountability

Previous issues of the Review have charted the introduction of new arrangements which developed the rather meagre system of accountability that has characterised the NHS for most of its life – an explicit system of corporate governance for NHS health authorities and trusts. This process took a step further in September 1997, with the issue of EL(97)55, *Corporate Governance in the NHS: controls assurance statements*, which required a new statement covering 1997/98 from board directors on the control standards operating in the bodies for which they are responsible. This was followed up in a further circular, *Corporate Governance in the NHS controls assurance statements 1998/1999 and 1999/2000* (HSC 1998/070). Apart from minor changes to the requirements for 1998/99, the key change was the introduction of a more comprehensive statement for 1999/2000 and beyond. From that year each health authority and trust will be required to have a strategy identifying all the key non-clinical risks it faces and the relevant actions to manage them, covering business planning, corporate strategy, environment

matters, human resources and service management. The Circular sets out both an outline statement relating to the adequacy of the financial controls each trust and health authority have in place and minimum control standards.

One notable omission from these arrangements, as the Circular itself notes, is any system of accountability for clinical activity, apart from those lying with the professions and applicable, as in the Bristol case, to the extremes of poor performance. As we have noted already, particularly in Section 1.5, *The New NHS* set out a series of proposals which, taken together, amount to a system of clinical governance explicitly designed to parallel the arrangements for corporate governance already in existence. In the words of the White Paper:

> *The performance of trusts will be assessed against new broad-based measures reflecting the wider goals of improving health and healthcare outcomes [and] the quality and effectiveness of service … The effect of [trusts'] new statutory duties will be to broaden their accountability which until now has rested largely on financial performance. In future they will also need to be able to demonstrate that they have necessary systems in place to assure quality. (p.48)*

The proposals for clinical governance combined with the clinical elements of the performance framework mean that for the first time a system of assessment of clinical work will be in place for the whole of the NHS.

The need for this was confirmed by Richard Smith, the editor of the *BMJ*, not in terms of serious failure but rather the generality of practice: '*The profession certainly needs to show that its members are keeping up with the latest evidence and maintaining their skills. The abundant evidence [is] that the practice of many doctors is not in line with the best evidence'.* (BMJ, 30 May 1998, pp.1622–3). In other words the profession appears toothless – unable to influence standards effectively despite the role of the Royal Colleges and other clinical organisations in the production of guidelines, the oversight of training and in continuing medical education.

As we have noted, the Government has shown itself keen to step into this gap with the array of measures outlined above. Nevertheless, *The New NHS* also makes it clear that it wishes to see professional self-regulation remain. A key element of self-regulation is the maintenance of professional standards and in particular the imposition of sanctions, including dismissal from the profession concerned. The existing arrangements within the medical profession were given their sternest test during the year as a result of events at the Bristol Royal Infirmary. Because of the vast amount of publicity it attracted, it became a test of whether the medical profession could regulate itself, i.e. take effective action against a senior member accused of poor performance.

Traditionally, the medical profession have been accountable only to themselves – what has been termed 'normative' accountability, directed solely to the ethical principles and codes of the profession itself. Such professional self-regulation – governed by the General Medical Council (GMC) – often appears to be a recipe for evasiveness and self-preservation to the lay outsider. But the justification has always been that only professional peers are in a position to be able to judge the competence of their colleagues. Specialist knowledge, which underpins any

'profession', is necessary to assess the competence or otherwise of its practitioners.

This system was itself in the dock during 1998 as the longest-running disciplinary hearing in the GMC's history took place. Three doctors from Bristol, two surgeons from the Royal Infirmary and one former chief executive of the trust, were charged with serious professional misconduct over the deaths of a number of babies during or after heart surgery. In June they were found guilty but only two of the three doctors concerned were struck off the medical register.

One of the striking features of the Bristol case was that the situation was known about – articles had appeared in *Private Eye* – but no one took effective action for several years. In the words of a leader in *The Lancet* (vol. 351, no. 9117, p.1669):

> there was no clear chain of command communication to ensure that the difficulties were remedied at the earliest possible point. If the organisations that regulate the medical profession do not put their heads together now and create a system to pick up – and deal with problems in clinical practice as they emerge, the Bristol story is bound to be retold elsewhere. Professional self-regulation cannot be left entirely to the disciplinary function of the GMC – by then it will often be too late.

The form the action eventually took failed to satisfy those most closely concerned – many potentially relevant cases were not considered. This may have been in part due to the desire of the GMC to ensure a 'conviction' and in part due to the precise nature of the charges. As noted in last year's Review, these arrangements are already being modified so as to allow the GMC to proceed against poor performance not, as in the Bristol case, unprofessional conduct alone.

In June 1998 the Secretary of State announced that there would be a public inquiry into paediatric cardiac surgical services at the Bristol Royal Infirmary under the chairmanship of Professor Ian Kennedy. In making this announcement the Secretary of State made it clear that the inquiry would, unlike the GMC hearing, look at all the facts of the case.

In theory, a Bristol case will be less likely to occur in the future, as the proposals for clinical governance are introduced. Trust boards and chief executives in particular will be held directly responsible for clinical performance, making it impossible, as one of the defendants did, to argue that as chief executive he was not responsible for what occurred. Furthermore, in principle at least, the main means by which poor performance is identified in practice, whistleblowing by colleagues as in the Bristol case, is to be made easier. In September 1997 the Minister for Health Alan Milburn announced that, as part of the new NHS human resources strategy, gagging clauses in NHS employment contracts would be outlawed. More generally, the Government plans to introduce a 'whistleblowers' Bill designed precisely to protect such actions: the Public Interest Disclosure Bill, due to become law in 1999. This will protect potential whistleblowers when they raise concerns through internal procedures if they reasonably believe the information tends to show a specified malpractice and are acting in good faith. For outside disclosures, the employee must additionally have no motivation for personal gain and must reasonably believe that the information is substantially true.

There are rival options in the Bill regarding compensation for victimisation or dismissal –

there could either be limited awards or the award could actually match the loss suffered by the whistleblower.

Although shifting the balance of costs and benefits in favour of the whistleblower, such legislation can do nothing to prevent the social ostracism and humiliation suffered and which in itself will remain a significant barrier against such actions. In the Bristol case, it was an anaesthetist, Stephen Bolsin, who exposed the failings in paediatric cardiac surgery and who subsequently decided to emigrate to Australia to find a new job, as jobs in this country proved hard to find. Whether the new legislation would have allowed him to comfortably remain in this country must be doubtful; whistleblowing will probably remain the province of courageous individuals unless and until the Government succeeds through the measures taken to introduce clinical governance, to alter the environment within which NHS staff work in a way which reduces the pressure to protect colleagues.

As these developments indicate, 'pure' self-regulation of the profession is being watered down. Furthermore, the GMC appear keen to demonstrate willingness in the new relationships with patients and the general public. In a new edition of its *Good Medical Practice*, it gives doctors guidance about what they should do, and not just about what they should not:

> *If a patient under your care has suffered serious harm, through misadventure or for any other reason, you should act immediately to put matters right, if that is possible. You should explain fully to the patient what has happened and the likely long- and short-term effects. When appropriate you should offer an apology ...*

If a patient under 16 has died you must explain, to the best of your knowledge, the reasons for and the circumstances of, the death to those with parental responsibility. Similarly, if an adult patient has died, you should provide this information to the patient's partner or next of kin, unless you know that the patient would have objected. (p.7)

The guidance goes far beyond what is required in legislation.

The GMC guidance and that from the Senate of Surgery cited in Section 1.4 do not, however, deal with one of three key areas of clinical discretion – the use of resources. The issue here is not one of professional misconduct as currently conceived but rather a matter of how broadly the professional role should be defined. As has often been acknowledged by commentators on the mechanisms of rationing health care, clinicians make the vast majority of decisions of this kind on a day-to-day basis. These decisions include how much time to spend with patients, the number of diagnostic tests to undertake, which patient should be admitted next from a waiting list, whether a new drug offers sufficient prospect of benefit, and so on.

Of those who accept that some responsibility for the *allocation* of resources also lies with clinicians, some go so far as to argue that the fundamental tenets of medical practice need redrafting. For example, in June the outgoing Chief Medical Officer, Sir Kenneth Calman, wrote in *The Potential for Health* (Oxford University Press 1998) that the Hippocratic oath should be reformulated to take into account the medical profession's responsibility for the whole community and not simply the individual patient being treated. In a key passage, Calman suggests the following element of what he terms a new 'promise':

I will recognise that the decisions I make will have consequences for the patient, the community and for resources. (p.223)

Although this was a personal proposal, and did not have official sanction, it reflects a wider concern that clinicians should become more accountable about how they decide what to do with the resources at their disposal. What form this accountability will take, and the extent to which it will be internal or external to the professions is far from clear.

As the changes to the composition and role of the GMC and the other development described here indicate, the leadership of the medical profession in particular has recognised that times have changed. Whether they have yet moved far enough is another matter. While the Bristol case did demonstrate a willingness to grasp a particularly difficult nettle, the outside perception, as Rudolf Klein notes elsewhere in this volume, was that the inquiry was too narrow in its scope and too lenient in its judgement. Frank Dobson's statement that he thought all three doctors should have been struck off may have been unwise coming from a Secretary of State, but it probably reflected a commonly held view.

Performance indicators

Shortly after the White Paper was published, the Government issued *A National Framework for Assessing Performance*, which set out their approach to managing the NHS in more detail. It emphasises various principles from the White Paper, including, once again, 'to renew the NHS *as a genuinely national service*' and '*to shift the focus onto quality of care*'.

To achieve this it proposed an enlarged and reformed set of performance indicators which moved away from measures of performance which simply counted activity or financial performance – a characteristic of earlier performance indicator sets. Six areas within which these indicators would operate were set out (see Box).

All performance indicators are to some degree an exercise in quantification. If Government wishes to find out how well an organisation is doing in relation to an objective, or how various parts of an organisation are faring relative to each other, then some kind of numerical judgement must be made.

Otherwise, rigorous and systematic comparison is difficult – one cannot judge whether Health Authority A is doing better than Health Authority B without quantifying *something*.

But here the difficulties start, and although the expanded indicators received a reasonably warm welcome, in part because of their inclusion of measures bearing on clinical activities, there are also many concerns about the whole approach. It is clearly awkward to put a number against something as nebulous as a health improvement,

The New Performance Indicator Framework

Six areas are identified by the new Government within which a modified set of performance indicators would measure the success, or otherwise, of the NHS. They are:

- ●Health improvement
  - the overall health status of populations, reflecting social and environmental factors and individual behaviour as well as care provided by the NHS and other agencies

- ●Fair access
  - access to elective surgery
  - access to family planning services
  - access to dentists
  - access to health promotion
  - access to community services

- ●Effective delivery of appropriate health care
  - health promotion/disease prevention
  - appropriateness of surgery
  - primary care management
  - compliance with standards

- ●Efficiency
  - maximising use of resources

- ●Patient/carer experience
  - accessibility
  - co-ordination and communication
  - waiting times

- ●Health outcomes of NHS care
  - NHS success in reducing levels of risk
  - NHS success in reducing levels of disease, impairment and complication of treatment
  - NHS success in optimising function and improving quality of life for patients and carers
  - NHS success in reducing premature deaths

and as a result performance indicators have tended in the past to focus on the easily measurable patients with operations cancelled, day case rates, etc. That remains true of the new proposals.

'Output' measures which do form a part of the current set – survival rates in avoidable deaths, for example – have been chosen on the basis that data are relatively easily available. They are far from representing the full range of clinical outcomes. The danger, then, is that the attention of providers and policy-makers will become unduly focused on those aspects of the NHS activity which are more easily measurable, at the expense of possibly more important elements which are harder to measure – such as a patient's satisfaction with an outcome, for example.

Another difficulty becomes apparent when the purpose of the indicators is to allow comparison of various parts of the system. Thus, in the consultation document an example is given of performance in relation to care of elderly people. Most of the elements look at how various health authorities' 'rate' according to an indicator in each of the broad categories. It is virtually impossible to look at a graphical representation of an indicator without coming to the conclusion that some are doing worse than others – that some are at the top or bottom of a 'league table'.

But 'league table' comparisons are controversial, principally because of the operation of confounding factors – circumstances more or less beyond the control of those working in the NHS. Thus, we need to be sure that case-mix, severity, environmental factors and so on are all accounted for before comparisons can be properly made. There is also the question of chance: one's

position in the league may simply be luck, and once appropriate statistical confidence limits are built in, apparently significant variations in performance become rather less so.

Given all these problems, is the Government misguided in adopting this strategy? Should it instead concentrate at the 'other end': on improving our understanding of what systems and configurations of service seem to produce better outcomes? The Government would argue – and the previous one did so in relation to health and other services – that to 'suppress' such information, no matter what the difficulties, is simply not an option in a democracy, and that accountability to the public demands that some effort is made to understand better how the system is working.

Perhaps, then, the crucial factor is how they are used. As long as their purpose is purely as an indication of where further investigation may be required, then the problems outlined above are not insuperable. They may be a valuable method of establishing where unacceptable behaviour is taking place, or where good practice can be learnt by others. They should, in short, be 'tin-openers' (to cans of worms) not 'dials' (of performance). The question remains whether such caution will be exercised when the desire is for quick answers and immediate improvement.

The remit of the Commission for Health Improvement suggests that it will operate on the basis of the tin-opener approach, i.e. that it will investigate and work with the organisations where poor performance has been identified before recommending to the Secretary of State a more rigorous course of action. But the Secretary of State will have the power to remove trust chairs and non-executives 'where there is evidence of systematic failure', exactly as Frank Dobson threatened to do in relation to one specific indicator – length of waiting list for elective care, as noted in Section 2.1. If the Secretary of State does in fact take action in this way, in relation to a measure of performance which few in the Service believe to be sensible, then the risk of the measures proposed in the Framework will seem a real one. As a result, their introduction will appear to be a threat rather than a means of improving performance.

Ombudsman

Clinical self-regulation is also being eroded from another quarter, as the Health Service Commissioner begins to investigate clinical matters. In fact, the *Health Service Commissioner's Annual Report for 1997–98* (The Stationery Office 1998) reported in detail on two significant changes bearing on his new role which had been instituted in April 1996. The first, the introduction of a new NHS complaints procedure, was considered in Section 1.4. We look here at the second, the extension of his jurisdiction to investigate complaints about the exercise of clinical judgement and about the actions of family health service practitioners.

This has two elements. The first involved a significant shift in the way family health services have to deal with complaints. Whereas previously complaints were dealt with through the statutory arrangements for considering whether a practitioner was in breach of his or her NHS terms of service, now family health service practitioners come within the Commissioner's jurisdiction and are required to have and to publicise their own in-house complaints procedure as part of the general reform of that system.

The Commissioner's overall conclusions on how it was working were as follows

- *Some GPs consider that the lack of any legal obligation to provide reasons for removing a patient from their list is of itself sufficient ground to excuse them from offering any explanation. It is not. As their representative body says in its own guidance, it is only common courtesy to do so.*

- *Some GPs too readily regard the fact that a complaint has been made as sufficient evidence that doctor–patient relationship has broken down, rather than considering the patient's concern and trying to meet it or explain why it is unfounded.*

- *Some GPs appear to act precipitately to remove a patient from their list, rather than taking time to consult colleagues, reflect on alternative courses of action, or discuss the problem with a patient.*

- *Above all, the right of patients to complain when they believe they have cause must not be inhibited by fear that, as a consequence, they or their family will find themselves facing a change of doctor. Unless that fear is removed, the new NHS complaints procedure in general practice … will be seriously undermined.* (p.11)

Overall, however, as measured by a simple volume of complaints, the operation of the scheme within family health services seems to be rather more satisfactory than those of hospitals. The ombudsman reports that in 1996/97, 36,990 complaints were made against family practitioners, compared with almost 93,000 against hospital and community services, despite the much higher levels of contacts with the former.

Higher apparent levels of satisfaction – or lower levels of overt dissatisfaction – may actually mask nervousness about damaging relations with a person one has to see quite regularly, and who may practise conveniently close to the patient's home. In this way, GPs are in a position of considerable informal strength *vis-à-vis* their patients, in a way that hospital consultants are not. The role of the Commissioner could well prove important in the future in mediating this relationship when it goes wrong.

The second arm of the Commissioner's new role relates to clinical complaints. He could not investigate any events that happened before April 1996; as a consequence he started his first investigation in May 1997; and by the end of 1997/98, 26 clinical investigations were under way but none had been completed.

The Commissioner is not entitled to investigate matters where a person has a remedy in the courts, unless to seek such a remedy would in his judgement be unreasonable. The guiding principle, however, is not to throw out any complaint which could technically be resolved in the courts – e.g. those alleging negligence – but only those where the complainant appears to be seeking financial compensation or damages. The Commissioner considers his role to be adjudicating where:

- a complainant is seeking an explanation for what he or she believes has gone wrong; or
- to find out 'what really happened'; or
- to have where appropriate the satisfaction of an apology and evidence that actions are being taken to prevent similar misfortune.

Clinical complaints currently under investigation by the ombudsman

- That the care and treatment at birth caused or contributed to the brain damage of a baby
- That there were unacceptable delays in arranging admission to a hospital of a patient who later died of meningitis
- Alleged failures in care and assessment which caused delay in discovering perforated oesophagus following an endoscopic examination
- That insufficient clinical attention was given to the information provided that a patient with a dislocated elbow was receiving anti-coagulant therapy, resulting in internal bleeding, the need for several operations, and some permanent impairment
- That a diagnostic investigation (ultrasound) was cancelled, although it would have led to earlier discovery of a cancer which proved fatal
- That a psychiatrist inappropriately diagnosed and treated a patient later found to have a schizo-affective disorder

Although none of the investigations has been completed, some of the complaints clearly involve very serious matters – the Box gives some examples.

For all clinical complaints the Commissioner must appoint professional (i.e. clinical) advisers, typically from within the specialty concerned. To some degree, then, the outcome of a complaint will still remain influenced by the professionals themselves, with all the attendant dangers of self-protection which already damage public confidence. However, the Commissioner is quite clear that the final decision will be his alone and, given that technical matters will inevitably require advice from those expert in that field, such a situation may be unavoidable. Perhaps the final assessment of this particular reform must wait until we can see how many times the Commissioner is prepared to find against the profession. In any event he believes, from experience of 1997/98, that in the future the majority of complaints he deals with will involve clinical matters, which quite apart from the impact on the profession, will have a profound impact on the work of the Commissioner.

The Select Committee on Public Administration also reviewed the work of the Commissioner, in the context of the general standard of administration in the NHS and the accountability of those who manage it. As noted in Section 1.4, their overall conclusion was strikingly severe, referring as it did to 'recidivist trusts' whose record had been poor over a considerable period of time.

One such 'recidivist' trust was the University College London Hospitals Trust. The case cited in the ombudsman's report for 1996/97 involved failure to deal sensitively and appropriately with the relative of a dying man. But it transpired that this complaint was only one of six concerning poor complaint-handling by the trust between 1994 and 1995. At one point the ombudsman was investigating five complaints against the trust. Although the chair of the trust also chaired the Complaints Panel – 'to send out a signal' that the trust was taking matters seriously – according to the Select Committee report, this did little to alter the way the Panel worked (it met only quarterly during this period of the ombudsman's investigation). Furthermore, in June 1995 the Complaints Panel heard that 44 of the 79 complaints from March to May of that year remained unresolved, and not one complainant had received a reply.

The trust argued that they were operating in a turbulent environment arising from the creation of the trust out of a number of separate hospitals. But the Select Committee felt that there was a more serious fault in the operation of NHS accountability, as the chair had claimed that, regardless of the failures identified above, it would not fundamentally 'affect my decision to continue as chairman of the trust':

> We believe his [the chairman's] confidence to be completely unfounded. The evidence we heard, and the events of the case, made us believe that he should not have continued … It is essential that NHS bodies are made properly accountable when they fail; if prompt action had been taken in this case, we believe it would have sent a message to the NHS in general which would have had a galvanising effect across the institution. (para 19)

This draws attention to the requirement for proper control and, where necessary, sanctions to be exercised for accountability to work properly – it is not sufficient for people simply to 'account' for actions and then continue as if nothing had happened. In this case, both accountability and control were missing. But how should the chair have been 'removed'? This would appear to be a job for the Secretary of State, although the Committee refrained from specific reference to that individual. However, the problem of 'overload', as we further discuss below, means that in practice it is unlikely that such inaction and incompetence over a significant period will be discovered, and the requisite action taken, until it is too late.

Openness

One of the key concerns to emerge from the Bristol case was the lack of robust accessible evidence of clinical outcome with which it might be possible to 'benchmark' the performance of individual clinicians and trusts in various parts of the NHS. Medical audit has always been a 'private' activity among the clinicians concerned, and thus any statistical evidence that death rates, for example, were higher than they ought to be relies on whistleblowing to be brought to wider attention.

But 'government' openness was given a boost in December 1997 with the publication of the White Paper, *Your Right to Know: the Government's proposals for a Freedom of Information Act*. The proposals were summarised in another document, *Code of Practice on Access to Government Information – 1997 Report*, which annually reviews the progress of the Code which the Act is set to replace. The key changes which the latter proposes over the former are:

- unlike the Code the proposed Act will apply to almost all public authorities across the country, including the NHS (which is currently subject to separate codes); local authorities; and some private sector organisations which carry out public functions;
- whereas the Code only allows access to information, the proposed Act will provide access both to information and to the actual records held by organisations;
- instead of the Code's 15 'exemptions', public authorities will only be able to withhold information if disclosure would cause harm to one of seven specified 'interests'. Moreover, in most cases the test will be one of 'substantial' rather than 'simple' harm;
- the Act will be policed by a new independent information commissioner. The commissioner will have wide-ranging powers, including a legally enforceable power to order disclosure

(whereas under the Code it was only possible to *recommend* disclosure).

The Code's 15 exemptions, and the Act's proposed seven 'interests', are as listed in Table 2.11.

In the proposed Act, it is the last 'interest' which provides the greatest opportunity for Government to retain an element of secrecy in the conduct of their business. This is for two reasons: first, the 'integrity' of decision-making could be interpreted widely, including anything which would prevent Government from making 'good' decisions; second, it is subject to a 'simple' rather than 'substantial' harm test:

> *factors which would need to be taken into account in determining whether this test would prevent disclosure of information are likely to include:*
>
> – *the maintenance of collective responsibility in government;*
> – *the political impartiality of officials;*
> – *the importance of internal discussion and advice being able to take place on a free and frank basis;*
> – *the extent to which the relevant records or information relate to decisions still under consideration, or publicly announced. (Your Right to Know, para. 3.12)*

The test of the Act's success, of course, will be whether it makes a significant difference to the quantity and nature of information disclosed in practice. The 1997 Report notes that the number of requests under the Code in 1997 remained much the same as in 1996, and that the number of Code requests remains far below levels of Freedom of Information applications registered in countries with statutory regimes.

Table 2.11

Code's 'exemptions'	Act's 'interests'
Defence, security and international relations	National security, defence and international relations
Internal discussion and advice	Law enforcement
Communications with the Royal Household	Personal privacy
Law enforcement and legal proceedings	Commercial confidentiality
Immigration and nationality	The safety of the individual, the public and the environment
Effective management of the economy and collection of tax	Information supplied in confidence
Effective management and operations of the public service	The integrity of the decision-making and policy advice processes in government (subject to the weaker 'simple' harm test)
Public employment, public appointments and honours	
Voluminous or vexatious requests	
Publication and prematurity in relation to publication	
Research, statistics and analysis	
Privacy of an individual	
Third party's commercial confidences	
Information given in confidence	
Statutory and other restrictions	

Sources: *Your Right to Know,* Cm 3818, and *Code of Practice on Access to Government Information,* 2nd edition, Office of Public Service, 1997

That this continues to be the case several years after its introduction is almost certainly indicative of the Code's underlying limitations as a non-statutory openness arrangement whose operation is (in the views of many applicants) essentially dependent on the goodwill of the department or agency. (p.4)

Alternatively, it could be that the British public are so used to the culture of secrecy that they will take many years – Act or no Act – to get used to new rights to information. However, a report from the Association of Community Health Councils for England and Wales on access to medical records (Health Surveys no. 1) found that, although the Access to Health Records Act provides for patients having access to their records, some GPs have been imposing inappropriate charges for access itself, for photocopying and for explaining the records to their patients. One obstacle, in other words, has replaced another.

Something that remains unclear is the extent to which the Act will affect the disclosure of information such as that in the Bristol case.

Presumably, clinical audit data will remain with the individuals concerned. But under clinical governance arrangements, the chief executive and board will be accountable for the quality of clinical care and will expect greater access to the types of information which will allow them to discharge that responsibility.

This information may well then be covered by the new Act, with important implications for public scrutiny of the performance of individual consultants. For their part, this may encourage clinicians to become more secretive about clinical information, on the grounds that too much openness will encourage people to cover up their mistakes rather than own up to them. The Act will provide more detail on precisely which bodies, and who within them, are to be covered.

One formal change to 'openness' in the NHS had already been signalled by Frank Dobson announcing in June 1997 that all trust, as well as health authority, meetings must in the future be held in public (Department of Health 97/148, 3 June 1997). Following this announcement, Alan Milburn outlined in more detail the changes the Government proposed:

- *secret NHS trust board meetings will cease; three days' notice of time and place must be given; that agendas and papers must be provided; that newspapers are enabled to report on the meetings; and that committee proceedings are treated as proceedings of the body and public access be given although closed sessions will still be allowed for some confidential matters such as patient or personnel issues;*

- *no management information will be classified as 'commercial in confidence' between NHS bodies;*

- *reports from committee hearings set up to hear appeals from certain doctors and dentists who believe they have been unfairly dismissed will now be made available to the parties involved in the appeal.*

(Department of Health 97/371)

These changes were finally ratified in February 1998. In a separate development, from April health authorities will be required to publish their inspection reports on nursing homes and private hospitals and clinics.

The significance of changes to board meetings had already been discounted by community health councils, who argued that important business simply goes on elsewhere. Their concerns were raised in January with reports that some authorities were deciding matters of local interest, such as hospital closures, in secret sessions:

> *there are problems with the legislation because it gives [the boards] a broad discretion. We [CHCs] believe new guidance is needed, not just for HAs but for regional offices who seem to be encouraging HAs to breach the law.*

(Health Service Journal 8 January 1998, p.5)

An informal survey by one ex-trust board member also raised questions about whether the regulations outlined above were being followed:

without supporting papers (at five of the nine meetings attended) my being there was almost useless. Many board members spoke quietly and many sat with their backs to us … At one meeting, I had hardly any idea what was being discussed. When people said things like 'I think the report is self-explanatory', or 'You will see what the position is on page five' the sense of exclusion was almost complete.

(*Health Service Journal* 19 March 1998, p.31)

From this point of view, a 'freedom of information' Act is likely to be more significant for the accountability of the service than open meetings. It is likely, nonetheless, given the general apathy of most members of the public when it comes to matters of public policy, that success of such an Act will depend on those who have a direct interest in it actually using the system, and on how forcefully the news media pursue documents and information which might expose unwelcome practices.

Board membership

It has long been felt that effective accountability within the NHS depends in part on those appointed to public boards broadly representing in socio-demographic terms the populations they serve. Last year we reported on the first full survey of all public appointments to NHS boards and found that, contrary to expectations, the proportion of women and minority ethnic members was not very different from the population as a whole – 40 and 5 per cent respectively. However, this obscured variations from one area to another, and failed to reveal how many women or minority ethnic members gained 'chair' status, for example.

New figures published in *Department of Health Public Appointments Annual Report 1998* showed that the number of board members in these categories was growing. Table 2.12 shows the overall position at 1 March 1998.

The number of appointments made since 1 May 1997 in each category was 52 per cent women and 9 per cent from minority ethnic groups.

Under the Nolan rules, all candidates should be selected on merit, but they must also satisfy the Government that they are personally committed to the NHS and can bring a user's perspective to it, as well as in aggregate increasing the number of women and minority ethnic members. In order to satisfy this difficult set of criteria the Government invited local councils and Members of Parliament to offer nominations, as a means of expanding the potential pool – over 1,800 were supplied. This caused something of a spat between Frank Dobson and the then shadow Secretary of State John Maples, who claimed that Parliament had not been kept fully informed of these changes. Although the allegations were effectively refuted by the intervention of the Commissioner for Public Appointments, Sir Leonard Peach, the accusation was in fact devised to raise the issue of 'political' appointments. Nominations from councils were overwhelmingly likely to be of Labour sympathisers.

Political 'activity' must now be declared by new appointees, and the new figures support the claim of political 'bias'. Of those appointed since 1 May 1997:

- 615 declared no political interest;
- 26 were active on behalf of the Liberal Democrats;

Table 2.12 Composition of boards

	Minority ethnic groups (%)	Women (overall) (%)	Women (chairs) (%)
Health authorities	6.3	40.5	40.8
NHS trusts	7.4	43.7	28.4
Special health authorities and dental practice board	10.5	36.8	21.4
Executive non-departmental public bodies	9.2	33.7	28.6
Total	**7.5**	**42.3**	**30.6**

Source: *Department of Health Public Appointments Annual Report 1998*, p.v

- 29 were active on behalf of the Conservatives;
- 208 were active on behalf of Labour;
- 4 other.

Many of these serve their communities as councillors: 111 of those declaring support for Labour, for example. Whether this 'bias' is inappropriate, however, is less obvious. Commitment to the NHS might necessitate rather more Labour than Tory appointees. More generally, for a legitimately elected government to implement its proposed reforms to the NHS it could be argued that a board membership broadly in sympathy with those aims is required.

Overview

The developments described in this section can be seen as a desirable rounding out of the way that the NHS accounts to the nation at large for the way it uses the funds allocated to it and the quality of the service it offers. In particular the degree of discretion enjoyed by the medical profession in respect of both will be reduced.

But while this may seem desirable, there are risks not so much in what the Government is trying to do but in the way it is going about it. Most of the reforms in train involve greater activity by the centre: the introduction of performance indicators, the activities of the National Institute for Clinical

Excellence (NICE) and the Commission for Health Improvement (CHIMP), the activities of the ombudsman and so on. Furthermore, the introduction of Primary Care Groups reporting to health authorities can be seen as a means of corralling otherwise independent GPs into the mainstream of NHS accountability.

All this can be defended both on straightforward accountability terms – by making GPs, for example, more directly answerable for their use of public funds than previously – and in terms of geographical equity, which requires a single point of reference and control at the centre. But the pressure on the centre is growing and will increasingly do so as national service frameworks for care provision along the lines of Calman-Hine come into place.

We noted in Section 1.3, reports into two major failures in screening programmes. In his October 1997 report on events at Kent and Canterbury NHS Trust, *Review of cervical screening services at Kent and Canterbury Hospitals NHS Trust*, William Wells isolated the following key problems:

- poor and confused management at the trust;
- warnings about understaffing and poor training, and other matters, went unheeded over many years;

- the remoteness and apparent lack of interest in the cytology screening programme by its consultants;
- lack of a clear line of accountability on both management and quality assurance for the national Programme through the NHS Executive and Health Authority to the trust.

The fact that this was a national programme implies a greater responsibility on national agencies, with all the attendant responsibilities for ensuring that quality is up to scratch: this plainly did not happen in the Kent case. Wells recommended in his report that:

> management of the … Programme should be strengthened by incorporating responsibility for issuing guidance, quality assurance and performance management of local implementation into the regular accountability structure of the NHS Executive. (p.39)

But although this specific recommendation seems sensible, the implication of following it across the full range of clinical activity where, as in the case of the National Service Frameworks, the centre has a key role, is enormous in terms of the strain put on the capacity of the centre to monitor and respond. And other trends are adding to this pressure. As noted above, where poor performance of a trust becomes apparent, it is the Secretary of State who has the ultimate sanction of dismissal of the chair and non-executives. With more openness and rigorous scrutiny of board performance, it is likely that demands for such severe action will become greater. But can the Secretary of State and his advisers manage, in a practical sense, to monitor the many hundreds of such people and their performance?

The Select Committee on Public Administration noted in its second report on the ombudsman:

> these powers [of dismissal] are rarely used but they exist. The Ombudsman told us that he could not think of a case where the powers had been used in response to one of his Office's investigations. Of course the Secretary of State also has to consider with enormous care the extent to which blame can be pinned to any single individual. Yet such care and consideration should not inhibit his ability to take salutary action where it seems justified. (para 101)

In the following paragraph the Committee continues:

> We believe that the central management of the NHS should take a closer interest in the performance of NHS bodies across the country. (para 102)

But the Committee also notes Sir Alan Langland's doubt about the extent to which the NHS Executive, for its part, could monitor an organisation of the size of the NHS in detail.

The response of this Government, and others before it, to many of the ills of the NHS has been to strengthen central powers, and with it the requirements of central accountability. This has been deemed necessary to retain a proper sense of a *national* health service. It is inevitable that accountability 'upwards' will form some part of any institution financed largely from general taxation; it is equally inevitable that some form of central direction will be necessary in an increasingly open and visible service if a sense of geographical fairness is to be retained. The question is: is the centre up to it?

Part 3 Overview

Our Review began by citing the Government's aim of making the NHS the best health care system in the world. Fired by that ambition, it is scarcely surprising that the list of initiatives started under the new Government is immense. The Government has acknowledged that the changes it wishes to see cannot be realised overnight. *A First Class Service* refers to a ten-year programme for modernising the NHS. The White Paper also emphasises the need for a change in culture, also by its nature a slow process.

Despite these sensible qualifications, *The New NHS* sets out a demanding schedule for change on the ground, as do the subsequent circulars which form part of the implementation process. The Government is impatient for results – as the succession of measures targeted on waiting lists indicates.

As the generally favourable reception to the White Paper suggests, most of the Government's proposals, or at least its aspirations, have been welcomed: an explicit concern with equity and with clinical quality and accountability, continuing emphasis on primary care-led purchasing, maintenance of the distinction between purchasing and providing, explicit concern with the way that specific services are designed, better links between health providers and between health and social care, and more emphasis on health as opposed to health care – all these represent areas of broad consensus.

But that consensus does not necessarily embrace the way the Government has gone about pursuing these broad aims. *Implementing the White Paper* identifies a series of practical obstacles which suggest that rapid change will be difficult. These obstacles fall into three main groups:

- management capacity
- knowledge base
- incentives to change

We consider these in turn.

Management capacity

The White and Green Papers and the series of consultation documents which have emerged in 1998 represent an enormous workload, both locally and at the centre.

The key change in the central role, already begun under the Conservatives, is that the NHS Executive, or the Department of Health, has become committed to achieving specific outcomes – cuts in numbers waiting, cuts in management costs, increases in efficiency, reductions in mixed-sex wards, and so on. The White Paper and subsequent circulars and consultation papers make no substantive mention, however, of what the proposals taken as a whole mean for the central role, in terms of time, skills and technical developments.

At local level, the new agenda creates a range of new tasks, such as the management of clinical performance or the development of health improvement programmes, which will involve vast amounts of time, much of it in what is often the most demanding but unrewarding of activities, inter-agency work. Moreover, local management will in many parts of the country have to deal with pressures from service configuration, as well as changes in the structures of health authorities and trusts, which will both absorb management time and reduce management capacity.

In this omission, the new Government continues the mistake of its predecessors in failing to acknowledge that management of a health care system is a creative task, not an overhead to the system which adds no value of its own. Consequently, it continues with the arbitrary policy of reducing management expenditures while increasing what management has to do. These cuts, as the figures given in Section 2.1 show, are severe and not only will they have a direct effect on numbers of staff but also an indirect effect through the process of responding to the need to make reductions.

Knowledge base

The key theme of much of *The New NHS* and *A First Class Service* is the proper application of existing knowledge. The role of NICE, for example, as noted in Section 1.5 is to remove the confusion that has arisen because different bodies have come to different recommendations. Similarly, the national service frameworks are intended to be based on an assessment of all the relevant evidence.

While there is an obvious attraction in the notion of a central assessment of the best available evidence, it ignores what is apparent in many parts of the NHS – that the right sort of evidence is not available. This, in turn, reflects a fundamental bias in the way that the knowledge relevant to the delivery of clinical services is derived towards the specific intervention rather than the system of care.

This bias is slowly being corrected, but in the meantime there remain huge gaps in knowledge about the best way of designing and delivering services, or improving health by other means. There is implicit in *A First Class Service* a form of technical arrogance, to the extent that its proposals imply that solutions can be found which are both reliable and stable enough to form the basis of detailed implementation plans such as those involved in national service frameworks. Although the Paper refers to the possibility that more research may be required, overall it exudes confidence that answers can be found.

There are some areas of clinical activity where professionals can have justified confidence that they know 'what works' and reasonable people would agree that it should be generally applied.

In cases such as these the logic of national frameworks and guidelines is compelling. Equally, however, there are many areas where 'what works' is not so clear. Furthermore, frameworks or programmes of care require the identification of the best combination of interventions, all of which may work to a greater or lesser degree when considered in isolation but not necessarily as well when viewed as a whole. Furthermore, service innovation will reveal new areas of ignorance as they point the way to new combinations which have never been the subject of systematic research.

The gaps are even greater and more obvious in the areas of organisation and management. The more the centre seeks to 'performance-manage' the NHS, and personal social services, the greater the understanding it requires of how the system it intends to manage responds to the policies imposed upon it. The management of waiting lists during 1997/98 provides an excellent example of failure to do so. Even if the Secretary of State was right to conclude that waiting lists were coming down in the second quarter of 1998 (more precisely, the months of May, June and July – to ensure that a large reduction could be announced, a non-standard 'quarter' was used), neither he nor anyone else could know what the effect of that achievement had had on the other services nor on real waiting times for access to care, i.e. times including waits outside hospital.

This kind of 'system' knowledge has been systematically undervalued throughout the life of the NHS: the R&D initiative has so far done little to correct that bias – the long-awaited programme into service delivery and organisation is yet to emerge. Under the Conservatives, the key mistake was to pretend that the 1990 system was self-regulating when it was not. The new arrangements are clearly not self-regulating and hence do require 'system' knowledge as well as better monitoring and analysis of the data collected. The first timid recognition of this can be found in the attempts, referred to in Section 2.1 to introduce a system approach to waiting-list management and winter pressures which explicitly acknowledges the linkages between the various parts of the health care system. The difficulty is that many of the underlying relationships are not understood.

Incentives to change

As noted in Section 1.1, *The New NHS* states that New Labour has found a new, or third way, of running a national health service, rejecting command and control on the one hand and market processes on the other. According to *The New NHS*:

> there will be a 'third way' of running the NHS – a system based on partnership and driven by performance. It will go with the grain of recent efforts by NHS staff to overcome the obstacles of the internal market. Increasingly those working in primary care, NHS Trusts and Health Authorities have tried to move away from outright competition towards a more collaborative approach. Inevitably, however, these efforts have been only partially successful and their benefits have not as yet been extended to patients in all parts of the country. (p. 10)

Here and in other parts of the text the emphasis is on co-operation, collaboration and partnership. The White Paper does not analyse these notions nor discuss the conditions which will promote them. In respect of trusts, however, it indicates the intention to impose:

a new statutory duty for NHS Trusts to work in partnership with other NHS organisations. The duty of partnership will require their participation (alongside Primary Care Groups, universities and Local Authorities) in developing the Health Improvement Programme under the leadership of the Health Authority. In turn, the Health Improvement Programme will set the framework for the services NHS Trusts provide and the detailed agreements they make with Primary Care Groups. (p.45)

The perceived need to impose a duty to co-operate might stem from the belief that co-operation between health service organisations is not something that can be assumed to be a natural phenomenon. Unfortunately, just as *Working for Patients* did not rest on an analysis of the conditions required for effective competition, *The New NHS* does not rest on an analysis of the conditions which promote co-operation. However, it does suggest that incentive structures may be helpful:

Increasingly, clinical teams will develop and agree the new longer term service agreements with Primary Care Groups. Clinician to clinician partnership will focus service agreements on securing genuine health gain. The efficiency incentives that come with budgetary responsibility will be reinforced by longer term service agreements that allow a share of any savings made to be redeployed by the clinical teams, in a way consistent with the NHS Trust's priorities and the local Health Improvement Programme. (p.49)

Furthermore:

there will be **clear incentives** *to improve performance and efficiency. Health Authorities which perform well will be eligible for extra cash. NHS Trusts and Primary Care Groups*

will be able to use savings from longer term agreements to improve services for patients. (p.19)

The incentive model underlying these proposals is essentially that of 'carrot and stick', to use the terms of the Secretary of State's announcement of the extra funds for waiting lists. But, as the excerpts from the Audit Commission and Clinical Standards Advisory Committee reports cited in Section 1.2 indicate, the critical need is that the incentives facing the various agencies involved in complex care programmes should be aligned so that co-operation is mutually beneficial. Neither the White Paper nor any of the subsequent papers acknowledge how difficult this task is – it is over a decade since the Audit Commission identified perverse incentives within community care. Arguably, despite the transfer of social security funds to local authorities, they have got worse.

The White Paper is on surer ground when it goes on to assert that:

it will be increasingly important for the staff of NHS Trusts to work efficiently and effectively in teams within and across organisational boundaries. Integrated care for patients will rely on models of training and education that give staff a clear understanding of how their own roles fit with those of others within both the health and social care professions. (p.46)

The White Paper is almost certainly right to suggest that training and education are the key to change but it has little of interest to say about what changes are required in that area – a human resources strategy, although promised, has yet to appear. However, the timescale within which changes in training and education will be able to have an impact is somewhat slower than that envisaged by the Government. The Government is clearly intent on pressing ahead with national service frameworks, including, as one of the first two, mental health where the need for changes in organisation, management and training is extensive and the difficulty in getting the right balance between health and social care interests also well documented. The history of the NHS and of health and social services is that collaboration cannot be taken for granted: even the introduction of duties is insufficient – that too was tried in the 1970s.

Already however the signs of what the new driver will be are apparent:

> there will be **clear sanctions** when performance and efficiency are not up to standard. Health Authorities will be able to withdraw freedoms from Primary Care Groups. They, in turn, will have a range of new powers to lever up standards and efficiency at local NHS Trusts and as a last resort will be able to change provider if, over time, performance does not meet the required standard. And the NHS Executive will be able directly to intervene to rectify poor performance in any part of the NHS. (p.19)

The New NHS does recognise that incentives may help to guide performance in the desired direction. However, it does not consider specific ways in which behaviour might be changed by such means. Instead, it sets out in outline a system of monitoring and control, backed by sanctions, as outlined in Section 1.5.

Even without this new apparatus, the Secretary of State has shown that the means for more command and control are already at his disposal in his actions in relation to waiting lists, by the targeting of funds and the threats of dismissal

aimed at board non-executives. Thus the White Paper itself, but also the Government's own predilections, open the way for an NHS which is subject to much greater direction than ever before. The structure of control which the Chancellor announced with the comprehensive spending review will mean that the pressure for 'better' measurable performance will increase even further.

But the Government does not see it that way. In a speech in June 1998, Alan Milburn set out his definition of the third way:

- Clear national standards for quality and access, reinforced by monitoring arrangements.
- Local responsibility for delivering services, backed by a performance management system 'that counts the things that matter'.
- Open benchmarking.
- Public involvement and scrutiny to hold local services accountable.
- Incentives for the best performers.
- Intervention and penalties 'to sort out failure'.

(*Health Service Journal*, 25 June 1998, p.5)

What this represents is a command-and-control system. Within it, there is no role for local judgement about what to do: there is no form of accountability other than to the centre. It flies in the face of much of the Government's own rhetoric. This Government, like the previous one, has not understood its own reforms.

Conclusion

The Government's broad aims command widespread support. The danger in the present situation is that the cost of pursuing a small number of its specific targets will be too high, not simply in terms of direct costs but also in terms of the indirect costs, such as the absorption of clinical time in organisational issues. These costs will take time to become apparent but eventually they will emerge.

Under the previous Government, the need to demonstrate clear improvements from the new arrangements, even before they had had time to take effect, led to the emphasis on central targets – the purchaser efficiency index and Patient's Charter requirements. This Government has already adopted the same approach to waiting lists, introducing new mechanisms and imposing strong pressures on trusts to meet one specific target. The risk was already apparent in mid-1998 that the emphasis on this one highly visible target, on which the prestige of the Government as a whole was attached, was distorting other priorities.

So in the end the central critique of the Government's many proposals may be that they are mutually inconsistent. *The New NHS* recognises, admirably, the responsibility of the Department of Health to ensure that individual policies are mutually consistent. Unhappily, it does not spell out what this means in practice, understandably so in view of its difficulty – nor have any subsquent official papers. Unhappily also, the performance framework does not apply to it so there is no explicit test of whether it has succeeded or not. Its failure will make itself known – the only question is when.

Part 4 Calendar of Events

May 1997

1 **Government**: Labour wins General Election.

19 **Pay:** Secretary of State announced the end of current arrangements for local pay.

20 **Fundholding:** Secretary of State announced new financial arrangements for GP fundholding: subsequent guidance issued in EL (97)33. Eighth wave of fundholding deferred.

22 **Cancer/finance:** £10m allocated to diagnosis and treatment of breast cancer.

27 **Information technology:** Frank Burns seconded to lead review of Information and Management technology.

June 1997

10 **Private Finance Initiative:** three-point plan for improvement of Private Finance Initiative announced.

11 **Efficiency:** NHS Efficiency Task Force established.

12 **Winter planning:** health authorities instructed to give priority to emergency admissions.

19 **Fraud:** prescription fraud scrutiny report published.

20 **London:** review panel announced, under chairmanship of Sir Leslie Turnberg.

25 **Health Action Zones:** notion of health action zones set out by Secretary of State as co-operative health partnerships.

26 **GP commissioning:** applications requested for GP commissioning pilots.

July 1997

2 **Finance:** Chancellor announces extra £ 1.2bn for NHS in the UK.

3 **Private finance:** 14 hospital projects financed through the Private Finance Initiative given the go-ahead.

7 **Public health:** elements of new public health strategy announced, including review of health inequalities by Sir Donald Acheson.

11 **Paediatric intensive care:** plans for a nationwide mobile intensive care service for children announced, following publication of report from National Co-ordinating Group.
Clinical performance: announcement of intention to publish clinical performance indicators.

16 **Fundholding:** introduction of common waiting lists and maximum waiting times for fundholders and non-fundholders announced.
Private finance: National Health Service (Private Finance) Act received Royal Assent.

21 **Public health:** Healthy Living Centres announced.

30 **Hospital building:** contract concluded for first major health project financed through the Private Finance Initiative, at Dartford and Gravesham.
Accountability: trusts instructed to hold board meetings in public.

August 1997

6 **Patient's Charter:** new drive to end mixed-sex wards announced.

19 **Public health:** £19m allocated to improve hygiene in butchers' shops.

29 **Winter planning:** guidance issued on winter planning.

September 1997

9 **Dentistry:** Investing in Dentistry programme announced.

11 **Finance:** committee appointed to advise on allocation of financial resources, covering both primary and secondary care.

12 **Mental health:** Independent Reference Group established to vet hospital closures, and other issues.

20 **Hospital doctors:** code of practice on use of locum doctors in hospitals published.

22 **Mergers:** targets set for management cost savings from trust mergers of £0.5m within the first two years of going ahead.

23 **Clinical education:** changes announced in funding arrangements, following introduction of university tuition fees.

25 **Accountability:** NHS instructed to remove 'gagging' clauses in staff contracts.

29 **Accountability:** guidance issued on controls assurance statements in EL(97)55.

30 **Primary care:** approval given to first round of commissioning pilots
Clinical education/finance: £50m made available for professional training and facilities.

October 1997

8 **Patient's Charter:** review of Charter announced, led by Greg Dykes.

14 **Finance/winter pressures:** £300m extra finance for the NHS in the UK allocated for winter pressures.

17 **Fraud:** appointment of fraud 'supremo' announced.

18 **Fraud:** measures announced to prevent and reduce fraud by NHS dentists.

19 **Patient's Charter:** new standard for A&E immediate assessment published.
Fundholding: guidance issued for fundholding in 1998/99 designed to reduce management costs and give health authorities greater budgetary control.

21 **Winter pressures:** Secretary of State announces strategy for tackling winter pressures.

23 **Specialised services/finance:** £12m announced for NHS 'centres of excellence'.

30 **Health Action Zones:** £30m allocated for Health Action Zones.
Nursing: recruitment advertising costing £2.15m announced.

November 1997

3 **Screening:** Secretary of State ordered reorganisation of breast and cervical screening programmes.

4 **Finance/intensive care:** £5m allocated for children's intensive care.

18 **Waiting lists:** waiting-list action team appointed.

28 **Medical Workforce:** third report from the Medical Workforce Standing Advisory Committee published.

December 1997

4 **Long-term care:** Royal Commission into Long-Term Care established, with Sir Stewart Sutherland as chairman.
Finance: action announced to reclaim costs of traffic accidents from insurers.
Public health: European ban agreed on tobacco advertising and sponsorship

5 **Hospital building:** formation of NHS Capital Prioritisation Advisory Group announced.

9 **White Paper:** *The New NHS* published.

10 **Patient information:** report on protection of confidential information by Dame Fiona Caldicott published.

17 **Screening:** action plan to strengthen cervical screening announced.

18 **Public health:** £300m of Lottery money announced for Healthy Living Centres.

22 **Management costs:** additional savings of £80m announced.
Finance: £47.6m allocated to modernise 16 hard-pressed health authorities.

23 **Primary care:** 94 first-wave primary care pilots announced.

January 1998

1 **Dentistry:** funding announced for NHS dentistry.

7 **Fraud:** family health services fraud initiative announced, including setting up of fraud hotline and internet site.

19 **Staff involvement:** Task Force established on involving staff in improving efficiency and working practices.

20 **Learning disability:** guidance issued on rights of access to NHS services.

21 **Performance indicators:** consultation paper, *A National Framework for Assessing Performance*, issued.

29 **Pay:** pay increases announced for NHS Pay Review Body staff.

February 1998

3 **London:** report of review panel, chaired by Sir Leslie Turnberg, on London's health services published: recommendations accepted by Government.

5 **Public health:** green paper, *Our Healthier Nation*, published.
Finance/ethnic minorities: £1.3m allocated to improve health of minority ethnic groups.

18 **Patient's Charter:** renewed drive announced to end mixed-sex accommodation.

25 **The New NHS:** Guidance for implementing *The New NHS* and *Our Healthier Nation* issued in HSC 1998/021.

March 1998

2 **Charges:** prescription charge raised to £5.80.

6 **Accountability:** guidance issued on personal liability of non-executive directors of trusts in HSC 1998/010.

17 **Finance:** Chancellor announces additional £500m for NHS in the UK.

18 **Waiting lists:** strategy for waiting-list reduction set out by Secretary of State.

23 **London:** White Paper on Greater London Authority published.
NHS Direct: pilots launched in three areas.

31 **Health Action Zones:** first round of Health Action Zones announced.

April 1998

7 **Hospital building:** 11 major hospital developments given the go-ahead.

9 **Waiting lists:** performance fund for authorities hitting waiting list targets announced.

16 **National Service Frameworks:** the first two areas for National Service Frameworks announced, coronary heart disease and mental health, under leadership of Professor George **Alberi** and Professor Graham Thorneycroft respectively.

17 **Accountability:** guidance issued on controls assurance statements.

21 **Screening:** first report of National Screening Committee published.

23 **Dentistry:** new strategy for NHS dentistry announced.

28 **Finance/waiting lists:** £288m allocated to reducing waiting lists.

29 **Litigation:** Secretary of State sought suggestions to help cut down litigation against the NHS.

30 **Fraud:** responsibilities of health authorities in relation to fraud set out in HSC 1998/076.
Waiting lists: Peter Homa appointed as 'list buster'

May 1998

8 **Finance/Primary Care Groups:** £22m allocated for development of Primary Care Groups.

15 **NHS Direct:** second wave of pilots announced. **Dentistry:** 15 pilot schemes announced.

18 **Finance/waiting lists:** allocation of £65m for primary and community services announced. **London:** announcement of single London office as from 1 April 1999.

19 **Mental health:** Independent Reference Group issued report on future shape of mental health services.

21 **Waiting lists:** Secretary of State announced that 18-month target has been met.

28 **Fraud:** James Gee appointed fraud 'supremo'.

29 **Procurement:** efficiency review of NHS procurement announced.

June 1998

8 **Self-care:** first national home health booklet launched.

9 **Clinical performance:** plans announced for publication of clinical indicators at hospital level and to make participation in confidential enquiries compulsory.

10 **Carers:** development of a carers' strategy announced. **Management costs:** proposals for Out of Area Treatments announced to replace extra-contractual referrals.

18 **Clinical performance:** public inquiry announced into paediatric cardiac services at Bristol Royal Infirmary.

29 **Primary care:** second wave of primary care pilots announced.

July 1998

1 **Quality of care:** consultation paper, *A First Class Service*, published.

6 **NHS Direct:** £14m announced to extend NHS Direct.

13 **Finance:** Chancellor of the Exchequer announced results of the Comprehensive Spending Review.

15 **Finance:** Secretary of State announced some of the uses to which the extra funds made available to the NHS will be put.

23 **Fraud:** recruitment drive for fraud unit announced.

29 **Mental health:** Secretary of State set out 'third way' for mental health services.

August 1998

4 **NHS Direct:** second wave of sites announced, extending numbers covered to 19m.

5 **Finance/cancer:** £10m allocated to bowel cancer.

6 **Primary care:** formation of 480 Primary Care Groups announced.

10 **Pay:** reform of consultants' distinction awards scheme announced.

11 **Health Action Zones:** second round of Health Action Zones announced.

13 **Primary care:** guidance issued in HSC 1998/139 on development of Primary Care Groups.

18 **Waiting lists:** fall in numbers recorded on waiting lists announced.

24 **Screening:** cervical screening action team report published.

ANALYSIS

Does the public mind having to wait?

Jack Kneeshaw

Throughout the 1990s, successive Governments have attached great importance to waiting lists (i.e. the number of patients waiting for hospital treatment) and time spent waiting for elective treatment in the NHS. Since the General Election in May 1997, waiting lists in particular have assumed a new level of political significance. The Labour Government has committed itself to reducing their size by some 100,000 as 'a first step'. In his speech to the NHS 50th Anniversary Conference, Tony Blair recently made the claim:

> I am proud of the pledge we made on waiting lists. People are fed up with waiting. They wait for a GP appointment. They wait in the GP surgery. They wait for a prescription. They wait for outpatients. They wait to have tests. They wait for results. They wait for their operation. They sometimes even wait to be discharged.

Despite the increased amount of attention given to the issue, however – and despite the proliferation of opinion surveys on health care issues in recent years – little is known about the public's opinions on waiting in the NHS. The public's views on waiting lists and waiting times have been examined by researchers in previous editions of *Health Care UK* (1994/95 and 1996/97) but no systematic study has ever been undertaken of how attitudes have changed over the years and what factors determine them.

This article aims to fill that gap. It begins with a brief description of how actual waiting times for different NHS services have changed and, where relevant, the numbers waiting. It then draws on British Social Attitudes (BSA) surveys to describe shifts in the public's attitudes towards waiting in the period 1987–96 (1996 being the most recent year for which the data have been published). The article also examines in closer detail those changes in public opinion that seem most difficult to explain: the increasingly *lower* levels of dissatisfaction with waiting lists and the public's enduring dissatisfaction with waiting in casualty, which continues despite recorded improvements in the accident and emergency (A&E) service.

Next, in order to see whether media coverage has an effect on public opinion, we conduct an analysis of articles published in *The Independent* since 1989, examining trends both in the coverage and in the presentation of waiting in the NHS for that newspaper. Two rival explanations

Table 1 Waiting in the NHS, 1988–97

	1988	1989	1990	1991	1992	1993	1994	1995	1996	1997
United Kingdom										
Size of national waiting list (000s)	837	876	912	910	910	1020	1040	1010	1090	1158
Mean waiting time (months)	9.3	8.8	8.0	6.4	4.8	4.8	4.4	3.9	4.0	4.6
England										
Number of patients waiting more than 18 months for hospital admission (000s)						21			nil	
Percentage of patients assessed immediately in A&E						75			94	
Percentage of outpatients seen within 30 minutes of appointment time						80			90	

Sources: Health Committee, *Public Expenditure on Health and Personal Social Services* (annual reports); Department of Health (press releases)

are examined here. One is that the public's views simply respond to real changes in waiting times and the numbers waiting – that is, as waiting lists increase in size or as the average waiting time increases in length, public perceptions shift accordingly. A second explanation, however, might be that public attitudes are informed and led by the media. Previous research by Judge *et al.* has claimed that public opinion on the NHS is in part affected by media coverage of the topic.[1]

In view of the Government's current commitment to reducing the numbers on the waiting list, we also consider whether levels of dissatisfaction are linked to the length of the list as well as the time people spend on it. Finally, by means of a multivariate analysis, we assess the importance of the public's evaluations of waiting in the NHS as part of the public's overall level of satisfaction with the Service.

Waiting in the NHS: official figures

From the early 1990s onwards – and certainly since the introduction of the *Patient's Charter* – waiting, as a feature of the NHS, has changed in two distinct ways. First, the number of people waiting for elective treatment has risen steadily. Between 1988 and 1997, the national waiting list increased from 837,000 to 1,158,000 – a 38 per cent increase. In contrast, however, time spent waiting to be admitted has fallen.

Table 1 outlines these two features in greater detail. While waiting lists have increased, time spent waiting for hospital admission and the numbers waiting longer than 18 months for admission have decreased. At the same time, the percentage of patients assessed immediately in casualty and the percentage of outpatients seen within 30 minutes of their appointment time have risen.

By far the most significant of these changes relates to the time spent by people waiting to be admitted to hospital, displayed in Table 1 as the mean waiting time. While the average waiting time was as high as 9.3 months at the end of 1988, it had fallen to just 4.6 months by December 1997. In addition, the number of people waiting for more than 18 months to be admitted to hospital also fell sharply between 1992 and 1996, especially in England. To sum up, in the second half of the 1990s people are waiting for shorter periods of time (on average) before being admitted, and fewer are having to wait for what the *Patient's Charter* considers an unreasonable length of time (18 months and over).

Other improvements have been more marginal. According to the previous Government's figures, the percentage of outpatients seen within thirty minutes of their appointment time increased in England from 80 to 90 per cent between 1993 and 1996. The corresponding figures for Wales and Northern Ireland were 85 to 90 per cent and 80 to 81 per cent respectively: small but important improvements.[2] Similarly, the percentage of patients assessed immediately in casualty departments rose in all parts of the country. This particular improvement should probably be noted with caution, however. The term 'assessed immediately' has almost certainly been taken to mean different things in different casualty departments. In some cases, assessment has consisted of little more than an acknowledgement of the patient's presence.[3] It might be, therefore, that improvements in this area are more illusory than real. Our analysis in a later section of this paper suggests that any measured improvements have not yet fed into the public consciousness.

> **Box 1** *The Patient's Charter*
>
> In 1995, the Government revised the *Patient's Charter* so that it included the following commitments:
>
> 1. Waiting time for elective admission guaranteed to be less than 18 months.
> 2. An expectation that operations will not be cancelled on the day of admission or, if a cancellation occurs, the patient can expect to be admitted again within one month.
> 3. Nine out of 10 patients can expect to be seen within 13 weeks of referral (the 'waiting time standard').
> 4. *All* can expect to be seen within 26 weeks of referral.
> 5. Patients can expect to be seen immediately – and be assessed – in casualty departments.
> 6. Patients can expect to be seen within 30 minutes of appointment time in outpatient departments.
>
> **Source:** *The Patient's Charter and You*[4]

Trends in public attitudes, 1987–96

Given these observed changes, how satisfied has the public been with waiting in the NHS over the past decade? Data from the BSA surveys suggest that dissatisfaction with waiting in the NHS has, in fact, been quite substantial since it was first measured in 1987. The brief summary of the data in Table 2 makes this clear.

For every category of waiting, consistently over half of those people questioned have responded that improvement has been needed. The average figures for the period, displayed in the final column of Table 2, bear these levels of dissatisfaction out. In particular, they indicate that waiting lists and waiting time have aroused

Table 2 Percentage of the public feeling that waiting in the NHS needs improving for six aspects of waiting, 1987–96

Attitudes towards:	1987	1989	1990	1991	1993	1994	1995	1996	Avg. 1987–96
Waiting lists	86.9	84.8	82.6	84.3	78.1	77.1	74.6	76.5	**80.6**
Waiting time (before admission)	83.6	85.9	82.7	83.7	78.7	80.1	76.2	78.8	**81.2**
Waiting areas (casualty)			57.4	59.1	55.6	53.5	55.0	55.7	**56.1**
Waiting areas (outpatient)			52.5	55.1	49.3	50.0	50.0	48.7	**50.9**
Waiting time (casualty)				73.5	70.1	70.4	70.7	72.7	**71.5**
Waiting time (outpatient)				80.0	73.9	70.0	67.7	68.1	**71.9**
N	1281	1307	2430	2481	2567	2929	3135	3103	

Data: BSA. (Questions on 'waiting' in the NHS did not appear on the BSA survey before 1987. BSA surveys did not take place in either 1988 or 1992.)

Note: Per cents are calculated by collapsing the two response categories 'need a lot of improvement' and 'need some improvement' into a single measure.

Box 2 British Social Attitudes survey

Since 1987, the BSA survey has explored public attitudes towards several facets of waiting in the NHS. Six aspects in particular have been measured: respondents' attitudes towards waiting lists for non-emergency operations (since 1987); attitudes towards waiting time before hospital admission (since 1987); attitudes towards waiting areas, in both casualty and outpatient departments (since 1990); and attitudes towards time spent waiting in casualty and outpatient departments (since 1991).

---

the greatest dissatisfaction, with more than four out of five members of the public recognising a need for improvement in these areas.

Other aspects of waiting have attracted almost as much public concern. Throughout the period, more than seven out of ten people have regarded time spent waiting in both casualty and outpatient departments to be in need of improvement. Only when it comes to waiting 'areas' (the physical surroundings in which the patient waits) has public dissatisfaction been

toned down. There, public opinion seems more finely balanced between those feeling that improvement is necessary and those feeling satisfied with the present state of the service.

Despite the fact that public dissatisfaction has run at a high level, the figures in Table 2 uncover other important developments in public attitudes towards waiting in the NHS. Not the least of these developments has been the fact that although the public has shown a significant degree of dissatisfaction with waiting, the level of dissatisfaction has, in fact, decreased since it was first measured in 1987. The public is less dissatisfied with waiting in 1996 than it was in 1987.

Figure 1 displays these changes in public attitudes towards waiting. In all but two of the categories (waiting areas and time spent waiting in casualty), the public's satisfaction scores for 1996 are higher than they were in 1987. Indeed, between 1987 and 1994, public attitudes towards every aspect of waiting improved to some degree. Only in 1995 and 1996 did these improvements appear to slow

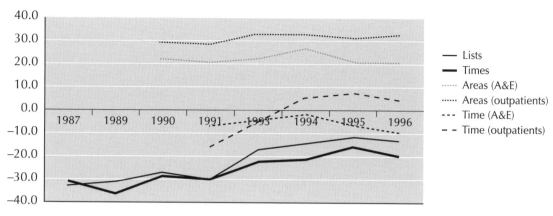

Data: BSA.

Note: 'Satisfaction' scores are generated by subtracting the percentage responding 'need a lot of improvement' from the percentage responding 'satisfactory' or 'very good'.

Fig 1 Changes in public satisfaction with waiting, 1987–96

down, and only where attitudes towards waiting in casualty were measured did the public's more positive attitudes suffer a notable decline.

For the most part, then, these figures sit neatly with the idea that public opinion reflects the objective reality of waiting in the NHS. The real improvements in time spent waiting that we noted in the previous section appear to have had some influence on public opinion. As there has been a decrease in the average time spent waiting for hospital admission, assessment in casualty and treatment in outpatient departments, the public has generally displayed lower levels of dissatisfaction with waiting.

Two paradoxes?

Despite this apparent endorsement for the theory that public opinion changes according to the actual reality of waiting, the public's attitudes have *not* mirrored reality in two key areas. First, the public has shown less dissatisfaction with the problem of waiting *lists* throughout the 1990s despite the fact that the national waiting list has increased in size over the past decade. Second, attitudes towards waiting in casualty barely changed between 1991 and 1996 (see Table 2) despite the improvements shown in the official data (see Table 1). How may we account for these particular opinions which appear to be at odds with the official statistics?

Box 3 Public opinion by sub-groups of the population

In keeping with virtually all measures of public opinion, there are differences in evaluations of waiting when we separate the public into sub-groups. Table 3 displays these differences for attitudes towards waiting lists and waiting time specifically.

cont.

Box 3 *(cont.)*

Table 3 Public evaluations by sub-group, 1996

	Waiting lists			Waiting time			Ratio 1:3
	1.Need lots of impr.t	*2.Need some impr.t*	*3.Satisf./ very good*	*1. Need lots of impr.t*	*2.Need some impr.t*	*3.Satisf./ very good*	
By gender:							
Male	38	39	20	39	40	18	**2.0**
Female	31	45	22	38	40	20	**1.7**
By age:							
17-24	39	41	18	39	42	18	**2.3**
25-34	36	42	20	39	42	17	**2.0**
35-44	39	40	20	44	40	15	**2.4**
45-54	38	42	18	45	37	17	**2.3**
55-59	28	47	21	34	46	16	**1.7**
60-64	31	40	26	39	37	22	**1.4**
65+	26	44	25	28	41	27	**1.0**
By region:							
Scotland	27	42	29	27	44	26	**1.0**
Wales	37	39	20	44	31	22	**1.9**
North	34	41	23	38	41	20	**1.7**
Midlands	30	48	20	37	42	20	**1.7**
South	35	41	21	37	42	18	**1.8**
London	45	41	11	53	34	11	**4.4**
By class:							
AB	33	44	21	37	41	19	**1.7**
C1	32	46	20	37	39	22	**1.7**
C2	38	39	20	40	41	16	**2.1**
DE	36	38	22	41	39	17	**1.9**
By recent experience:							
Inpatient past 2 years	37	39	22	41	39	19	**1.9**
Not	33	45	20	37	42	19	**1.8**
By private health:							
Private	38	44	16	43	41	14	**2.7**
Not	34	42	22	38	40	20	**1.7**

Data: BSA 1996.

Note: The composite ratio is calculated by dividing the mean percentage responding 'need a lot of improvement' (across both waiting lists and waiting time) by the mean percentage responding 'satisfactory/very good'.

cont.

Box 3 *(cont.)*

Several sub-groups of the public display obvious differences in attitudes; others, however, show no apparent variation. Taking the ratio displayed in the final column of Table 3, it would seem that variation in a respondent's gender, class and whether or not a respondent has recent experience as an inpatient makes minimal difference to a respondent's evaluations of waiting.

In contrast, a respondent's age seems to have an effect on attitudes. Table 3 indicates that dissatisfaction with waiting *decreases* with age, with the effect appearing to speed up for respondents aged 55 and over. A similar difference in opinion is found between those members of the public with private health insurance and those without. As seems intuitive, those with private insurance are far more likely to regard waiting in the NHS as a problem than those who rely exclusively on the Health Service.

The most substantial differences in public opinion, however, are seen to relate to the respondent's region. Satisfaction with waiting seems to vary widely throughout the UK, with Scotland showing relative satisfaction at one end of the spectrum and London displaying huge dissatisfaction at the other. The London figures deserve special attention simply because of the magnitude of dissatisfaction in the capital. They reinforce the belief, reported in other research, that Londoners are generally more dissatisfied with the NHS than their fellow countrymen and women.[3]

Attitudes towards waiting lists

Table 4 provides a more detailed account of attitudes towards waiting lists and waiting time. As was evident from our earlier analysis, public dissatisfaction with both aspects of waiting has been substantial yet when we track the public's attitudes year by year, it is apparent that fewer people are dissatisfied as we move through the 1990s. For both categories of waiting, the proportion responding 'needs a lot of improvement' has dropped noticeably in recent years. Indeed, for waiting lists, the ratio of those responding 'needs a lot of improvement' to those responding 'satisfactory' or 'very good' has fallen from 4.1:1 in 1987 to just 1.6:1 for 1996.

Table 4 Evaluations of waiting lists and waiting time, 1987–96 (%)

	1987	1989	1990	1991	1993	1994	1995	1996	Diff. 1987–96
Waiting lists									
1. Need lot improvement	42.8	44.1	42.1	43.5	35.4	33.9	31.9	34.4	**-8.4**
2. Need some improvement	44.1	40.7	40.5	40.8	42.7	43.2	42.7	42.1	
3. Satisfactory/very good	10.4	13.3	15.1	13.4	18.4	19.5	19.8	20.9	**+10.5**
Ratio 1:3	**4.1**	**3.3**	**2.8**	**3.2**	**1.9**	**1.7**	**1.6**	**1.6**	
Waiting time									
1. Need lot improvement	44.6	48.1	43.0	43.5	39.9	38.6	35.4	38.6	**-6.0**
2. Need some improvement	39.0	37.8	39.7	40.2	38.8	41.5	40.8	40.2	
3. Satisfactory/very good	13.8	12.3	14.7	14.0	17.7	17.7	19.2	18.8	**+5.0**
Ratio 1:3	**3.2**	**3.9**	**2.9**	**3.1**	**2.3**	**2.2**	**1.8**	**2.1**	

Data: BSA.

Table 5 Evaluations of waiting in casualty and outpatient departments, 1991–96 (%)

	1987	*1989*	*1990*	*1991*	*1993*	*1994*	*1995*	*1996*	*Diff. 1991–96*
Time spent waiting in casualty									
1. Need lot improvement				30.3	30.5	28.0	30.2	33.2	**+2.9**
2. Need some improvement				43.2	39.6	42.4	40.5	39.5	
3. Satisfactory/very good				23.4	25.3	26.2	23.9	23.6	**+0.2**
Ratio 1:3				**1.3**	**1.2**	**1.1**	**1.3**	**1.4**	
Time spent waiting in outpatient departments									
1. Need lot improvement				33.8	28.3	22.1	20.8	24.5	**-9.3**
2. Need some improvement				46.2	45.6	47.9	46.9	43.6	
3. Satisfactory/very good				17.8	22.5	27.4	28.1	29.0	**+11.2**
Ratio 1:3				**1.9**	**1.3**	**0.8**	**0.7**	**0.8**	

Source: BSA.

The drop in dissatisfaction with waiting lists cannot be explained by the objective reality of increasing numbers waiting for treatment, however. If changes in public opinion are caused by real changes in the performance of the NHS, we would expect attitudes towards waiting lists to have displayed greater dissatisfaction at the end of the period. The fact that they have not requires an alternative explanation.

The most plausible alternative would seem to be that changes in attitudes towards waiting lists are caused not by changes in the *number* of people waiting for treatment but by changes in the *time* people spend waiting. That is, the reality of declining waiting times may be causing the changes in the public's attitudes to both waiting lists *and* waiting time. While it would appear that public attitudes do not react to real changes in the waiting-list total, it is quite conceivable that the reality of declining waiting times features in the minds of respondents who say that waiting lists are less of a problem than they were. After all, for those members of the public who have undergone hospital treatment, experience of waiting is based almost entirely on time spent waiting – most patients have no real way of knowing how many others are waiting with them. It should not surprise us, therefore, if the public's views on waiting lists were at least partly a function of the public's own experience of time spent waiting.

Attitudes towards waiting in casualty

The failure of attitudes towards waiting in casualty to show a sustained decrease in dissatisfaction seems easier to explain. Table 2 demonstrated that public perceptions of time spent waiting on hospital premises have shown large levels of dissatisfaction. Table 5 examines public opinion on this question more closely. For casualty departments, large percentages of the public have expressed the need for improvement in time spent waiting. This is despite the fact that more patients are supposedly being 'assessed immediately'.

The most straightforward explanation for continued public dissatisfaction in this area is that

Table 6 Coverage of waiting in the NHS in *The Independent*, 1989–98

Reference to waiting lists or waiting times ...	1989	1990	1991	1992	1993	1994	1995	1996	1997	1998*
Headlines	6	12	24	17	9	8	5	3	9	8
Articles	102	126	213	173	121	130	111	131	166	79

Source: The Independent.

* The 1998 figures are accurate to the end of May. If coverage continues at the same rate for the remainder of 1998, the headline and article totals will reach 19 and 190 respectively. This level of coverage would not have been seen since 1991–92.

the previous Government's efforts to get more patients assessed immediately has hidden the fact that patients are probably not being treated any faster. It would seem that being 'assessed' immediately is not regarded by the public as the same as being 'treated' immediately. Despite improvements in official figures, therefore, the time that patients spend waiting in casualty continues to be judged unfavourably.

This is best demonstrated by contrasting public opinion on time spent waiting in casualty with time spent waiting in outpatient departments (also displayed in Table 5). For outpatient departments, the percentages reporting 'satisfactory' or 'very good' almost doubled between 1991 and 1996. This would suggest that the recorded improvements for time spent waiting in outpatient departments are of greater substantive significance to the public than the seemingly more illusory improvements recorded for time spent waiting in casualty.

Changes in media coverage

Notwithstanding our earlier findings, it seems unlikely that shifts in public opinion on waiting can be explained *completely* by the real changes in either waiting times or waiting lists. Because the public does not have perfect information on these

figures – and because the public gains some of its information via its own experiences – we should examine other potential factors that may account for opinion change. Previous research suggests that the public's attitudes on health care issues are in part a response to the way the NHS is covered by the media. In a study on the effect of media coverage on public opinion on the NHS in the last quarter of 1991, Judge *et al.* tentatively suggested that 'there are fluctuations in opinion which seem to relate to the changing media agenda and to the reflection by the media of the political debate'.[1] From the limited amount of evidence available to us, this argument seems plausible.

The evidence for this argument comes from a content analysis of articles published since 1989 in *The Independent*, the only national paper which provided a suitable database for this period. To derive the data presented in Table 6, we have simply counted up the number of headlines and the number of articles that have included the words 'waiting lists' or 'waiting times'. The numbers in the table are quite striking. Since coverage of waiting in the NHS reached a peak in 1991, the issue would seem to have steadily fallen out of the media spotlight to the point that in 1996 *The Independent* carried only three headlines related to the subject. The fall in

Table 7 Positive and negative presentation of waiting in the NHS by headlines in *The Independent*, 1989–98

	1989	1990	1991	1992	1993	1994	1995	1996	1997	1998*
Waiting lists and waiting time										
Positive			3	4		1	2	1		1
Activity	1		4	1	1	1			2	2
Other		1	3							
Negative	5	11	14	12	8	6	3	2	7	5
Total	6	12	24	17	9	8	5	3	9	8
% Negative	**83**	**92**	**58**	**71**	**89**	**75**	**60**	**67**	**78**	**63**
Waiting lists only										
Positive				2	4			1	1	1
Activity	1		4		1	1			2	2
Other		1	2	10						
Negative	5	11	13		8	6	2	2	3	5
Total	6	12	21	14	9	7	3	3	5	8
% Negative	**83**	**92**	**62**	**71**	**89**	**86**	**67**	**67**	**60**	**63**
Waiting time only										
Positive			1			1	1			
Activity				1						
Other			1							
Negative			1	2			1		4	
Total			3	3		1	2		4	
% Negative			**33**	**67**		**0**	**50**		**100**	

Source: The Independent.
* As with Table 6, the 1998 figures are accurate to the end of May.
Note: Positive = favourable report of Government's handling of waiting, usually based on decreasing numbers waiting or falling waiting times; Activity = report of Government action or initiative; Other = report of other activity, usually a report of Opposition strategy; Negative = unfavourable report of Government's handling of the issue, usually based on increasing numbers waiting or lengthening waiting times.

the number of articles that contained a reference to waiting lists or waiting times is almost as striking. Again, coverage peaked in 1991 only to fall away over the next five years.

We present in Table 7 a more detailed account of *The Independent's* coverage of waiting lists and times, which shows how these topics have been presented over the past decade. The evidence again seems to support the findings by Judge *et al.*[1] that changes in media coverage have some effect on public opinion. Not only has coverage of the issue of waiting declined in terms of sheer volume since the start of the decade, the tone of the media's coverage would also seem to have become less negative. It would appear that public dissatisfaction with waiting in the NHS has, generally speaking, decreased at the same time as waiting has been covered less frequently by the media, and as the issue of waiting has been covered less negatively.

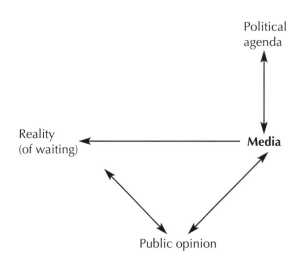

Political
agenda

Reality
(of waiting)

Media

Public opinion

Fig 2 The possible role of the media in shaping public opinion

Of course, it would be wrong to conclude that the media have simply 'driven' public opinion as if they were an autonomous force. Almost certainly, the media have *reflected* the reality of waiting, just as public opinion would appear to have done. The media have also *reacted* to government initiatives and the agenda set by particular ministers. That said, once the media pick up the issue, how they *report* the issue helps set the parameters of the political debate. For this reason, it would be equally wrong to regard the media as merely a reactive force. Instead, the media's role in influencing public opinion would seem to involve not only the *reporting* of actual changes and government initiatives but also the *presentation* of this information. As Figure 2 suggests, it is this presentation of reality which helps to supplement the public's beliefs.

If we take this view, changes in the media's coverage and presentation of waiting in the NHS may be a useful predictor of change in public attitudes. The media's ability to emphasise or de-emphasise an issue may well interact with the public's view of reality. Figure 3 overleaf represents diagrammatically the two explanations for attitude change at which we have looked so far in this paper: attitude change as determined by actual change and attitude change according to media presentation.

The evidence presented in Figure 3 suggests that changes in public opinion on waiting have probably been a function of both real changes *and* media coverage. However, in the specific case of attitudes towards waiting lists, public opinion appears to have been heavily influenced by the media's apparent lack of concern with this particular issue. It is clear that the decline in public dissatisfaction displayed in section (a) of Figure 3 closely resembles the decline in media coverage but bears little relation to the reality of an increasing waiting list (both shown in section (b) of the diagram).

In the case of public opinion on waiting time, Figure 3 suggests that both the reality of falling waiting times (section (2c)) and the lower profile given to the subject by the media (section (1c)) appear to have helped to lower levels of public dissatisfaction (section (a)). Indeed, as we noted earlier, the reality of falling waiting times may well have influenced public evaluations of waiting lists.

What does seem clear from Figure 3, however, is that the actual size of the waiting list has not impacted upon public opinion *directly*. The rising line depicted in section (2b) does not correspond either to media coverage or public opinion. In fact, if we took the increasing size of the waiting list as an indication of public dissatisfaction during the 1990s (as the Labour Government seems to have done), we would be misled.

(a) Change in public attitudes

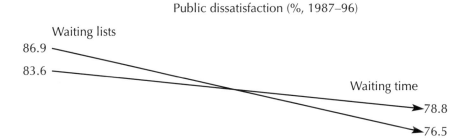

Public dissatisfaction (%, 1987–96)

Waiting lists
86.9
83.6

Waiting time
78.8
76.5

(b) Change in media coverage/presentation vs. change in objective reality (for waiting *lists*)

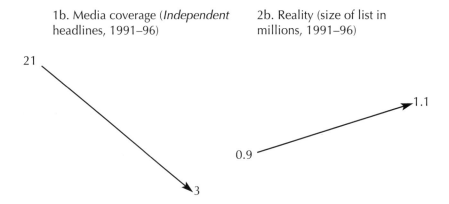

1b. Media coverage (*Independent* headlines, 1991–96)

2b. Reality (size of list in millions, 1991–96)

21

3

0.9

1.1

(c) Change in media coverage/presentation vs. change in objective reality (for waiting *time*)

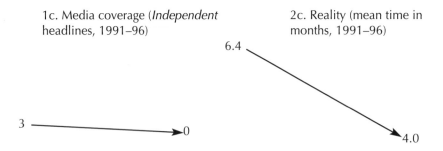

1c. Media coverage (*Independent* headlines, 1991–96)

2c. Reality (mean time in months, 1991–96)

6.4

3

0

4.0

Fig 3 Alternative explanations for attitude change: Media presentation vs. objective reality

Table 8 Level of satisfaction with the NHS, 1987 and 1996 (OLS regression)

Explanatory variable	1987	1996 (3-variable)	1996 (7-variable)
Four-point scale of satisfaction with:			
Waiting lists	**.20** (.11)*	**.21** (.13)*	**.17** (.10)*
Waiting time	**.21** (.13)*	**.31** (.19)*	**.26** (.16)*
Waiting areas (A&E)			**.05** (.03)
Waiting areas (output)			**.00** (.00)
Time spent in A&E			**.05** (.03)
Time spent in output			**.12** (.07)*
Quality of hospital treatment	**.41** (.26)*	**.27** (.17)*	**.24** (.15)*
(Constant)	.95	.89	.76
Adj. R2	.15	.18	.18

Data: BSA, 1987 and 1996.
* $p < 0.05$.
Note: The dependent variable is a five-point scale of satisfaction with the NHS. The model controls for respondent's age, class, gender, region, recent use of NHS and health insurance arrangements. B (slope) coefficients in bold. Standardised coefficients in parentheses.

The size of the waiting list may well have an effect if media coverage of the issue alters, however. In this case, the effect would be *indirect*. As the final columns in Tables 6 and 7 indicate, media coverage of waiting lists appears to have increased since the 1997 General Election. If the hypothesis that media coverage accounts for some of the change in the public's attitudes is correct, we might expect that public dissatisfaction with waiting lists has increased since it was last measured. The 1997 and the 1998 BSA survey data, when they become available, should confirm or disprove this theory.

Public attitudes and public policy

At the beginning of this paper, we noted the present Government's emphasis on the number of patients on the waiting list. This preoccupation with numbers waiting appears to be almost entirely a response to the Government's own perception that this particular feature of the Health Service represents the public's gravest concern. We now turn to examine whether this assumption is supported by the survey evidence. The findings that we have already presented would suggest that the Labour Government has seriously misread public opinion on this issue. The evidence is not conclusive but it is certainly compatible with the idea that the public responds more to objective changes in time spent waiting than to changes in the waiting list total. One way of confirming this belief is to 'model' the public's overall satisfaction with the NHS. By means of a multivariate analysis, we can attempt to measure what effect changes in the public's evaluations of waiting (lists, times, areas) have on changes in the public's more general satisfaction with the way the health service is run. We can also include in our model public attitudes to other features of the NHS, as a means of placing the significance of attitudes towards waiting in comparative perspective. For this reason, we have included the public's level of satisfaction with hospital treatment as a variable in the analysis. Regression analyses were run for both 1987 and 1996 and the results are set out in Table 8.

Box 4 Multivariate analysis

OLS regression is a statistical technique used to estimate the individual impact of particular variables on a dependent variable when all other variables are controlled for.

Taking the 1987 data first, we can see that the public's evaluations of waiting (both for lists and time) were positively correlated with NHS satisfaction (that is, a rise in satisfaction with waiting prompted a rise in satisfaction with the NHS). However, the public's assessment of the quality of hospital treatment was a more powerful predictor of overall satisfaction with the Health Service (its B coefficient of .41 was about twice as large as the individual coefficients for the waiting variables). In other words, in 1987, the public's satisfaction with the NHS appeared to depend more upon its satisfaction with the standard of hospital treatment than it did with its perceptions of waiting.

The 1996 data provide a startling contrast. In the first place, we are now able to include all six 'evaluation of waiting' variables in our analysis. Nonetheless, the inclusion of the extra four variables added little explanatory power to the model. Attitudes towards waiting in casualty and evaluations of waiting areas in outpatient departments, while positively correlated with NHS satisfaction, produced very small B coefficients which, in addition, were not statistically significant. Attitudes towards time spent waiting in outpatient departments, however, were statistically significant and produced a moderate B coefficient indicating that the public's assessment of the time spent waiting as an outpatient is fairly important when the public comes to assess the NHS.

Second, however, and of greater significance, are the changes in importance of the public's attitudes towards each of waiting lists, waiting time, and the quality of hospital treatment. To be strictly comparable, we should analyse only the first two columns of Table 8 to assess trends between 1987 and 1996 so that like is compared with like. The data suggest that while attitudes towards waiting lists hardly changed in their ability to explain overall NHS satisfaction, attitudes towards waiting time appear to have become increasingly important (B coefficient of .31). This would seem to be mainly at the expense of attitudes towards the quality of hospital treatment (B coefficient of .27).

These findings suggest that, quite apart from variations in public dissatisfaction with waiting in the NHS and variations in media coverage, perceptions of waiting are an increasingly important factor for the public when it comes to making overall judgements about the way the NHS is run. It seems likely that people's expectations have been stimulated by the *Patient's Charter* initiative to the extent that the public assesses the performance of the NHS according to a mental 'scoresheet', with increasing emphasis attached to Charter guarantees. In this sense, the present Government may be correct in focusing on the problems caused by waiting for treatment. In another sense, however, it seems that the Government's concerns are off target. It is the public's attitudes towards *time* spent waiting that appear to be important, as research carried out for the previous Government prior to the 1995 revisions of the *Patient's Charter* suggested.[2] Indeed, evaluations of time spent waiting have assumed a level of importance that was previously assumed only by the public's perception of the quality of hospital treatment.

Conclusion

Throughout the period 1987–96, public dissatisfaction with waiting has run high: roughly four out of five members of the public have held the belief that 'some improvement' in the management of waiting lists and waiting times is necessary.

Nevertheless, we have also seen that the general level of dissatisfaction with waiting seems to be declining. Paradoxically, the most significant decline in the level of dissatisfaction with waiting occurred at a time when the size of the waiting list was actually increasing. We have attempted to account for this paradox by suggesting – as Judge et al.[1] have done previously – that media coverage of the issue has some effect on public opinion. From the evidence examined in this paper, it would seem that changes in the coverage and presentation of waiting in the NHS do impact on the public's attitudes. As coverage of the issue of waiting for hospital treatment declined in the mid-1990s so too did public dissatisfaction.

At the same time, it would be surprising if the public's evaluations of waiting are not influenced by its own experience of time spent waiting for hospital treatment. Indeed, the public's evaluations of time spent waiting to be admitted to hospital would appear to be vitally important. While attitudes towards waiting have seemingly become increasingly important indicators of the public's overall level of satisfaction with the NHS, it is evaluations of *time* spent waiting that account for most of this effect. Even if the public is less dissatisfied with waiting than it was in 1987, it seems to place more importance on the time spent waiting for treatment in its overall judgement of the NHS than ever before. This central message does not seem to have fed into the Labour Government's thinking as yet. As a consequence, it is probably fair to conclude that the Government's focus on reducing the size of the waiting list as a means of placating the public is based on a faulty assessment of what the public actually wants.

References

1. Judge K, Solomon M, Miller D, Philo G. Public opinion, the NHS, and the media: changing patterns and perspectives. *BMJ*; 304:892–5.
2. *The Citizen's Charter – Five years on.* London: HMSO, 1996.
3. See evidence cited in Harrison A (ed). *Health Care UK 1995/96.* London: King's Fund, 1996.
4. *The Patient's Charter and You.* London: HMSO, 1995.

Acknowledgements

The author would like to acknowledge the technical assistance of Jonathan Burton (Institute of Social and Economic Research, University of Essex) in the preparation of these data.

Regulating the medical profession: doctors and the public interest

Rudolf Klein

On 13 October 1997 began what was to become the longest, most emotionally charged and perhaps most important case in the history of the General Medical Council (GMC). It concluded on 18 June 1998, after 74 days of hearings, when the GMC's Professional Conduct Committee found two cardiac surgeons at the Bristol Royal Infirmary and the medically qualified chief executive of the Bristol Royal Healthcare NHS Trust guilty of serious professional misconduct. So ended the case of the Bristol three.

But the end of the hearings case did not mean the end of the story. It marked the beginning of a wide-ranging debate about the adequacy of the existing machinery of professional self-regulation and the relationship between that machinery and the Labour Government's proposals for ensuring quality in the National Health Service (NHS). Specifically, it raised the question of whether the medical profession could be trusted to protect the public by ensuring the competence of its members. What did the case of the Bristol three tell us about the ability and the willingness of doctors, both individually and collectively, to monitor and police the practices of their colleagues and about the problems involved in doing so?

This article explores the issues raised by this question. First, to set the scene, it examines the role, functions and activities of the GMC: the apex and guarantor of the machinery of professional self-regulation. Second, it analyses in detail the Bristol case, using the transcripts of the proceedings: although the case received much media attention, the length and complexity of the trial meant that much of the evidence given never emerged into public view. Third, it discusses some of the issues highlighted by the evidence. Finally, it considers the wider implications of the case for future public policy.

The role and functions of the GMC

The crucial role of the GMC, from which all its other responsibilities flow, is to maintain a register of duly qualified doctors entitled to practise medicine. On the one hand, it controls entry into the profession – it validates the qualifications of those seeking to become registered and supervises medical education. On the other hand, it controls exit from the profession: it is responsible for disciplining, and if necessary removing from the register, doctors deemed unfit to practise. In all this, professional self-interest is assumed to be in harmony with the public interest. Doctors achieve a monopoly over certain activities, with the economic advantages that such a monopoly gives them, while the public are assured that they will be treated by competent practitioners. Or, as the Merrison Committee put it when reporting on the future of the GMC in 1975, the system of regulation can be seen as 'a contract between public and profession, by which the public go to the profession for medical treatment because the profession has made sure that it will provide satisfactory treatment. Such a contract has the characteristics of all freely made contracts – mutual advantage'.[1]

Both the composition and the role of the GMC have been evolving. The GMC remains, as it was in its origins, a body representative of the medical profession. Half its members are elected by the profession, with a further quarter nominated by the undergraduate medical schools and the royal colleges. The proportion of lay members has, however, been increasing and now stands at a quarter: lay members are, further, represented on the committees responsible for discipline, such as the Professional Conduct Committee, which heard and determined the Bristol case. Similarly, and most importantly, the GMC has over the past two decades expanded its definition of what is meant by 'fitness to practise' and by conduct liable to incur a charge of serious professional misconduct, which, as in the Bristol case, may lead to erasure from the register.

Following 1978 legislation incorporating the recommendations of the Merrison report, the GMC introduced special procedures for dealing with doctors whose physical or mental health put their patients at risk. More recently, it has elaborated the notion that doctors must not only avoid certain forms of conduct liable to bring the profession into disrepute – which encompasses such traditional professional sins as sleeping with patients or falling foul of the criminal law – but also have a positive duty to maintain their competence. This new and enlarged definition of proper professional conduct is set out in the 1998 edition of *Good Medical Practice*,[2] the GMC's handbook defining the duties and responsibilities of doctors: a summary of the GMC's philosophy as it has evolved in the 1990s.

Good Medical Practice urges doctors to 'recognise and work within the limits of your professional competence', 'take part in regular and systematic medical and clinical audit' and 'keep your knowledge and skills up to date throughout your working life'. Moreover, the responsibility for ensuring good quality practice is both individual and collective. A medical practitioner 'must protect patients when you believe that a doctor's or other colleague's health, conduct or performance is a threat to them'. In such circumstances there is a duty to report the facts to the employing authority, a local medical committee or a regulatory body. The emphasis throughout is that a doctor's prime duty is to his or her patients: a duty which includes treating every patient politely as well as listening considerately and respecting their views. This represents a crucial shift from the traditional view that the main objective of the GMC's disciplinary code and proceedings is to protect the profession against conduct by its members likely to bring it into disrepute, although nothing, of course, is more likely to bring the profession into disrepute than a failure to maintain standards of practice. Competence rather than chastity – to caricature only a little – has become the touchstone of good medical practice. Protecting the public rather than punishing doctors is the dominant concern.

This shift from a profession-centred to a patient-centred definition of professional responsibilities – and therefore of professional misconduct – reflects the GMC's reaction to both past criticisms that it has been too much of a cosy club protective of medical interests[3] and rising public demands for it to deal with complaints about the adequacy of treatment. Over the past ten years the number of cases received and considered by the GMC under its conduct procedures has roughly tripled, increasing by more than 20 per cent in 1997 alone. In 1997 the GMC recorded 2,687 incidents of alleged misconduct against 2,507 doctors. Of these 62 per cent were about treatment as against, for instance, 8 per cent about personal behaviour (including the doctor's personal state of health) and 6 per cent about dishonest or criminal actions.[4] The complaints are then filtered through a screening process which eliminates most of them either because they fall outside the GMC's remit or for lack of evidence. In some cases (about 90 in 1997) warning letters are sent to the doctors concerned. Only a very small proportion (43 in 1997) lead to a hearing before the Professional Conduct Committee. Investigations of the cases and the collection of evidence are contracted out by the GMC; the recommendation of the Merrison Committee that the GMC should have its own investigatory unit has so far not been adopted.

The proceedings of the Professional Conduct Committee are governed by statute.[5] In effect, they are very like a criminal trial. Both the case of the GMC and that for the defence are presented by counsel. Broadly speaking, the rules of criminal justice apply, so determining what evidence is or is not admissible. The case is heard by a panel of GMC members, assisted by a legal assessor; in the case of the Bristol doctors, the panel consisted of the GMC's President, Sir Donald Irvine, five medically qualified members and two lay members. The members of the panel may question witnesses but have to do so with circumspection; half way through the Bristol case, the defence argued, unsuccessfully, that the President's line of questioning showed that he was prejudiced and therefore should disqualify himself. Appeals against the decisions of the Committee can be made only to the Privy Council.

The nature of the proceedings have two consequences. The first is that, in a complex and long-drawn-out case, hearings can be very expensive: the Bristol case cost something approaching £3,000,000 (with the legal costs of the doctors being met by their medical defence societies). The second, crucial for the interpretation of the proceedings, is that the rules under which the GMC works meant that the case revolved around specific charges, involving specific patients, against the doctors concerned. The proceedings therefore offered what was inevitably a powerful but selective searchlight; the charges did not involve all the deaths at Bristol but only those where the evidence appeared to be strongest. For in no sense did the proceedings amount to a general inquiry into the conduct of the doctors concerned, let alone into the conduct of others who may have had a contributory responsibility. This explains the anger of some of the parents and the widespread sense of public frustration left by the Bristol case – the sense that it had raised more questions than it had answered about the delivery of safe medical care – and the subsequent decision of the Secretary of State for Health, Frank Dobson, to set up a public inquiry. The GMC had sought such an inquiry at a much earlier stage but failed to persuade Mr Dobson's predecessor of the need to do so.

The other crucial point to note is that GMC hearings were investigating the conduct, not the performance, of the doctors: i.e. whether the doctors concerned had breached the GMC's code of conduct, not whether they were technically competent. As from 1 July 1997 the GMC has had the power to investigate 'seriously deficient performance' – whether or not doctors are failing to meet the professional standards appropriate to the work they are doing[6] – and has set up panels of assessors to carry out this task. But given that the charges against the Bristol doctors referred to a period before 1997, this new power could not be invoked. So, although the hearings of the Bristol case involved lengthy and detailed consideration of the individual operations carried out, the question being asked was not whether the surgeons had carried these out competently but whether they had drawn the appropriate conclusions from the outcomes. The charge against the surgeons – as we shall see in the next section – was not that they were technically incompetent but that they had failed to examine their own results critically and to draw the appropriate conclusions about the limits of their own skills, and that it was this double failure that led to the death of a number of babies and small children. And by finding the surgeons guilty of professional misconduct on these charges, the GMC gave the most powerful expression yet to its view that the protection of patients requires all doctors to review their own practices critically and routinely: that it is the duty of doctors to internalise, as it were, performance assessment. If the scope of the GMC's trial was narrow, constrained as it was by the legal framework in which the GMC works, the implications of its findings for the medical profession were wide and profound.

The Bristol case

Exceptionally, the Bristol case was not triggered by a complaint to the GMC – the usual starting point – but was instigated by the Council itself, prompted by the publication of an article by Lord Rees-Mogg in *The Times* in April 1996. The charges, eventually considered by the Professional Conduct Committee, related to a series of operations on babies and small children carried out by two cardiac surgeons – Mr James Wisheart and Mr Janardan Dhasmana – between 1988 and 1995. The third doctor, Dr John Roylance, was the District General Manager of Bristol and Western Health Authority and subsequently Chief Executive of the Bristol Royal Healthcare NHS Trust. His case raises rather different, if related, issues and is considered separately below. The specific paediatric cardiac operations considered by the GMC formed only a very small part of the workload of the two surgeons.

At issue were 15 operations for the corrections of atrioventricular septal defects (AVSD) in the case of Mr Wisheart, and 38 arterial switch operations in the case of Mr Dhasmana (the numbers changed slightly during the course of the trial as the charges were amended). The overall record of the two surgeons was not examined, for the reasons given in the previous section, by the Professional Conduct Committee. The last of the operations took place in January 1995 and ended in the death of the child being operated on. One of the questions examined during the trial was whether the operation should have been carried out in the first place: the GMC determined that it should not. Thereafter the trust commissioned an external review of its record.

Concern about the mortality levels in paediatric surgery at Bristol had first been voiced in 1990 by Dr Stephen Bolsin, a recently appointed consultant anaesthetist. Dr Bolsin reiterated his concerns in the years following. Subsequently, Professor Angelini, a cardiac surgeon who came to Bristol in the 1990s, also raised the issue as did some (but by no means all) senior clinicians. In 1992 *Private Eye* ran a series of three stories about the high mortality rate. In 1994 Dr Peter Doyle of the Department of Health, prompted by Dr Bolsin, sent a letter expressing some anxiety to the Chief Executive.

Much of the hearings before the GMC were taken up with examining who said what to whom when. Recollections of conversations that had taken place years earlier were, unsurprisingly, rather hazy and interpretations as to what had been said turned out to differ greatly. As a result, there were sharp conflicts of evidence on some points. Similarly, there was much dispute about the nature and validity of the figures produced by those voicing concern, and the extent to which attempts had been made to check the figures with the surgeons concerned.

The hearings confirmed that the mortality rate of the operations in question was high for both surgeons: not only much higher than that recorded at the best centres in the UK but higher even than the national average. In the case of Mr Wisheart, indeed, it was considerably higher even than that of his colleague, Mr Dhasmana, when carrying out the same type of operation. But the precise number of 'excess deaths' at Bristol – that is the number of babies and small children who would have lived if their operations had been carried out elsewhere – was not established during the trial, though the GMC decided that both

surgeons should have stopped operating sooner than they did. Nor, probably, could it be established by any form of inquiry or investigation.

This is for two reasons which emerged during the course of the trial. First, there are the problems stemming from the statistical interpretation of results based on a small number of cases: much time was devoted during the trial to arguments about which cases should be included in the series for analysis and how the mortality rate should be calculated. Second, and most important, there is the problem of comparability: the defence made much of the argument that the Bristol results could not be compared with the national figures because they included a disproportionate number of complex and difficult cases.

Much of the trial was therefore taken up by cross-examinations of expert witnesses designed to establish whether the poor results – and no one disputed that the results were, at face value, poor – could be explained by the specific circumstances of each patient's condition: an argument which could not be resolved conclusively because the national statistics, as the expert witnesses agreed, did not stratify for risk. Similarly, there was much argument, and little agreement, about the extent to which poor results could be justified in terms of the 'learning curve': i.e. the time taken by a surgeon to acquire familiarity with a new procedure (new to that surgeon, that is, though not necessarily new to surgeons practising elsewhere). The notion of the 'learning curve', the evidence made clear, is ill defined and elastic. Additionally, the defence sought to demonstrate that there were contributory environmental factors specific to Bristol but outside the control of the surgeons, such as inadequate diagnostic information, the lack of a dedicated team and a site split between the Royal Infirmary and the Children's Hospital. However, when a specialist paediatric surgeon took up his post in 1995, the results improved dramatically, although none of the evidence given during the trial suggested that the environment had been transformed.

But if such environmental factors did exist, whose responsibility – if not that of the surgeons – was it to decide whether or not it was in the best interests of the patients to carry on with the operations? In asking this question, we come to the crux of the GMC case against the two surgeons. For the findings of the Professional Conduct Committee were not – as already stressed in the previous section – that they were incompetent to carry out the operations. They may or may not have been incompetent: the expert witnesses (paediatric cardiac surgeons and cardiologists from centres with outstandingly good records) made little or no criticism of the two surgeons' technical skills when painstakingly going through the details of each operation, and this remains an open question. Rather, the findings revolved around the failure of the two surgeons to show critical awareness of their own performance and the consequent risks to patients.

The point emerges clearly when we consider the findings of fact at the end of the case, i.e. the charges that were found proved (a number of charges were found not to be substantiated). These can be summarised under the following three headings:

- first, the surgeons had been made aware of concerns about the level of mortality by their colleagues at Bristol Royal Infirmary. But they had continued to operate without conducting

any sufficient analysis or audit of their own surgical performance;
- second, they had failed to seek adequate retraining, assistance or advice;
- third, they had consequently failed to pay sufficient regard to the safety and best interests of the patients concerned when deciding whether to operate.

In addition, the Committee found that Mr Wisheart had given misleadingly optimistic information about the risks involved to the parents of some of the children, based not on his own record (a 50 per cent mortality rate) but on the national average (20 per cent). Further it found that Mr Dhamana had agreed to carry out the last of the operations, in January 1995, in circumstances when the best interests of the patient would have suggested that the patient be referred elsewhere for surgery.

Both surgeons were found guilty of serious professional misconduct. Mr Wisheart, by then retired with a distinction award, was directed to be struck off the register. Mr Dhasmana was allowed to continue practising but his continued registration was made conditional on his not undertaking any paediatric surgery for three years (subsequently, however, his contract was terminated by the trust).

The GMC's decision in the case of Mr Dhasmana was sharply criticised as over-lenient by the Secretary of State for Health in a television interview.[7] However, the evidence makes it clear that the two cases were substantially different. Mr Dhasmana was concerned about his performance and on two occasions visited one of the country's leading centres of paediatric surgery in order to improve his skills. As the President of the GMC put it, in giving the Committee's judgment, 'It is clear that you made some effort – though an insufficient one – to address the problems which you were recognising'. Further, he did not carry the additional responsibilities which flowed from Mr Wisheart's position of medical director of the trust and the senior surgeon in the team.

The case of the third doctor appearing before the GMC, Dr Roylance, revolved around a different issue. This was whether as a doctor, who happened to be chief executive, he had a responsibility to act on the expressions of concern about the performance of the two surgeons. Why, until January 1995 when the external review was commissioned, had he not taken action? Here two lines of argument emerged from his defence during the case. The first was that the expressions of concern were ambiguous. Dr Roylance had interpreted the various representations made to him as the routine kind of shroud waving of consultants seeking to gain extra resources: it was in any case, common ground that Bristol's performance in paediatric cardiac surgery was less than optimal, which is why plans were being advanced for appointing a new specialist surgeon and for building new facilities. The second was that, as chief executive, Dr Roylance was no longer acting as a doctor but was quite deliberately (and properly, the defence argued) delegating responsibility for quality issues to his medical colleagues. In effect, this meant that he was delegating responsibility to Mr Wisheart, as the trust's medical director, who was assuring the board that all was well with paediatric cardiac surgery.

The Professional Conduct Committee rejected these arguments. Box 1 sets out the judgment as given by the President on the final day of the case.

Box 1 The responsibilities of the Chief Executive

In giving judgment, Sir Donald Irvine, President of the GMC, said:

The public expects members of the medical profession to put patients' needs first. This applies not only in the consulting room and the operating theatre, but in other areas where doctors' actions or inactions may affect the welfare of patients ... Your own evidence demonstrates that you chose, over a long period, to ignore the concerns which were being brought to your attention, preferring to leave these matters to the consultants concerned. Yet, faced with information suggesting that children were being placed at unnecessary risk, you took no adequate steps to establish the truth. You knew that your medical director was at the centre of many of these concerns, yet you took no adequate steps to obtain impartial advice from appropriate specialists.

Accordingly, it found Dr Roylance, by then retired, guilty of serious professional misconduct and directed that his name be erased from the register. Subsequently Dr Roylance – alone among the three doctors – decided to appeal to the Privy Council against the decision.

Issues raised by evidence

It was not just three doctors who were on trial before the GMC. It was, in effect, an institution: the Bristol Royal Infirmary (BRI). For the evidence strongly suggests that the conduct of the three doctors reflects a wider institutional malaise.[8] The BRI of the first half of the 1990s emerges from the evidence as a rather introverted and complacent institution, dominated by a number of long-established consultants who were reluctant to question the performance of one of their number. It seems to have been no accident that the 'whistle-blowers' were relatively recently appointed consultants, just as it was no accident that their warnings aroused resentment rather than prompting action. Dr Bolsin was described by the GMC's own counsel as 'maladroit' in the way he voiced his concerns and Professor Angelini's style appears to have raised hackles, but the evidence strongly hints that the institutional ethos was such that anyone who criticised his colleagues was stereotyped and dismissed as a trouble maker. As one consultant anaesthetist (again a newcomer) put it when giving evidence, 'In general surgeons do not take kindly to being told by anaesthetists that they are not doing a very good job or that they could be doing their job better. You have to find someone who will listen to you before it becomes a worthwhile dialogue and there was, I believe, a culture in that trust that would not foster that process'.

Lack of institutional self-criticism was also reflected in the failure of the audit machinery to review the performance of the paediatric cardiac surgery. The GMC hearings did not and could not – given the constraints on the nature of the proceedings – directly address the operations of the audit machinery. But while the surgeons concerned did scrupulously examine the outcome of individual operations, they failed adequately to discuss their overall results with their colleagues (and the publication of the *Private Eye* articles, based on leaked figures, appears to have put a stop to any systematic and regular self-examination). As one expert witness – a paediatric surgeon who had refused the offer of a post at Bristol – put it, there is always in such cases a risk of 'self-delusion or self-persuasion' (see Box 2). And the trust's audit committee failed to provide any corrective balance. For three years, the committee received

Box 2 Surgical self-delusion

Giving evidence, Mr Martin Elliott, consultant paediatric surgeon at Great Ormond Street, pointed out:

It is possible to delay confronting poor results by conferring 'special' features on any case that dies (too old, too small, too complex, too infected, etc.) thereby rationalising a poor series … If you operate on a child and it dies, your first reaction as a surgeon is to blame yourself. I have never met a surgeon who does anything else, never. You blame yourself and look through all the features that might be your own fault. If you do not find one or if you find something else that the child has died of, an unsuspected or an undiagnosed pre-operative problem, you will ascribe the cause of death to that and so, in a series of patients, you are likely to say 'the last one had this additional complication but when the other ones are OK, the ones I did earlier on when they did not have those complications are all right' so you prolong the series and eventually one can imagine oneself entering a situation when you have gone perhaps one beyond what you might have done but I think that the method of analysis then becomes what is important. You need to be protected from that view.

nothing from the cardiac surgeons but apparently took no action as a consequence. In addition, there seems to have been confusion as to which clinical directorate was responsible, compounded by the reluctance of the directors concerned to take action.

Institutional complicity also raises a question of personal responsibility. The cardiologists continued to refer to the two surgeons; the anaesthetists continued to assist at the operations on the babies and small children. So, too, did the nurses. If there is a collective team responsibility for maintaining standards – if doctors have a duty to act if they think their colleagues are putting patients at risk – then in many ways it is surprising that only the two surgeons and the chief executive appeared before the GMC. The fact that the GMC sent warning letters to three other doctors – two cardiologists and an anaesthetist, who as a result did not appear as witnesses – suggests that the Council itself was well aware of the wider implications of the case. However, the case leaves open the question of the quality and nature of the evidence required before doctors have a duty to report their concerns about colleagues. At Bristol there was a great deal of what was described as 'corridor conversation' about poor results in paediatric cardiac surgery. But, as some witnesses argued in self-exculpation for not doing more, there was a conspicuous absence of agreed 'facts', which, in turn, would indicate that no one was taking responsibility for determining what those facts were.

The Bristol case raises a further question about another dimension of institutional behaviour. One of the characteristics of paediatric cardiac surgery at Bristol was, as already noted, the small number of the procedures involved. For example, only 15 AVSD procedures were carried out at Bristol between 1990 and 1994, compared to the 30 carried out annually by a paediatric cardiac surgeon called to give evidence. The results of that surgeon witness were – unsurprisingly, given the evidence that quality is often (though not invariably) associated with quantity – much better than those at Bristol. So why was Bristol, a late comer in developing the procedures in question and lacking a specialist paediatric surgeon, engaged in carrying out the operations in the first place as distinct from referring patients to one of the specialist centres whose record was so

much better? It is difficult to resist the conclusion that the driving force was institutional imperialism: that Bristol, a prestigious teaching hospital, was determined to assert its role as a major player in this field – without much regard for its appropriateness for doing so.

A final institutional factor was the role of the trust board. This was the dog that did not bark. Members of the Board were not on trial before the GMC. So no evidence directly bearing on the actions of non-executive members of the board was put before the GMC. However, the available evidence suggests that the board remained passive throughout. Given the publication of the *Private Eye* articles – which at the very least should have alerted the Board to the fact that there was sufficient dissent and concern among members of staff to cause them to leak information – this is surprising, to put it mildly. Even more surprising, however, is the apparent passivity of other actors in the health care arena – the Department of Health itself, the regional authority and, above all, the royal colleges – who must have been aware of the disquiet about Bristol's record but who failed, on the evidence given to the GMC, to raise the alarm: the one departmental civil servant involved, Dr Doyle, acted in his personal capacity as a doctor but chose not to make it an official matter. No doubt the inquiry commissioned by Mr Dobson will illuminate these matters.

Leaving aside the specific institutional factors involved in Bristol, the hearings also underlined a more general problem. This is the lack of accepted standards, the expert witnesses agreed, against which doctors themselves and others can judge their performance. The fact that a surgeon's results are below average does not, of itself, necessarily indicate that they are unacceptable:

someone, after all, must always be below average. It is therefore difficult to know when relatively poor performance becomes unacceptable performance. The next and concluding section examines the implications of this and other general issues raised by the Bristol case.

Implications for public policy

At the end of the proceedings the President of the GMC, Sir Donald Irvine, identified some of the main issues raised by the case (see Box 3). The list illustrates both the importance of the role of the GMC and its limits. The GMC plays a crucial role in setting the agenda for the medical profession. However, the implementation of that agenda largely depends on the medical profession as a whole: on changing the attitudes not only of the royal colleges and the medical schools but of individual doctors. The GMC may provide the ethical framework within which the profession works but changing practice will require doctors to internalise the values embodied in that framework. So, for example, the GMC's new performance assessment procedures will give it a powerful new weapon to deal with doctors whose skills or techniques are deficient. But the impact of this new procedure will largely depend on the willingness of members of the profession (and others) to identify doctors whose performance appears to be inadequate and to modify their inbuilt tendency to protect colleagues:[9] a tendency common to all professions.

Some changes are already in train. For example, the collection of data about the outcomes of paediatric cardiac surgery has been improved, so that it is possible to compare the performance of different units.[10] But many of the issues identified by the GMC will require more fundamental changes still. For example, the Bristol case

Box 3 Wider issues raised by the Bristol case

At the end of the case, Sir Donald Irvine made the following statement:

Having concluded our determination in respect of the three doctors, the Committee wishes to identify a number of issues which arose during the course of the inquiry. These wider issues concern the practice of surgery and of medicine generally, and will have to be addressed by the medical profession. The issues include:

- *the need for clearly understood clinical standards*
- *how clinical competence and technical expertise are assessed and evaluated*
- *who carries responsibility in team-based care*
- *the training of doctors in advanced procedures*
- *how to approach the so-called 'learning curve' of doctors undertaking established procedures*
- *the reliability and validity of the data used to monitor doctors' personal performance*
- *the use of medical and clinical audit*
- *the appreciation of the importance of factors, other than purely clinical ones, that can affect clinical judgement, performance and outcome*
- *the responsibility of a consultant to take appropriate actions in response to concerns about his or her performance*
- *the factors which appear to discourage openness and frankness about doctors' personal performance*
- *how doctors explain risks to patients*
- *the ways in which people concerned about patient safety can make their concerns known*
- *the need for doctors to take prompt action at an early stage where a colleague is in difficulty, in order to offer the best chance of avoiding damage to patients and the colleague, and of putting things right.*

challenges the assumption that all surgeons should be free to try out a new procedure, whatever the risks to the patients being used as teaching material for this process of self-education, as distinct from being let loose on patients only after being trained by a surgeon already experienced in using the procedure in question. Similarly, it challenges the assumption that individual hospitals should be free to carry out procedures in penny packages when the evidence suggests that good outcomes depend on concentrating expertise in high turnover units.

In all this the underlying issue is the relationship between professional self-regulation and public policy. How much can, and should, be left to the profession? And how far can, and should, the State intervene directly to shape medical practice? Where should the boundary be set? The public impact of the Bristol case – which attracted unprecedented media coverage – has put pressure not only on the medical profession but also on the Government to act. For one paradoxical effect of the GMC's decision to bring the Bristol doctors to book – in itself a powerful message to all doctors about their duties to patients – has been to raise doubts about the profession's own capacity to protect the public. The visibility given by the GMC trial to medical failings may, perversely, fuel demands for stronger government intervention rather than being seen as evidence of the profession's own determination to deal with doctors whose performance is unsatisfactory. Indeed one effect of the case is likely to be that other examples of medical failures will be given even greater prominence in the media than would otherwise have been the case: a succession of medical scandals appears to be in the pipeline. Greater visibility for the activities of the medical profession and a willingness to expose

inadequacies may in the long run earn it greater public trust; in the short term, however, the result may be to fuel public anxieties and demands for more State intervention.

The present Government is already committed to a more interventionist policy stance flowing from its emphasis on quality in *The New NHS* and *A First Class Service*.[11,12] The details of the proposed changes are reviewed elsewhere in this volume (see Section 1.5 of the Review). Here it is sufficient to note how some of the proposed new institutions and mechanisms have the potential to address some of the issues raised by the Bristol case. On the one hand, the National Institute for Clinical Excellence could develop the benchmarks or standards against which the performance of individual doctors can be measured. On the other hand, the Commission for Health Improvement could address the kind of problems of institutional failure identified in the Bristol case. Similarly, while the publication of outcome statistics would not necessarily identify poor performers, given the problems of giving meaning to the data, they could act as alarm bells triggering off more detailed inquiries.

Finally, and most importantly perhaps, there is the proposal for giving chief executives a statutory responsibility for the quality of the services provided to patients. At present chief executives and boards are accountable for everything that happens in the service – except what matters most to patients, *i.e.* the quality of the medical care that they get. In the Bristol case, there would have been no formal machinery for disciplining the chief executive if he had not happened to be medically qualified. Thus the proposal would appear to complete the chain of accountability in the NHS.[13] However, it is not clear how practice will match theory. Will chief executives (and their boards) be accountable for setting up the appropriate machinery of clinical governance[14] designed to ensure quality control? Or will they be accountable for ensuring that good quality services, however measured, are actually delivered? Will they, to come to a central issue raised by the Bristol case, take the assurances of the medical director or will they be expected to conduct their own, independent reviews and test the data generated by audit?

To ask these questions is to underline the interdependence of public policy and professional self-regulation. The aim of public policy is to make the medical profession collectively more accountable for its performance. The aim of professional self-regulation is to make individual practitioners more accountable to their peers. In an important sense, the success of the former strategy depends crucially on the latter: on institutionalising professional self-regulation at the local level.[15] Control over the performance of the medical profession collectively is a complement to – not a substitute for – control by the medical profession of the quality of care delivered by its members. And the precise balance between the two will depend on the extent to which the medical profession demonstrates that it can be trusted to deliver its part of the bargain: trust that, as the GMC has realised, must be earned rather than taken for granted.

References

1. Committee of Inquiry into the Regulation of the Medical Profession. *Report*. Merrison AW (Chair). London: HMSO, 1975 (Cmnd 6018).

2. General Medical Council. *Good Medical Practice*. 2nd edition. London: GMC, 1998.

3. Stacey M. *Regulating British Medicine*. Chichester: John Wiley & Sons, 1992.

4. General Medical Council. *Work of the Conduct Procedures*. Report to the Council. London: GMC, 19 May 1998.

5. Statutory Instrument No 2255. *Medical Profession. The General Medical Council Preliminary Proceedings Committee and Professional Conduct Committee (Procedure) Rules*. London: HMSO, 1988.

6. General Medical Council. *When Your Professional Performance Is Questioned. The GMC's performance procedures*. London: GMC, November 1997.

7. Warden J. Dobson criticises GMC. *British Medical Journal* 1998; 316(27 June):1925.

8. Klein R. Competence. Professional self regulation and the public interest. *British Medical Journal* 1998; 316(6 June):1740–2.

9. Rosenthal M M. *The Incompetent Doctor*. Buckingham: Open University Press, 1995.

10. Treasure T. Lessons from the Bristol case. *British Medical Journal* 1998; 316(6 June):1685–6.

11. Secretary of State for Health. *The New NHS: Modern – Dependable*. London: The Stationery Office, 1997 (Cmnd 3807).

12. Secretary of State for Health. *A First Class Service. Quality in the new NHS*. London: Department of Health, 1998.

13. Day P, Klein R. *Accountabilities*. London: Tavistock, 1987.

14. Scally G, Donaldson L. Clinical governance and the drive for quality improvement in the new NHS in England. *British Medical Journal* 1998; 317(4 July):61–5.

15. Irvine D. The performance of doctors 11. Maintaining good practice; protecting patients from poor performance. *British Medical Journal* 1997; 314(31 May):1613–15.

Should the NHS have a computing strategy?

Justin Keen

Not long ago, information and communications technologies (ICTs) were located firmly on the periphery of many clinicians' and managers' concerns. But now, the Government is committed to major investments in the infrastructure of NHS computing and telecommunications, and the NHS is to be put under considerable pressure to deliver and use new large-scale systems. ICTs will therefore be a priority for everyone.

This article raises a number of questions about current trends in the use of ICTs, and the nature of NHS Executive policy in this area. It starts by outlining policy developments for ICTs throughout the 1990s and then points to the political imperatives that will drive ICT investments. Notwithstanding the strength of this imperative, the new strategy will have to deal with the problem that it is often difficult to construct business cases for ICT investments, and also with a number of issues relating to structure and ownership, at both national and local levels. The latter is analysed by focusing particularly on centre-local relationships, the long-term trend towards integration of formerly disparate sources of information, and the possible future move away from the traditional face-to-face clinical encounter which the rise of telemedicine will involve.

It seems likely that the top-down, directive thrust of earlier strategies will be maintained after 1998. Two points follow, namely that the respective roles of the centre and the NHS need to be more clearly defined, and the actions of the centre will need to be carefully handled in order to avoid stifling local initiatives: the more dependent we become on ICTs, the more likely it is that stifling local ICT initiatives will have repercussions on other parts of the Government's agenda. Important points on this agenda involve cross-sectoral partnerships, so the way forward for ICTs presumably will mean supporting cross-sectoral work patterns. The implication is that we should stop thinking about NHS computing in isolation, and instead work out how best to use ICTs in the development of these new extra-NHS relationships.

Background: new boundaries for old?

The development of ICTs and of ICT policies within the NHS over the last 10–15 years can usefully be conceived as involving changes in three areas:

- the number of NHS actors deemed to be involved;

- the integration of disparate systems and sources of information; and,
- the increasing separation of the parties involved in health care in time and space.

Until the advent of the personal computer in the early 1980s, the use of computers in health care had been the preserve of relatively small numbers of people working on mainly administrative tasks, typically on free-standing mainframe computers in regional health authorities or patient administration systems in hospitals. Computers were introduced alongside information systems based on paper, which were themselves fragmented: medical records were separate from nursing and other clinical records, and virtually all clinical records were separate from administrative data, collected both for local purposes and for central returns. There was minimal 'horizontal' transfer of data between the different parts of the NHS, outside clinician-to-clinician letters and phone calls. Computers were also regarded as an add-on to the 'real' information systems and networks in hospitals, surgeries and elsewhere. Most information goes nowhere near a computer, comprising as it does the conversations, arguments and rumours that give the NHS its singular character: this point can easily be forgotten in discussions about ICTs.

Policy documents published from the mid-1980s onwards[1,2] began to give shape to the direction of national computing policies, and led to a period of piloting of systems in the period to 1991. These included, in separate developments, the piloting of hospital information support systems (HISS),[3] management budgeting and case-mix systems for hospitals,[4] and administrative systems for GPs.[5] There were also initiatives in community services, but these were once again the Cinderellas of a policy story: there has been dispiritingly little progress in the last 15 years.[6]

The publication of *Working for Patients* in 1989[7] led to a review of ICT policy, on the basis that the proposed quasi-market would require a transformation in the volume and nature of information produced by both purchasers and providers. Moving the information around would, it was felt by civil servants, require ICTs. Perhaps the most remarkable aspect of ICT policy in this period, though, was the fact that it so studiously ignored the logic of the White Paper.[8] The 1990 document *Framework for Information Systems*[9] betrayed little awareness of *Working for Patients*, and focused instead on the continuing implementation of systems within organisations, with HISS the jewel in the crown, though there were to be limited administrative links in some areas, notably between GP practices and (the then) family practitioner committees. But there was scarcely a reference to the information that might be needed in a quasi-market.

As recently as 1992, then, the picture was that:

- the number of groups presumed to be affected by ICT policies had increased over a period of years, perhaps most importantly in the inclusion of GPs, but most people in hospital and community units were unaffected, unless they happened to work in one of the limited number of pilot sites, or had a personal interest in computers;
- there was very limited co-ordination of policies or systems, no obvious link between ICTs and information systems, and ICT policies were separate from the information policies embodied in *Working for Patients*;

- the rise of networking was not yet a policy option, so there was little serious thinking about using ICTs to transform the organisation of services in time and space.

The legacy of the pre-*Working for Patients* thinking is still with us today, two major White Papers later. This is expressed partly in the fact that many of the systems promoted in the 1980s are still in place, and some of them are still favoured by policy-makers: HISS is one example, GP computing another. Indeed, hospitals and GP practices that implemented systems early on now have ageing systems, and the time has come for replacement. Just as importantly, there is the legacy of serious problems in the purchase and implementation of systems, leading to critical reports of conflicts of interest in Wessex,[10] the failure of the HISS programme[11] and now the problems with the Read Codes[12] by the National Audit Office. Many NHS bodies have, understandably, been cautious in their approach to ICTs.

The 1992 IM&T Strategy

The 1990 Framework did not, apparently, meet the requirements of the (then) NHS Management Executive, who requested a new strategy. This led to the publication of the NHS *Information Management and Technology (IM&T) Strategy* at the end of 1992.[13] The Strategy had many different components, which together were intended to provide the opportunity for electronic communication between any two points within the NHS. There would be a dedicated national network (NHSnet, now provided through Private Finance Initiative contracts, with the contractors aiming to make good their investments through charges for network use). The network would link a series of databases located in general practices,

NHS trusts, health authorities and elsewhere, which would store a variety of clinical and administrative data. In order that the different systems could talk to one another, there were to be national data and systems standards.

The 1992 Strategy was a turning point. The previous lack of co-ordination in ICT policy was ended, and the Strategy set out an overall direction for future developments. The details were a little hazy, but the clear implication was that most NHS staff would have access to the NHS network, the individual computing initiatives would all be linked, and the possibility was opened up of exchanging data so that the geographical location of sender and receiver was irrelevant.

In the event, implementation was slower than the NHS Executive originally hoped. Concern was expressed about the Strategy by a number of people inside the Service and by academic commentators, notably about the failure to demonstrate that the investments made had been worthwhile,[14] and about the absence of safeguards for access to confidential information about patients (and, one guesses, the performance of doctors).[15] Ray Rogers, the former Executive Director of the Information Management Group within the NHS Executive, claimed that the Strategy would save £100m per annum,[16] but after six years there is no firm evidence that any money has been saved. Crucially, it has been difficult for health authorities and trusts to make ICT business cases that can compete successfully with other capital bids: the projected paybacks are too long, or not great enough, or both.

Yet progress *has* been made. At the time of writing, most GPs have made the limited administrative links to health authorities, though they cannot exchange clinical data with other sites. The NHSnet is in place and health authorities, trusts and some GPs have joined it. Many of these links are to just one or a handful of places in an organisation: most people in a trust do not have direct access to the network. Fears about confidentiality seem to have been assuaged.[17] As in 1992, then, the picture is mixed, with progress in some areas, but difficulties being encountered elsewhere. It seems reasonable to say that:

- ICT policy from 1992 recognised the importance of including many different groups, though GPs were for a long time viewed as inhabiting a separate universe, and community services remained on the fringes of central consciousness;
- the creation of the NHS network provided the potential for the free flow of information between many points in the NHS. At the same time, however, the 1992 Strategy served to emphasise the separation between ICTs and information policy and practice, and the division between clinical and administrative information. ICTs were added to, rather than integrated with, existing information systems;
- the slow progress meant that there was little evidence of ICTs being used to support or create new relationships in time and space.

There is, again, a legacy of systems in place that will influence the course of future policies. This is encapsulated in the creation of the NHS Clearing Service, which was introduced after the 1992 Strategy, in somewhat belated recognition of the idea of using ICTs to support contracting. The Clearing Service is a centralised service designed to route contractual and extra-contractual (i.e. administrative) information from providers to purchasers. Data from all NHS bodies would go over NHSnet to the Clearing Service, where they would be re-routed to the appropriate purchaser, and sent back out over NHSnet. The result, in an NHS moving away from a market-inspired model, is that sending a message a mile from a hospital to a health authority means sending it via a centralised system. This is another – this time highly centralised – system that constrains the options available for future policies.

In the same period, there were also wider, more 'secular' developments in computing, which complicate this picture. One of these was the development of local solutions, sometimes prompted by perceived failure of the centre to make progress. This is particularly true of GP computing, which has a long history of interesting local initiatives by GPs and others, and where there is now a considerable reservoir of knowledge and experience, which has not been fully exploited by the Executive. Another development was the rise of the Internet, which provides an alternative source of information and communication. Those people who are not attracted by NHSnet can, if they wish, use the Internet.[18] The Internet also raises questions about costs and ownership: if there is a choice between the Internet and NHSnet, what are the advantages to the NHS Executive and to NHS users of each system? As we shall see below, we do not know the answer to this question.

The current policy environment

Statements by the Prime Minister and others during late 1997 and 1998 provide us with a good sense of the future thrust of ICT policy. *The New NHS*[18] signalled a decisive move away from administrative concerns and towards clinical ones. Technologies new to the NHS such as telemedicine (in essence, clinical work conducted via electronic media) and electronic patient records (EPR) will be central to developments. The NHS Direct telephone service is to be extended across the UK. There have also been hints that GPs may receive subsidies to help them to implement new computer systems, in part to help them to participate in primary care groups. And, as the preceding account suggests, it seems likely that existing initiatives including a national NHS network and – rather surprisingly – the Read Codes will be retained and promoted.[19]

Now is therefore an odd time for the NHS: on the one hand there is a patchy history, by no means all bad but not entirely positive either; on the other hopes are now being pinned on ICTs as the way forward. The political imperative is to put past frustrations aside and get it right this time.

The political imperative

At the NHS Confederation Conference to celebrate the 50th anniversary of the NHS in July 1998, Prime Minister Tony Blair spoke about the promise of telemedicine, which in his view would help to revolutionise the delivery of NHS care.[20] This is a sure sign that ICTs are firmly centre stage, and becomes even more interesting when seen in context, because this was not an isolated statement. In October 1997 Mr Blair announced that by 2002 25 per cent of all transactions between individuals and Government would be via ICTs – using telephones, computers, and possibly via TVs at home.[21] Changes in the delivery of social security benefits will probably account for a substantial proportion of the 25 per cent, with NHS Direct providing another useful tranche of transactions. The Prime Minister's statement confirmed support for the government.

direct initiative[22] started by the last administration in 1996, whose broad aim is to integrate public services so that they are more user-oriented, whether that user be a private person or someone in business.

Even these statements have a wider context. The Government will strive for targets – 'visions' might be a better word – spelled out by the European Union in the Bangemann Report in 1994,[23] and by the G8 at its 1998 meeting.[24] Why we might need a new EU-wide or global network is not clear – we are asked to accept that it is inevitable and desirable. Efforts by the author to establish the existence of investment cases for these networks came to nothing: the Web sites for the EU Bangemann Initiatives and for G8 are worth a short detour, highlighting as they do the preference for rhetoric over evidence or a closely argued business case for ICTs.

It is useful to view NHS ICTs in this broad context, and see them as essentially non-rational investments, rather like the Channel Tunnel Rail Link, where it has become clear that the business case is not compelling. Non-economic factors – such as looking modern and progressive to our continental colleagues – come into play. On this view, ICTs are things that politicians want to support, whether or not there is a business case. ICTs are a UK *grand projet*.

But, like the NHS itself, the fact that ICTs are someone's vision does not mean they are a bad idea, or uneconomic. Is there in fact a good business case for a new round of investment?

The investment case

What might an investment case for the new ICT strategy look like? We do not know the detail, of course, so here I present a 'shadow' business case: my guess at what it might need to contain, taking a central view of the problem. It starts with the observation that resources will be committed to ICTs across the NHS: we know that much from the political imperative. Experience since 1992 shows that local business cases are difficult to make, so local sites will find it difficult to go it alone. It may be that the cases for the NHS network and other services purchased by the NHS Executive were stronger, but these cases have not been published. The rational challenge is to steer the allocation of resources in the right direction, so that the investment case adds up.

It is useful to think of two main sources of expenditure for ICTs, namely the NHS Executive and the NHS itself. These are linked, so that expenditure by the Executive changes the balance of costs and benefits in the NHS, and *vice versa*, as shown in Figure 1. To take a simple example, the provision of subsidies to GPs to purchase computer systems should mean that GPs do not have to spend as much themselves.

The question for the NHS Executive is: what should happen in the NHS Executive box, in terms of resources committed, systems implemented and so on, in order that investments would be worthwhile in the NHS box? That is, investing centrally should lead to a situation where local sites find that *their* benefits outweigh their costs. Ideally, putting an activity in the NHS Executive box should also reduce the *total* cost of doing something for the NHS as a whole.

There are a number of options for the NHS Executive here, including the following.

- Provide for infrastructure and services such as national networks centrally, so as to reduce investment costs or increase benefits for local sites.
- Directly subsidise local systems, as was done for GPs in the past.
- Take decisions about data and system standards, which gives local sites confidence in their investment decisions. For example, a centrally agreed standard for sending pathology information between any two sites would help all sites, as they could ensure that systems they purchased would adhere to the standard, and they could talk to any other site.
- Manage other parties, notably suppliers, so that their interests are more closely aligned with the interests of the NHS.
- Undertake evaluations, and hence demonstrate the costs and benefits of different investments.

These have all been used in the past and might be used again: as noted already, there have been hints about further subsidies for GP computing. The weakest area to date has been evaluation, perhaps not surprising if one believes that ICTs embody managerialist thinking.[25] That is, ICTs are something where the Nike maxim – 'just do it' – applies, whereas evaluation is for wimps who just want to stand in the way of managers managing. Perhaps this will change with the new strategy.

Fig 1 A simple model: the balance of expenditure for ICTs

So, to the investment case. The need for the NHS to make business cases for ICT investments has been a useful discipline, forcing people to look at real money: it is just that the local numbers tend not to add up. The key problem has been that we do not have a convincing conceptual framework for thinking about costs and benefits.[26] The central guidance has been disappointing, in spite of good intentions, and points the Service towards a view of ICTs as technologies which save money by replacing people or paper with systems.[27] This is a narrow view of what ICTs might do within organisations, and something more sophisticated is needed, which takes account of how ICTs really interact with organisations, and of economists' thinking about the costs and benefits of joining networks.

An alternative approach would involve the following steps:

1. Identify objectives that ICTs will help to achieve, such as better co-ordination of information flows between service providers.
2. Work out the 'theory of application' of the ICTs, that links the ICT interventions to specific costs and benefits that should be attained. For example, implementing a network might be conceptualised as leading to reducing administrative costs and/or increasing the speed of a service.
3. Identify costs and benefits associated with each intervention, and the conditions under which they will be incurred.
4. Construct a list of costs and benefits, which will include some due to direct substitution of paper with IT, and others due to economies of scope and scale.
5. Combine the figures.

Of course, this is easier said than done. In particular, the step that appears to have been missing in previous strategies is Step 2, developing understanding of the ways in which costs and benefits will be incurred. It is not really a simple step in a guide on investment appraisal, but a call to think about the nature of ICTs. This has not been done systematically in the past, but might go as follows.

Looking forward, at systems that will form part of the new landscape, such as telemedicine and EPR, there are several distinct theories in play. For example, one implicit assumption underpinning telemedicine is that it will produce positive returns to scale: any one specialist can treat people over a wider geographical area than hitherto, and this may save both the NHS's and patients' money – for example, in reducing investment needed in physical infrastructure.

The task then becomes one of working out whether such economies are likely to occur in practice, and how big they might be. The greater the number of users, the lower the costs and the greater the benefits to each individual user. In the early stages of development of a network, the (often high) investment and initial running costs have to be shared between a relatively small number of users. It is this initial cost hurdle, which some systems never overcome, that explains why some initiatives fail. But if the hurdle can be overcome, then increasing numbers of users can share the benefits flowing from the efforts of pioneers (see Figures 2 and 3).

Taking another example, the argument that implicitly underpins the promotion of the electronic patient record is that sharing of

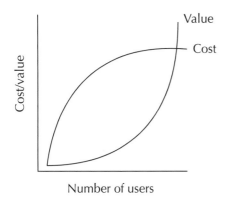

The costs of implementing the network are high initially, but the rate of increase in costs falls once the main elements are in place, and the additional cost of linking new users is relatively low. Conversely, the benefits are modest initially, but increase as the number of users increases. For the right design and implementation strategy, and sufficient users, the curves cross so that the value exceeds the cost.

Source: Keen J. Rethinking NHS networking.
BMJ 1998;316:1291–3

Fig 2 Change in cost and value of a network as the number of users increases

information will lead to better co-ordination of services, which will in turn lower costs, or increase the effectiveness of service delivery, or both. This is, then, an argument about the ways in which clinicians use information, and depends on them using the information in records in their decision-making. The evidence for or against this view is not clear-cut: people do use information when provided, but it seems that they are more likely to use it when they have incentives to do so, rather than simply because it is available. More positively, there are now many examples of local sharing of clinical information across professional boundaries, albeit without ICTs. There is some reason, therefore, for optimism even if many organisational barriers still have to be overcome.

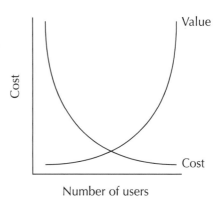

From the perspective of a GP practice, the marginal cost of using a network decreases as the network grows in size, because there are more users to share the investment and running costs – as long as any savings are passed on to users and not retained entirely by suppliers. The value of the network increases with increasing size, as the network allows users to benefit from new services that can be made available.

Source: Keen J. Rethinking NHS networking.
BMJ 1998;316:1291–3

Fig 3 Marginal cost and value for individual users, as the number of users increases

We could go further with our analysis if we had good data on which to base judgements about costs and benefits, and a better understanding of the ways in which ICTs actually work in health service settings. Unfortunately, we don't have good data, and understanding of modern ICTs in modern settings could be better. The NHS Executive will not, therefore, have this information either. What we can say, though, is that there are likely to be some activities which are properly undertaken by the NHS Executive. One example is standards setting, where it is easier for everyone in the Service if the Executive can set sensible standards for exchanging data and linking systems.[28] Another example is likely to be accreditation of systems, where the Executive can act on behalf of the whole NHS in discussions with suppliers. The devil is in the detail, of course, but it is important to note that the NHS Executive box in Figure 1 is far from empty.

Hopefully, the detailed investment case for the new strategy is being prepared for publication, and we can share in the results. It is difficult to see how the NHS can respond rationally to the new strategy if the central business case is not published. It would be odd to make sites develop their own cases in ignorance of central thinking, and odder still if the centre had not established that local sites could indeed construct robust cases. Publication would, at the very least, be good evidence of thinking about central–local co-ordination.

Structural change

Recent statements about the direction of ICT policy point to the possibility of an exciting future, but also to the deep tensions inherent in this area. Here, the three issues identified at the beginning of the article are returned to: centre–local relations, integration of information systems – contrasted with individualism, and the separation of relationships in time and space. It often seems as if ICTs accentuate these tensions: each attempt at integration brings us up against deep structural issues, that the NHS has in practice to work around rather than resolve.

Centre–local relations and beyond

The account to this point has suggested that ICT policy has often been something that is done to the NHS, and moreover done in isolation from other central policies. ICT policy has concerned itself with the 'supply' side of the problem, in providing and promoting systems, but not the 'demand' side – using them. In some ways this is understandable, if one thinks of people in the NHS Executive who can do little themselves to promote an information culture, and yet are under pressure to deliver to tight timescales.

The awkward fact is, though, that successive studies of management initiatives suggest that the NHS is not focused on information: historically, there have been only weak incentives to collect and analyse data, and much of the best work has resulted from local initiatives in clinical audit and other quality-oriented activities.[29,30] The result is that commitment is at best patchy.

These issues of local culture and incentives are really the proper object of a rounded ICT policy, since successful implementation must depend on receptive local environments. This goes beyond computers and networks, and includes elements of *The New NHS* such as the forthcoming NHS performance management framework, which needs ideally to be designed in such a way that NHS staff have incentives to collect data accurately and completely. The same goes for EPR, telemedicine and the rest: history tells us that they cannot simply be picked off shelves and then installed and used by everyone. There is a clear implication for ICT policy-makers here: the centre must not simply prescribe systems, because those systems will be injected into environments that may well not be receptive to them.

As if this were not enough, there are tensions within the more general policy framework of *The New NHS*. ICTs might on the one hand be used to support the centralising tendencies in the White Paper, including the creation of national service frameworks, the Commission for Health Improvement (CHIMP) and related initiatives. On the other, they might pick up on the comments about the need for a greater clinical focus in the application of ICTs and be used to support more local initiatives. This makes it very difficult to set a 'rational' ICT policy, whether one is in the NHS Executive or an embryonic primary care group (PCG).

Recognising the true nature of the problem means that one cannot simply identify the 'information needs' for the NHS from the centre. In practice there is no one locus or type of decision-making or requirement for information. Any one group of actors has many hats on and is subject to many different influences. Just think of GPs, who are to be clinicians, managers of their own practices and members of PCGs. The ways in which they might acquire and use information in all three areas is dynamic, and this suggests that there is little point in telling them what they can and cannot do. This is not so different from other infrastructure investments such as buildings: needs change over time, and one has to decide whether to provide for today or build in flexibility for future service developments.

The emphasis should, rather, be on enabling local people to develop flexible, local solutions – and the time to grow them. Sadly, given the comments about the political imperatives made earlier, there seems certain to be a mismatch here between the length of time required to move the NHS towards an information culture and the timescales available, with the 25 per cent transaction deadline being 2002, with the cultural change requiring rather longer than the time allowed by the Prime Minister's statements. Recognition of the 'true nature' of ICTs would *inter alia* lead to longer timescales for what are difficult organisational transitions. Some things just cannot be hurried.

These issues are not new, having been present through all previous ICT initiatives. However, now there are new structural issues coming to the fore, all of them stemming from the blurring of the boundaries between public and private sectors, and between the NHS and other parts of the welfare state. What might the effects be? One example is that use of the Private Finance Initiative in both primary and secondary care might have little effect on the willingness and ability of NHS staff to use ICTs; or, alternatively the presence of commercially minded contractors might help to promote their use. The signing of long-term contracts for ICTs might 'lock in' the organisation of services within the NHS, because extra-NHS requirements are not specified; or, contractors might be agile and respond quickly to changing patterns of delivery. We do not know. There seems to have been little discussion of the potential effects of changing ownership on attitudes and performance with information systems and ICTs.

Similarly, one might ask about the role of ICTs in supporting lateral relationships with organisations outside the NHS, since these sit at the heart of a number of government policies. There ought to be some thinking somewhere about ICT links to social services, housing departments, voluntary organisations and private nursing homes, to name just a few. Will there be joint networking initiatives? Will there be reporting of 'joint performance indicators' for accountability for cross-boundary resource use? Will there be new issues of security and confidentiality to tackle? Again, there seems to have been little discussion of these issues: it is not clear how EPR – to take just one example – will be integrated with cross-boundary strategies.

The most striking example of blurring, though, involves ICTs themselves. Over the last four years a number of NHS-wide ICT services have been contracted out to BT, AT&T and other companies. These are large and powerful companies, who have the muscle to get things done – which may well help propel the new strategy forward – but also have their own (proper, commercial) interests. ICTs are a prime example of a public-private partnership – it is just that they are not often viewed in this light. The debate is no longer just about centralisation/decentralisation, then, but about the triangular relationship between the contractors, NHS Executive and NHS. The Executive therefore needs to have strategies for managing the triangle, rather than the NHS alone. One would expect to see a regulatory regime put in place to ensure that NHS and patient interests are protected. We will have to wait and see if such a framework is put in place: this ought to have a central role in the new strategy.

Individualism versus integration

ICTs highlight the long-standing tension between the 'cult of the individual' and the desire for integration. There has until now been a strong tendency towards the use of ICTs to support *individuals* in their work. Within central policies, HISS, general practice and other systems are designed to support individual clinicians and managers – albeit by co-ordinating the flow of data on their behalf – rather than joint working. Arguably, much of the thinking about networking since 1992 has been based on the assumption that networks are there to serve many individual decision-makers. This is also true for more localised initiatives. The continuing support for decision support systems (systems designed to support specific types of clinical decision) within parts of the medical profession could, similarly, be interpreted as support for the view of the doctor as a discrete decision-maker. The nature of discussions about telemedicine at present suggest that it, too, is viewed essentially as a special type of individual decision support system – one clinician is the 'decision support system' for another clinician or for a patient.

There is another tendency, though, towards the *integration* of work practices, implicit in the promotion of case mix systems in the Resource Management Initiative, though less obvious since. Resource Management was an attempt to overcome the separation of information systems discussed earlier, in that case by linking clinical and management data within a single database, that both sides could then discuss and debate. The one current initiative which may have a more integrationist element is NHS Direct, which could be interpreted as a system for nurses and users to arrive at joint decisions about courses of action: whether this is how it actually works will come out of the current evaluation of the initiative. Now, with the rhetoric outside the world of ICTs all about integration, one might expect to find systems being designed to heal the rifts described earlier. It is possible that EPR will perform a similar role in the future, if it is used to integrate information across professional and organisational boundaries.

The problems here are, then, of mindset and of organisation. If ICTs are to be used to support more integrated working, then it will be necessary to address the problems described earlier, of the separation of ICTs and information systems. It will be necessary to integrate, at least to some extent, across professional and managerial boundaries: but the difficulties of bringing together ICTs with 'formal' and 'informal' information systems are serious management issues that go far beyond the boundaries of recent ICT policy thinking. Simply stating this as the problem hints at one reason why individually-focused systems might persist – the task is not at all trivial – and it is possible that EPR will end up supporting individuals rather than integration of data (and at least give a small boost to integrated practice). At present, there is little evidence that these deep issues are in fact likely to be tackled – and the individualistic mindset may therefore win out.

There is another worry here, which is that EPR could turn out be a solution to yesterday's problems. Hitherto, EPR might have been justified on the basis of integration within the NHS, but if working across organisational boundaries is really here to stay, then an NHS-focused solution will soon be inadequate to meet everyone's needs. The discussion now should be more about the design of networks, and who is linked to whom, than the content of NHS-only databases.

Changing relationships in time and space

There is, so far, little evidence that ICTs have changed relationships in time and space in the NHS or other health care systems, but it is predicted by some doctors, who among other things see it as necessary to support greater concentration of medical specialisation in ever fewer hospitals. It is also hinted at in discussions of NHS Direct, which may in time become a major 'electronic health service', where the physical distance between the professional and user could as easily be 10,000 miles as ten. There seems little reason, other than maintenance of restrictive practices, to keep the service based in the UK, if it can be shown that a service of similar quality can be provided more cheaply from elsewhere.

Before we go much further down this road, though, we might ask: is this what we want? Most of the current discussion of ICTs implies 2-way interactions, embodying the individualistic model of service provision. This might avoid taking on the messy governance issues required for integration, but may well lead instead to a faceless NHS, where the ties between professionals and patients are weakened. The alternative is, therefore, to retain the more humanistic face of medicine, and only use networks in clinical settings where circumstances give it clear advantages over face-to-face contact. It is a moot point who should decide between these alternatives: the choices call for some informed debate.

Conclusions

The arguments in this paper lead to two main conclusions. The first is that all of the noises coming from the NHS Executive and from politicians suggest that they are still inclined to instruct rather than co-operate. ICTs are likely to fall in with the centralising thrust of *The New NHS*. This tendency can be understood in terms of the wider pressures to get ICTs in place across Government, but means that there is little sensitivity to development of local culture and incentives to deliver on central directives. Such a policy is likely to fail. There must be a real danger that progress will again be slower than hoped: this might well only reflect the fact that the 'natural' pace of development is too slow for the central timetable.

The main consequence of a centralist approach is that the thrust of integration is likely to be at the centre rather than within the NHS. For example, performance indicators, national service frameworks and other management information fit a centralist model, whereas clinical information does not: perhaps this central information system will be integrated with NHSnet and other systems. It is doubtful whether this will help the NHS much, though, given that the NHS is unlikely to gain ownership of systems. The long-standing separation of ICTs and information systems will remain.

The second conclusion is that the world in which ICTs are implemented is becoming ever more complex and difficult. The way to address this complexity cannot any longer lie solely within the NHS. The era of NHS computing is over: we are now entering an era of working, over time, to provide locally integrated solutions across traditional boundaries. NHS computing is dead – long live NHS computing!

References

1. DHSS. *National Strategic Framework for Information Management in the Hospital and Community Health Services.* London: DHSS, 1986.

2. DHSS. *A new approach to information technology research and development in the hospital and community health services.* London: DHSS, 1987.

3. Audit Commission. *For your information: A study of information management and systems in the acute hospital.* London: HMSO, 1995.

4. Keen J, Buxton M, Packwood T. Complexity and contradiction in NHS computing. *Public Money and Management* 1991;11(3):23–9.

5. NHS Management Executive. *Integrating Primary and Secondary Health Care.* London: Department of Health, 1991.

6. Audit Commission. *Comparing Notes: A study of information management in community trusts.* London: Stationery Office, 1997.

7. Secretaries of State for Health. *Working for Patients.* London: HMSO, 1989 (Cmnd 555).

8. Keen J. Should the National Health Service have an information strategy? *Public Administration* 1994;72:33–53.

9. Department of Health. *Framework for Information Systems: the next steps.* London: HMSO, 1990.

10. National Audit Office. *The Wessex Regional Information Systems Plan.* London: HMSO, 1993.

11. National Audit Office. *Department of Health: the Hospital Information Support Systems Initiative.* HC 332, Session 1995–96. London: Stationery Office, 1996.

12. National Audit Office. *NHS Executive: the Purchase of the Read Codes and the Management of the NHS Centre for Coding and Classification.* HC 607, Session 1997–98. London: Stationery Office, 1998.

13. NHS Management Executive. *IM&T Strategy: Overview.* London: Information Management Group/NHS Executive, 1992.

14. Lock C. What value do computers provide to NHS hospitals? *British Medical Journal* 1996; 312:1407–10

15. Anderson R. NHS-wide networking and patient confidentiality. *British Medical Journal* 1995;311:5–6.

16. Committee of Public Accounts. *The hospital information support systems initiative.* PAC 7th Report, House of Commons (Session 1996–97). London: Stationery Office, 1996.

17. The Caldicott Committee. *Report on the Review of Patient-identifiable information.* London: Department of Health, 1997.

18. Secretary of State for Health. *The New NHS: Modern, Dependable.* London: Stationery Office, 1997.

19. Mitchell P. Log on and like it. *Health Service Journal* 1998; 2 April:16

20. See http://www.number-10.gov.uk/public/info/releases /NHS 50th Anniversary Speech, 2 July 1998

21. See http://www.number-10.gov.uk/public/info/releases /publications/infoagefeat.htm.

22. Central Information Technology Unit. government. direct. London: Stationery Office, 1996.

23. See http://www2.echo.lu/eudocs/en/bangemann.html

24. http://www.open.gov.uk/govoline/golintro.htm.

25. Pollitt C. *Managerialism and the public services* (2nd edition). Oxford: Blackwell 1993.

26. Keen J. Rethinking NHS Networking. *British Medical Journal* 1998;316:1291–3.

27. NHS Executive/Information Management Group. *Investment Appraisal of IM&T Projects*. Leeds: NHS Executive, 1993.

28. Ferguson B, Keen J. Transaction costs, externalities and information technology in health care. *Health Economics* 1996;5:25–36.

29. Mugford M, Banfield P, O'Hanlon M. The effects of feedback of information on clinical practice: a review. *British Medical Journal* 1991;303:398–402.

30. Keen J, Buxton M, Packwood T. Doctors and resource management: incentives and goodwill. *Health Policy* 1993;24:71–82.

The NHS: what business is it in?

Bill New

References to the NHS have, over the years, regularly trumpeted the objective of comprehensive NHS care – take the Royal Commission:[1]

> Our definition of this objective includes health promotion, disease prevention, cure, care and after care. The NHS was, from the first, designed to be a comprehensive service. (p.10)

This has now been taken for granted: the NHS will not pick and choose which health services it provides. We are all entitled to the full range. Instead, government policy has in recent times concentrated on getting the most out of the system – weeding out ineffective services or encouraging cost-effective use of resources. Two new agencies – NICE and CHIMP* – will have the job of ensuring that only properly evaluated and cost-effective services become a part of the NHS. All types of health care will continue to be provided, as long as they 'work' and do not cost more than other interventions that work.

But is 'comprehensiveness' quite so simple? This article will argue that it is not, that we need to incorporate thinking about the *types* of benefit

NHS services provide, as well as the quantity of that benefit, and that different agencies or combinations of agencies can be involved in producing health benefits, just as the NHS could be argued to produce non-health benefits.

The story starts with rationing. It is now reasonably well accepted that the NHS cannot provide everything which might benefit those who make claims on its resources. The process by which this mismatch between supply and demand is resolved – rationing or priority-setting – is the subject of a substantial literature. At the individual level, five methods – deterrence, delay, denial, deflection and dilution – are generally considered to cover the ways in which the Service can manage its limited resources.

But one issue is rarely analysed and poorly conceptualised. It is partly implied by 'deflection' – the idea that the NHS can shift a patient onto another agency. Underlying this possibility is the fact that there is nothing straightforward about the benefit called 'health'. That is, in general terms we know that the NHS can do things which improve our welfare – are 'beneficial' to us in this sense. But we can 'benefit' from a huge variety of

*The National Institute of Clinical Excellence and the Commission for Health Improvement.

goods and services – from anything, in fact, which improves what economists call our 'utility'. The question is: which types of benefits are the province of the NHS, and which are the proper responsibility of other agencies or of private individuals?

To clarify the point, consider two examples of beneficial services, both within the capabilities of NHS professionals to provide, which are clearly not appropriate for universal state subsidy: aromatherapy massage and bed-and-breakfast accommodation. The former is pleasantly relaxing, the latter necessary for people travelling away from home. But no one can seriously claim that they should be provided free at the point of use, on a universal basis. There are many other examples, however, which are less clear cut and these will be outlined in detail below. The general point is that there is a need to decide which services are *relevant* to the NHS and which are relevant to other agencies and the private sector.

But how do we recognise when a service is no longer part of core NHS provision? The key concept here is 'universalism'. If 'comprehensiveness' relates to the bundle of services provided by the NHS, 'universalism' relates to the bundle of people who have access to them. The defining characteristic of the NHS is that ability to pay should not be a relevant factor when deciding on admission for treatment. It is therefore 'universal' because everyone has access, regardless of their income, as long as they are judged to be in sufficient need. Furthermore, services are not charged for – i.e. there is a 100 per cent subsidy.

If this constitutes 'pure' NHS provision, there are also services which are provided by the NHS, but for which charges are levied. This may still incorporate a universal subsidy (now less than 100

per cent) if only a proportion of the cost of a service is charged to all. In other cases a means-test could come into play. These distinctions are elaborated in Table 1. Our concern is with the boundary between services provided at 100 per cent subsidy – access and time costs only – and all others: i.e. the boundary between the third column in the table and those to the right. This constitutes the boundary between a 'pure' form of universalism – what we immediately think of when we consider the NHS – and other standards of provision, whether administered by the NHS or not. Where does this boundary lie? Which services have moved across it over time, in either direction? Is there any coherent rationale for this movement, or for the overall configuration of services on both sides of the boundary? These questions form the basis of this article. [2]

It is important to distinguish these sorts of issue from those involving a judgement of cost-effectiveness. In these cases, a decision about whether to provide on the NHS is made on the basis of whether the *quantity* of benefit is sufficient to justify the cost. No judgement is being made about the type of benefit: it is assumed to be one relevant to the NHS. Occasionally, decisions of this type have to be made simultaneously with those according to relevance – *in vitro* fertilisation, for example, is often claimed to be insufficiently cost-effective and is also claimed to be not really a 'health' benefit.

Finally, there is a more general issue. Some health benefits – or 'outputs' – can only be provided by the NHS jointly working with other agencies, or on occasion by agencies working entirely independently of the NHS. On the other hand, some interventions – or 'inputs' – result in joint benefits, partly made up of a health element and partly relating to non-health improvements in

Table 1 Range of costs to users of various health-related services

Nature of cost to service user / Broad service categories	('Universal' state provision)			('Residual' state provision)	(No state provision)
	'Free'**	Access & time costs	Subsidised price to all (with additional means-tests)	Subsidised price to some (means-tests)	Market price only
Acute and 'community' services	Emergencies	Consultations, elective surgery, outpatients, 'community' services etc.	–	–	Cosmetic and infertility services*
Continuing care services	–	Long-term 'medical' care*	Aids and appliances	Long-term 'non-medical' residential or nursing care	–
Family health services	–	GP consultation	Prescribed drugs, dental care	Eye tests/prescriptions, spectacles, hearing aids, some self-care medication	'Medicines' on selected list (not available for NHS prescription)

* Depending on area – some health authorities have run down these types of care, as discussed further below.
** 'Free' is placed in inverted commas because it is recognised that even emergencies are subject to time costs, and individuals do not always get immediate treatment even after arriving at hospital.

welfare. A number of combinations of both are possible, and we make a tentative start in outlining all the possibilities.

But first we discuss the specific issue of which benefits are the business of the NHS, and which are not. The following provides a range of examples of where this question is proving controversial, including the historical context where appropriate. Some general comments are made in each case, reflecting the kind of arguments used for excluding or including these services in the NHS. These are not necessarily those of the present author – I will present a brief summary of my own view in the conclusion. The preliminary objective, however, is to show how the current debate is confused, or at any rate how the individual issues fail to be connected by a coherent conceptual thread.

Health, or something else?

The following section comprises a description of the situation in a number of service areas where provision on the basis of 100 per cent universal subsidy seems to be slipping away. The discussion may not be exhaustive, but most of the important services where this is an issue are covered.

Dentistry

The provision of general dental services was undertaken on the same principle as all other 'medical' services when the NHS began in 1948: available to all, free at the point of delivery and financed out of general taxation. The mechanism for remunerating dentists, on the other hand, was based on the pre-NHS 'fee per item' system. Thus patients had a choice of dentists, and dentists could accept or reject patients, and decide whether to treat any accepted patient wholly or partly on the NHS. Priority dental care provision for children and nursing mothers remained with local authorities until 1974.

One consequence of this remuneration system was that there was immediate pressure on the budget during the late 1940s, as incentives existed for dentists to undertake as many procedures as possible, particularly denture provision and extractions, in order to maximise their income. These procedures were all reimbursed through the Treasury. As a result, charges were introduced in 1951, initially for half the cost of dentures up to a total of £4.50 and then, the following year, a flat-rate charge of £1 per course of treatment, other than for exempt groups. The free examination was retained.[3] Fees were set centrally, so dentists were not able to compensate for any reduction in demand by increasing their prices (fees) within the NHS. Instead they had to undertake more procedures in order to maintain income – the so-called 'treadmill' system.

Until the mid-1980s treatment charges remained small, and for certain groups – expectant mothers, children and those on income support – there was, and remains, no charge. However, from this period on, charges to the remainder of the population became more significant. From 1984,

the treatment charge was £14.50, while the maximum chargeable for dentures rose to £110. In April 1985, the Government increased the treatment charge to £17.00 plus 40 per cent of all additional fees paid to the dentist up to a maximum of £115. In April 1988, treatment charges were fixed at 75 per cent of dental fees up to a maximum of £150; in April 1991, the latter fee was raised to £200.[1] By 1997, the proportion had risen to 80 per cent and the maximum to £330. Most significantly, dental examinations – which had remained free on a universal basis since the outset – became chargeable from 1 January 1989.

Thus there remains a minimal universal subsidy, but effectively adult dentistry has been removed from the mainstream of NHS provision. This is certainly not because it is an ineffective or cost-ineffective procedure. Yet for some reason, these increases in charges have been met with little public opposition. A procedure which corrects a fault in physiological functioning – often accompanied by extreme pain or discomfort and which prevents one of the most fundamental human activities, namely eating food – is apparently not considered by the politicians to constitute a central part of the Health Service.

Various theories have been suggested for this public and political ambivalence. One is that the deterioration of one's teeth, as with hair loss, is a normal part of a healthy – if ageing – existence.[4] In this sense, trouble with teeth is considered peripheral or external to health proper, even when some degree of pain is involved. Another possible explanation is that many of the most common procedures are relatively inexpensive in comparison to hospital-based procedures, and therefore non-exempt groups can pay out-of-pocket without insurance. Another factor may be that many procedures are perceived, possibly erroneously, as merely cosmetic. Finally, the existence of exempt groups, maximum charges and centrally set fees all soften the impact on the consumer. It remains to be seen if the finance of non-exempt dental care will gradually become entirely privatised.

Optical services

Until 1984, sight-testing and examinations, which were free, and the provision of spectacles and lenses, were carried out by optometrists or other types of qualified optician. After this date the market for the sale of spectacles was opened up, allowing unregistered (unqualified) opticians to sell prescription spectacles to the public. But this did not in itself alter the financial subsidy, which had operated as follows. Some spectacles frames and lenses had always been provided on the NHS, but from 1950 those requiring spectacles – apart from some exempt groups – were charged all but 25p of the cost of plastic frames, and then the following year 50p per lens and the full cost of the frame.[5] The lens charge increased twice until 1971 when the full cost was charged up to a maximum of £3.50. This maximum was increased periodically until 1985. Thereafter regulated charges were abolished and replaced with a voucher scheme for those on low incomes and children, which could be redeemed against the value of spectacles and contact lenses.[6] Finally, free sight tests were abolished except for exempt groups from April 1989 – the sight test fee charged under general ophthalmic services is set centrally, currently at £14.10.[7] This is the amount reimbursed to opticians for exempt groups only; all other patients pay an unregulated private market rate. As part of the Comprehensive Spending Review, it was announced that older people would be included as an exempt group.

A higher proportion of opticians' income than dentists' has derived from private practice over time, since people have always bought non-NHS frames and sunglasses – the Royal Commission estimated that 75 per cent of opticians' gross profit came from non-NHS activity in the late 1970s. In the late 1990s, this proportion is likely to be even higher following the withdrawal of NHS frames.

Thus a high proportion of the real cost of spectacles has, since the earliest days of the NHS, been financed privately, perhaps providing a clue as to why optical charging has been, with the exception of eye tests, even less controversial than that for dental care. The nature of the 'good' in question is also rather different – a pair of spectacles more closely resembles a 'product' like many others essential to a well-functioning life – like food and clothing – but which are not provided on a universal basis. The eye *test* was perceived as the 'medical' element and, unsurprisingly, the introduction of charges was fiercely resisted. Nevertheless, as with dental check-ups, the universalism of the service was fundamentally altered without apparent long-term political cost.

It may be that poor vision, like poor teeth, is considered a peripheral health matter – part of the normal process of ageing and consistent with being in good health. Prices, again, are relatively low and there are exempt groups. On the other hand, poor sight can be as physically disabling as a physical handicap and diseases of the eye may be missed in the early stages without regular checks – one rationale for keeping tests free. Thus it remains something of a mystery why universalism in sight-testing has gone the way of dentistry.

Chiropody

Chiropody involves care of the foot, including the treatment of walking disorders in children, fractures in athletes and joggers, bunions and hammer toes, foot ulcers, toenails and infections. State-qualified chiropodists have three years' full-time training and can use pharmaceutical preparations, local anaesthetics and mechanical and electrical techniques for treating foot problems.

However, chiropody services are mainly provided for certain priority classes of person within the NHS – elderly people, disabled people, expectant mothers, school children and some hospital patients.[8] According to an NHS Executive report,[9] this was not a formal policy – there was no specific requirement to restrict the service to these groups. It appears that chiropody services are implicitly rationed in favour of these groups, principally because they constitute the overwhelming majority of those in need. Others, in practice, pay for it themselves.

The report recommended that:

> basic foot care needs should be met by a wide variety of different helpers – for example, relatives, home carers, district nurses and carers in residential care homes and nursing homes. (p.10)

The authors were here acknowledging that some forms of foot care, such as toenail clipping, are not, or should not be, the province of the NHS, no matter how important they are to the well-being of the individual concerned.

Chiropody displays similarities to ophthalmic and dental services: a community-based treatment whose practitioners derive a significant proportion of their income from private practice, and whose services are not universally provided free at the point of delivery. They are all concerned with what might loosely be termed 'peripheral' complaints. However, this is an inherently vague term, and the gradual erosion of all these primary care services from core NHS provision does not appear to be backed by a coherent policy rationale.

Self-medication

In various circumstances, individuals are able or encouraged to take responsibility for treating themselves. In such cases the universal subsidy will not apply because the NHS is bypassed and treatment becomes a private matter. There are two possible reasons why this may happen.

First, if a drug or other form of treatment is on the 'selected list' then GPs cannot prescribe it. For some drugs this will be on cost-effectiveness grounds – for example, if a 'brand name' drug has an identical generic version which costs less. But in other circumstances the product will be something which is no longer considered to be a health treatment, such as toothpaste. Other examples in the past have included: honey, mustard and coffee; evening primrose oil capsules; 'diabetic' cherry cake; pesticides; moisturising creams; suntan lotions; and infant formulae.

The common feature of these products is that, even though they may promote good health, they are not considered to be relevant to a health *service*. The rationale is by no means clear, however: if toothpaste readily promotes dental health then its support by the NHS might be considered appropriate, as with other elements of public health promotion discussed below (including, in one case, the provision of free toothpaste for children in a classroom setting!). On the other hand, the type of benefit derived from these items, and their relatively low cost, could lead one to argue that such indirect health benefits are the responsibility of the individual in the same way that following a healthy diet is.

Second, 'self-medication' may include medicines *not* on the selected list (thus prescribable on the NHS), but for which we have sufficient everyday knowledge to be able to treat ourselves without the advice of a GP. Examples include painkillers, hay fever treatment, dermatological creams and antiseptic lotions. Some decisions about whether to treat oneself 'privately' with these items are dependent on the arbitrary level of prescription charges. That is, for those not in exempt groups it will often be more expensive to pay the prescription charge than to buy the item privately. On other occasions where this is not the case – for example, with a course of hay fever medication – it may be that the inconvenience, and perhaps embarrassment, of visiting a GP for a minor condition persuades many that they should pay for it themselves rather than take advantage of the universal subsidy.

This example reveals an important point about the need for health care. In general we have little information or knowledge about our condition or what to do about it, and thus need the advice and skills of medical professionals. This is not always the case, however, with some medical care being as straightforward and uncomplicated as many other consumer goods. In such circumstances, there may be no reason why we cannot buy and 'consume' it privately, without the advice of a third party. In practice, however, the NHS rarely withdraws entirely from the subsidy of such care.

Fertility and other sex-related therapies

In the acute sector, health authorities since the 1991 reforms have become more conscious of the possibility of not providing certain services at all. Again, not all these decisions were made on the basis of cost-effectiveness.

In vitro fertilisation provides one of the classic cases of confusion over what constitutes an NHS benefit. The case is well documented, with services available in some health authorities but not in others.[10] The reasons given by health authorities for not purchasing fertility treatment varied. Some took the view that the resources required by this expensive treatment would be better spent elsewhere; others that since it is available in the private sector, people could buy it for themselves. Such views, however, could equally be used for many other NHS treatments. But, in addition, underlying many of these rationalisations was an apparent assumption that money should not be spent on people who are not 'ill'. Predictably, other health authorities took the line that 'the pain of childlessness is every bit as great as that of osteoarthritis of the hip'.[11]

Other forms of sex-related treatment suffer from the same uncertainty. Gender reassignment – i.e. sex-changes – is undertaken only in certain areas by the NHS, as is reversal of vasectomy (a form of fertility treatment). Impotence treatment has also recently hit the news. Although it is reasonably well accepted to be a treatable condition, and one for which a GP will give advice, the introduction of a drug to treat this condition, Viagra, has caused a storm of controversy. Due for licence in the autumn of 1998, many commentators have questioned whether this is appropriate for NHS provision. There is certainly resistance to the drug being used to 'improve' sexual practice, as opposed to enabling some level of sexual functioning. Precisely where the former 'non-NHS-related' use becomes the latter 'allowable' use is hard to define.

One can speculate on the reasons for sex-related services being the subject of such controversy. On the one hand, inability to conceive children or to have sex does not hinder functioning in most daily activities. When it does prevent what is a normal, possibly fundamental, part of our lives, one could argue that sexual dysfunction or infertility represents the *absence* of a privileged and pleasurable activity, not the *existence* of distress, pain or physical handicap. Some might argue, on the other hand, that this is a narrow-minded point of view, and that sex and bearing children are every bit as important, and their absence just as likely to cause psychological distress, as the inability to climb the stairs because of an arthritic hip.

It is worth contrasting these cases with the free availability of contraception on the NHS, both on prescription and often no charge in family planning clinics held in primary care settings. It appears that having children when they are not wanted is an 'illness' to be prevented without question, whereas inability to conceive a longed-for child does not constitute ill health and should be tolerated by all concerned.

'Cosmetic' procedures

The other main controversial area of acute care involves those procedures which seek to alter the physical appearance of an individual. Interventions which have other therapeutic objectives – such as skin grafts for burns victims – do not fall into this category. Neither does reconstructive surgery to correct congenital abnormalities which impair normal physical

Box 1 Examples of cosmetic surgery not purchased by some health authorities

Adult bat ears
Breast augmentation
Cosmetic rhinoplasty
Tattoo removal
Removal of non-genital warts
Buttock lifting
Varicose vein surgery

functioning. Other examples, however, are less clear and comprise what may be classified as cosmetic surgery for aesthetic reasons.

There are a number of well-known examples. Tattoo removal is typical of the kind of procedure that many health authorities have considered not purchasing (see Box 1). Some of these issues are also relevant to dentistry – teeth whitening, for example.

On occasion the line between physical and aesthetic benefit is hard to draw, at least without entering the mind of the potential patient. A woman with large breasts may have severe back problems as a result; it is equally possible that a purely aesthetic concern exists. However, it should be clear that aesthetic benefits are potentially large – witness the size of the private sector market for such treatments and the 'effectiveness' that these procedures have demonstrated on television and film personalities.

But perhaps the most difficult issue is the line between aesthetic and psychological benefit. In many cases clinicians argue that the reason why aesthetic procedures are justified as an NHS procedure is that they are the only means of addressing the psychological trauma and distress which the physical 'abnormality' is causing. Appreciation of the existence of mental health problems has undergone a transformation in recent decades, with the realisation that the mind can become as sick as the body. Thus, a young man with a visible tattoo which is preventing him getting employment, or a woman whose appearance leads her to become the butt of persistent workplace humour, might both become, effectively, mentally ill. Where surgical treatments are available, they may be more effective, and cheaper, than conventional psychiatric treatment.

One response to this is to argue that the possibility of physical reconstruction is promoting a culture of psychological weakness. Although mental illness is indeed 'real', we should not encourage its manifestation by offering to correct physical differences which, in the past, people simply had to put up with. Even when extreme cases indicate that some surgical intervention is indeed warranted, this merely begs the question about where to draw the line between improving well-being and contentedness, and correcting a 'deficit' in mental health. This echoes the wider difficulty of establishing the extent to which health care should really pursue the World Health Organization's goal of complete well-being, or whether this objective could too easily become confused with the never-ending pursuit of absolute happiness.

Patient transport services

Although an emergency ambulance is taken for granted as a universal free service, other patient transport services are not provided on this basis for all journeys to NHS treatment, even if such transport is necessary in order to obtain care. As described in a National Audit Office study,[12]

patient transport journeys are divided into three categories:

- emergency – those made in response to 999 calls;
- urgent – those requested by doctors or others and which require a patient to be transported to hospital within a specified time;
- routine – those planned by the ambulance service and which involve the transport of patients between home and hospital, clinic and day centre.

All three categories are, on occasion, provided on a universal basis, with the first two normally offered in this way. However, there is another test noted in the National Audit Office report which applies to all journeys:

> *Ambulance services are required to provide or arrange the provision of suitable transport, free of charge, for any patient who is considered … to be medically unfit to travel by other means.* (p.6)

The report goes on to describe how 'medical need' can be interpreted more flexibly when patients do not have access to their own or public transport.

Whereas transport is not normally an activity with a positive health benefit, it is on occasion so closely tied up with treatment that it becomes an integral part of the health intervention, particularly in emergencies (in this sense, transport is a form of 'joint input' to that of the NHS, a point further developed below). Alternatively, when the medical condition makes travel impossible without professional help, the same principle applies. Otherwise, and in circumstances where mobility is not affected, transport is viewed in the same way as other 'products' which patients must buy for themselves, although the Hospital Travel Costs Scheme does provide financial help for those on income support.[13]

However, there is an uncertain area where travel to and from hospital is awkward, time-consuming and possibly expensive. If this transport is unavoidable as an element of the treatment of the condition, deciding when a universal ambulance service is still appropriate will be difficult. It is likely, in the flexible interpretation of medical need noted above, that ambulance operators carry out an informal means-test, agreeing to carry free those who have no private transport means and who are otherwise in financial difficulties.

Furthermore, there is the issue of improper use of the 999 facility. This led to the recommendation (not taken up) to institute a 'not life-threatening or serious' category of call which could be referred on to a 'social services professional, [or] trained help from a local voluntary group or organisation'.[14] This is an implicit acknowledgement that many types of condition – perhaps including some of those discussed elsewhere in this article – might be better dealt with by other agencies, as they may not be the business of the NHS.

Long-term and continuing care

In terms of expenditure, long-term care is by far the most significant service area of those reviewed here. Residential and continuing care services have always been split between the NHS, local government and the private/voluntary sector. In terms of provision, rather than finance, the trends are outlined in Table 2. The basic picture is clear: NHS and local authority 'Part III' provision is in long-term decline, whereas private, and to a lesser extent voluntary, sector provision is on the increase.

Finance is not organised along the same lines as ownership, however. Since 1948, local authority residential care ('Part III' residential homes) has been means-tested; other residential services were privately financed, either in the private or voluntary sectors. Nursing home care was for most of the post-war period privately financed (although the state was able to cover the fees of those in financial need under 'board and lodging'

Table 2 Provision of long-term care by *ownership* category of residence, number of places

Year	NHS beds general patients, elderly	Private/voluntary nursing homes or hospitals	Local authority Part III residential homes	Voluntary residential homes	Private residential homes
1976	55,600	–	110,796	32,789	26,412
1980	55,100	–	114,103	34,957	35,764
1982	55,100	–	115,493	36,743	44,346
1984	55,800	22,600	116,430	38,242	63,072
1986	55,300	33,900	115,609	36,000	92,605
1988	53,300	57,000	112,422	34,402	116,688
1990	48,700	89,600	105,380	34,960	145,457
1992	42,100	124,000	86,676	40,608	158,990
1994	37,500	148,500	68,899	45,513	164,208

Source: Adapted from Joseph Rowntree Foundation. *Meeting the Costs of Continuing Care.* York: JRF, 1996.

payments, a power seldom used before the 1980s). NHS care of all kinds has never been means-tested. This underlying financial framework remained unchanged for most of the post-war period, and thus the recent controversies over the NHS 'withdrawing' from long-term care are complex and require setting out in some detail.

The seeds of the problem were sown in 1948 with the state taking on responsibility for 'board and lodging' payments for those in private residences unable to pay their costs. In the early 1980s local DHSS offices, already entitled to pay these costs for those in independent residential and nursing homes, began to exercise this discretion more commonly, gradually increasing the demands on the DHSS budget.[15] In principle, each DHSS office locally set a single 'maximum' payment for these benefits, but these could be exceeded for those in residential and nursing homes if it was not reasonable to expect the claimant to move to cheaper accommodation. The growing pressure on the budget led to the system being formalised: three separate local 'maximum' payments were introduced in 1983 corresponding to the 'highest reasonable charge' in the area, one each for residential, nursing and ordinary board and lodgings. In 1985, as the budget continued to rise, national limits were set corresponding to the type of home and the dependence of the individual staying there. The effect of this increasing formalisation of a previously implicit policy was effectively to advertise the availability of these payments, and to encourage providers to charge the maximum allowable fees.

From the perspective of NHS and local authorities (the latter's residents could not claim under these rules), there now existed a clear and widely known incentive to move individuals into the independent sector as a means of reducing the pressure on their budgets. Although those individuals moved out of NHS provision would now be eligible for means-testing, most satisfied the criteria and so had their fees paid in full (there was a maximum savings eligibility rule in the mid-1980s of £3000 for social security payments). After the introduction of the 1993 community care reforms, local authorities took over responsibility for arranging and paying nursing and residential fees out of their own budgets, again according to national means-testing rules, which now included an upper limit on capital savings of £16,000. Thus, both systems had financial means-testing: the principal difference with the previous system was that now care needs were assessed within a capped budget – under the previous regime, the only 'test' was financial need.

Over time, however, the combination of an elderly cohort who increasingly owned their own homes, together with the boom in house prices during the 1970s and 1980s, meant that more of those who entered residential or nursing home accommodation were no longer eligible for financial support. The result was that many were faced with 'spending down' their capital assets rather than being able to pass them on as inheritance. At the same time, the 'care needs' test had replaced a simple financial needs test, so that fewer elderly individuals were assessed as entitled to a place, in turn increasing the burden on carers at home. And, regardless of these developments, health authorities were continuing to run down long term care provision. From an elderly person's point of view, the perception was that the financing of their care was being shifted from the state – either NHS or social security – onto them or their families. In fact no significant policy change to the financial subsidy had been made. The split between means-tested social/ residential care, and free NHS care, was effectively the same as it was in 1948. It was the financial wealth of elderly people, combined with the actions of administrators and professionals which had changed.

Nevertheless, the result was substantial uncertainty about the role of the NHS. The Service is allowed to provide nursing home care itself, or finance provision in the independent sector. In 1996 it did this for only 7 per cent of nursing home residents (3 per cent of all residents) but, more importantly, the provision that did exist was patchy. In March 1996, the National Audit Office published a report of a survey conducted during 1994 of all 101 health authorities existing at the time, to establish their contractual arrangements for 'continuous health care' for elderly people, such as nursing home care and community nursing.[16] The summary results were as follows:

- 17 health authorities said they do not currently have a policy in this field;
- 11 health authorities have not funded *any* continuous health care beds for 1994–95; more specifically, since 1993 in terms of funding for physically ill elderly:

  - 40 had not funded any nursing home beds
  - 14 had not funded any hospital ward beds
  - 5 had not funded any community nursing in patients' own homes
  - 4 had not funded any community nursing in residential care homes.

One case in particular – the so-called 'Leeds case' – brought these matters to a head. A severely brain-damaged man was discharged into a nursing home when he was no longer considered to be in need of acute care, and his family then presented with the prospect of being charged for his care. The Health Service Commissioner took the view that Leeds Health Authority's decision not to provide continuing care for such a patient amounted to a failure of service. The Government's response was to issue guidance – to be locally implemented – on the precise responsibilities of the NHS. The crucial passage indicates where a patient requires continuing inpatient care arranged and funded by the NHS:[17]

[if] he or she needs ongoing and regular specialist clinical supervision (in the majority of cases this might be weekly or more frequent) on account of:

- *the complexity, nature or intensity of his or her medical, nursing or other clinical needs;*
- *the need for frequent not easily predictable interventions;*
- *or because after acute treatment or inpatient palliative care in hospital or hospice his or her prognosis is such that he or she is likely to die in the very near future and discharge from NHS care would be inappropriate.*

It remains to be seen how successful this 'clarification' of the role of the NHS will be in the future in successfully establishing the boundary between universal health benefits and means-tested social ones and, in particular, what position nursing occupies in this spectrum.

Appliances and fabric supports

Finally, in this section, many appliances, wigs and fabric supports are charged for by the NHS. The Royal Commission noted that:

charges to NHS patients are also made for amenity beds, [and] for certain items such as wigs dispensed in hospital out-patients departments. (p.340)

HSG(97)16 gives details of charging policy for these types of item. 'Elastic hosiery' and 'other appliance and each quantity of a drug (including oxygen cylinders)' are charged at £5.65 – the standard prescription fee. There are, in addition to the normal exemption categories, conditions which exempt patients from the charge for an item specific to certain types of disease. But these are not comprehensive – for example, one exemption category includes those with a 'continuing physical disability which prevents the patient leaving home without the help of another person' but the category goes on to note that 'temporary disabilities do not count even if they last for several months'.

Charges are also made for:

- tights supplied through the hospital service;
- surgical brassieres;
- abdominal or spinal supports;
- various types of wig.

Some of these are clearly cosmetic, and issues of this kind were discussed above. However, an abdominal support is charged at £29.05, and in these categories there are no exempt groups as a result of medical condition (financial means, however, are taken into account). Here, once again, there seems to be a lack of clarity about whether such items should be considered a medical treatment; many would no doubt be surprised to find themselves charged for such items.

Concluding comment

This discussion has so far related to the beneficial services the NHS and its staff are capable of providing, and which have either gradually been withdrawn from the Service, or are provided patchily, or otherwise occupy a 'twilight zone' of uncertainty between the NHS and other agencies' areas of responsibility. This is because the particular benefits which are relevant to the NHS have never been comprehensively defined; instead it has been left to the professionals and managers to decide whether a need which *can* be satisfied *should* be satisfied by the NHS. The business of the NHS has always been implicitly accepted as simply that of promoting health or curing ill health. What this shows is that where a health benefit stops, and where general improvements in well-being, happiness or contentment start, is anything but clear.

The issue should not be confused with those relating to cost-effectiveness, or even effectiveness, which are questions of *quantification*. Whether or not to purchase betaferon, riluzol or tamoxifen, or recombinant factor VIII, or introduce screening programmes for particular age groups are issues relating to whether the *amount* of benefit is sufficient relative to the cost, or indeed whether there is any benefit at all. But, for whatever reason, no one disputes that treating multiple sclerosis, Alzheimer's, breast cancer or haemophilia is of central relevance to the NHS: these kinds of illness and their potential cures or treatments are clearly the *business* of the NHS – even if no effective treatment currently exists. For some other conditions – in particular those listed above – it is less clear.

Public health measures and a benefit-agency taxonomy

So far we have been examining one particular type of issue: the various types of benefit which the NHS is capable of providing, and whether they are all appropriate for 100 per cent universal subsidy. But these questions can be more complex even than outlined in the analysis thus far. For example, assuming a benefit *is* relevant to a health service, is the NHS always the best administrative agency to finance or provide it?

The question concerns those interventions aimed at preventing illness or promoting health. Such interventions are not typically confused with other kinds of well-being. In terms of the previous discussion, whereas then we were concerned with NHS inputs possibly producing non-NHS outputs, here the issue is the place of non-NHS inputs producing a clear NHS-type output. In addition, these are very often joint production activities – that is, promoting health is often tied up with another activity which is beneficial or pleasurable in its own right. Thus, either because they are not directly concerned with curing or treating a medical condition, or because they produce other forms of benefit in addition, these activities are often suited to settings outside the traditional confines of the NHS. Even so, all the examples given in Box 2 (on p.193) are at least partly funded by the NHS.

One can establish a number of categories of this kind of intervention. Those which seek to improve:

- the income levels of individuals, e.g. by providing Citizens' Advice Bureau advice on benefit eligibility;
- material conditions, such as housing;
- knowledge of healthy lifestyles, such as advice on cooking and nutrition;
- social networks and thus reduce social exclusion.

Although at first sight not typical NHS activities, these interventions do command, in principle at least, consensus that addressing the root cause of ill health should become a central part of health policy in the future. This is not just to prevent avoidable distress and disability, and to reduce the burden on future NHS budgets, but also to play a part in wider social policies to improve social conditions and reduce social exclusion.

There may, however, be a question about who pays for these projects. Many involve more than one area of expertise: a health element plus housing, legal, educational knowledge. It is possible that some of these interventions should be funded from within other budgets – local government, for example – if this allowed better integration of expertise. Indeed, with the growing acceptance that health outcomes are the result of multiple factors, it may be that in the future clinical health professionals should be employed in a wider range of agencies.

If we now move beyond thinking about public health specifically, we can see that there are a number of permutations of benefit and agency: benefits can be health-related or non-health-related, and sometimes a single activity can produce both; similarly, a health benefit can be produced by the NHS, by another agency, or by both working together. Table 3 offers some possible examples of types of activity which fit into these various categories. The columns relate to instances of the NHS working alone, or another agency working alone, or two or more working in combination. For each of these inputs there are a number of 'outputs' or benefit types along the rows of the table: a health benefit, a non-health benefit, or an outcome which provides both kinds simultaneously.

In the top left-hand corner, treatment for cancer is clearly a health benefit provided by the NHS (although other agencies may provide after care).

Table 3

Type of benefit or output \ Agency or 'input'	NHS	Non-NHS	Combination or 'joint' input
Health	Treatment for cancer	Traffic control measures	Care for mentally ill people; taxi to hospital
'Non-health'	Cosmetic (aesthetic) surgery	Residential care for elderly people	–
Combination or 'joint' output	Physiotherapy; complementary medicine; health visitors advising on housing needs	Swimming facilities; Citizens' Advice Bureau; healthy living centres	Public health initiatives to promote healthy eating

Treatments such as this are squarely the business of the NHS. Moving down the column we find a box which might also include other examples discussed in this article: perhaps the clearest example of a non-health benefit which could be provided by the NHS is aesthetic, cosmetic surgery. The final box in this column includes interventions which might provide both health and non-health benefits: physiotherapy may be relaxing, or invigorating, *in addition* to any physiological improvements it achieves; furthermore, some complementary medicine might improve health (if clinical trials so demonstrate), but it might also improve people's well-being, perhaps because they gain satisfaction from medicines made from 'natural' ingredients. And the example of health visitors in Box 2 fits here too.

The next column includes non-health agencies or inputs: traffic-calming measures reduce the likelihood of death or serious injury; residential care provides what is necessary for frail elderly people to enjoy a reasonable quality of life; and swimming facilities *both* produce a health outcome (protection against heart disease) and a non-health benefit (the enjoyment of splashing around in water). The Citizens' Advice Bureau (noted in Box 2) assists access to welfare benefits: the rationale is that this would indirectly result in better material conditions for the potential recipients, and thus a healthier environment; however, higher incomes also improve general well-being. Healthy living centres also occupy this point in the table: their aim is to promote an activity associated with good health (these activities – such as exercise classes – will typically involve a non-health benefit as well), but they are entirely funded from outside the NHS – from the lottery (see Section 1.3 of the Review).

Finally, the third column indicates where the NHS and other agencies need to work together: care for mentally ill people requires NHS and other agencies in combination to provide an adequate health benefit; a taxi to hospital, if NHS transport is not available, may still be a necessary part of the package of care required for a successful health outcome. And public health measures to promote healthy eating will involve NHS

Box 2 Examples of NHS-funded or partly funded schemes for improving or promoting public health

Citizens' Advice Bureau (CAB) services were provided in a general practice setting on a part-time basis; members of the primary care team referred people to the CAB service as deemed appropriate.

Health visitors discussed nutritional issues with mothers, including a completed questionnaire; they visited mothers for about an hour a fortnight over a 4–5 month period, provided lists of foods in desired categories and practical advice about shopping and cooking; other lifestyle skills were discussed.

School children received a 20-minute classroom-based teaching on oral hygiene and toothbrushing; take-home materials were provided for parents and children received a free toothbrush.

Health visitors assessed the medical condition of people who were applying to be rehoused; a medical environmental officer of health or GP gave recommendations to the housing department.

Well-woman clinic was set up on a deprived estate: access to services was on a drop-in basis; consultations could last as long as necessary; atmosphere was informal and relaxed; free tea and coffee were readily available; crèche facilities provided.

Norfolk Park Project: a part-health-authority-funded project to increase the amount of community involvement and activities, to decrease isolation, and encourage supportive networks to enable empowerment.

Plymouth and Torbay deprivation initiative: to encourage innovation and involvement from within the area toward raising health awareness and making services more responsive to need.

Sandwell Food Co-operatives Development Unit: part-health-authority-funded project to develop and sustain a network of community-based and run fresh fruit and vegetable co-operatives within the borough.

Stockport Community Health Workers: a health authority-funded project which recognises the importance of social support and networks, and aims to reduce inequalities in health by working in partnership with local residents, and by empowering groups which experience discrimination.

Sources: Arblaster L *et al. A review of the effectiveness of health promotion interventions aimed at reducing inequalities in health.* York: CRD, 1997. Laughlin S, Black D. *Poverty and Health, Tools for Change.* Birmingham: Public Health Alliance, 1995.

professionals and others working together to provide a health 'outcome' in combination with that purely related to the pleasure of food.

It is not at all clear where some kinds of care fit: for example, nursing care could be located anywhere in the table, depending on what it consists of. Some, such as the Royal College of Nursing, believe that nursing is *de facto* a health benefit; it is certainly one which is in practice provided by NHS staff in most cases. On the other hand, it could be argued that routine nursing care

– involving help with feeding, bathing, dressing and movement, for example – is a non-health output, and one which can take place in non-NHS residential homes. Nursing can be a joint input (district nurse working with social services) or result in a joint output (a patient's improved physical cleanliness and comfort may also be essential to their medical improvement). Perhaps this complexity explains, if not justifies, the Clinical Standards Advisory Group's[18] failure to discover:

> [a] rationale for the present situation in which the cost to the patient of nursing care depends on where the care is provided, that is, it is free at the point of contact if it is provided in hospital, in the patient's own home or in a residential care home, but not if it is provided in a nursing home. (p.33)

Table 3 is an attempt to demonstrate how the production of health, and other, benefits requires more careful categorisation than has hitherto been offered. Specifically, thinking must move away from simply considering the quantification of benefits – i.e. the issues of cost-effectiveness. We also need to consider the qualitative nature of welfare-improving interventions, and how these can comprise either health-related benefits or benefits which might be better understood as relating to other areas of well-being; sometimes an intervention might produce both types. Furthermore, we need to understand better the ways in which various agencies combine to produce health (and other) benefits. Sometimes, non-NHS agencies produce what seem to be unambiguously health-related benefits, leading to questions of which budget should finance these activities. A precondition for answering this question, and others like it, is greater conceptual clarity. The preceding categorisation has offered a tentative step along that path.

Conclusion

There are a number of points to make in conclusion. First, debates about the boundary of NHS provision are accompanied by conceptual muddle. Although the health and social care divide is an issue which has exercised policy-makers and analysts for some time, this debate has been confused by claims that comprehensiveness was being eroded in the NHS, and that 'cradle to grave' care was being withdrawn. The truth is more complex, with 'comprehensiveness' ultimately an unhelpful term which encourages the belief that the NHS should provide anything which offers a benefit, whether this is relevant to universal state intervention or not. Furthermore, the apparent changes we have seen in the provision of residential care have more to do with wider changes in the socio-demographic profile of the population and with the discretionary actions of administrators and professionals than with fundamental changes in the scope of the NHS.

Furthermore, the residential care issue has not been linked with related issues across the whole NHS. The question 'what business is the NHS in?' is not just one of cost-effectiveness. The latter is a matter of *quantification*, revolving around questions of *how much* we are getting out of the Service. The quite separate issue considered in this article is concerned with *qualitative* matters: which of the 'good things' the NHS and its staff are able to provide, should it provide? The issue arises from the possibility of skilled professional people, and the facilities at their disposal, being used to ends which are *not* necessarily commensurate with the objectives of universal public funding, or, conversely, failing to pursue ends which *are* commensurate with those objectives. The problem originates from the lack of any precise statutory specification as to what those objectives are. In fact, the NHS Act 1977 merely states that it is the duty of the Secretary of State to 'provide hospital accommodation … medical, dental, nursing and ambulance services … such facilities for the prevention of illness, the care of persons suffering from illness and the after care of persons who have suffered from illness as he considers appropriate'. No further specification of what constitutes 'illness' is made.

Second, this conceptual muddle is significant, not just because it leads to uncertainty about the role of the NHS but also because it leads to geographical inequity. Health authorities are able to decide what 'counts' as NHS care in many cases, and one health authority will decide differently from another. Thus infertility will be available in one town but not in a neighbouring one.

Third, this has implications for NICE. This new agency will need to understand the distinction between issues of quantification and those of a qualitative nature if it is to undertake its role successfully. This may require its remit to be extended. NICE will consider quantification issues, with part of its purpose to remove geographical inequities in the availability of new technologies – for example, by recommending that a new drug is not sufficiently cost-effective to be generally prescribed on the NHS. But variability occurs not just as a result of different judgements about cost-effectiveness, but also on many of the issues described above. If NICE proves a success, there will be a strong case for extending its terms of reference to include questions of which services are relevant to the NHS.

Fourth, given the range of agencies which can be involved in the production of health benefits,

sometimes in combination with other types of benefit, there is a growing issue about how these interventions should be paid for. Healthy living centres exemplify this kind of problem: why should activities which produce an unequivocal health benefit – as with many public health measures – be funded from lottery money?

Finally, a big question remains: how should judgements about the boundary of NHS activity be made? One approach is to shift from thinking about defining 'health' according to colloquial and everyday understandings of its meaning, and instead focus on the characteristics which make services appropriate for non-market provision by a state-run institution. Specifically, these would include characteristics relating to market failure and equity. If we consider what makes health care 'special' in general terms, we can isolate three key characteristics:

- uncertainty – we do not have certain prior knowledge of when ill health will strike;
- information imbalance – between the patient and the health care professional;
- fundamental importance.

Most health care services satisfy all three of these, but some do not. For example, residential care is of fundamental importance but does not suffer from information imbalances (we are good judges about our residential needs and what to do about them – untrue for most health care). On the other hand, cosmetic treatment does suffer from information imbalances (witness the lack of knowledge about silicone implants) but is not of fundamental importance – serious problems are more properly thought of as psychiatric illness, as noted above. Services such as these should be 'outside' NHS responsibility. This approach is

Table 4 Examples of services which should be 'outside' NHS responsibilities, and those which should be 'inside'

'Out'	'In'
• Residential care for the elderly	• Continuing medical care
• Routine nursing home care for the elderly	• Medical or specialist nursing services for those in residential care
• Cosmetic dental treatment; provision of spectacles and hearing aids	• Curative dental treatment (including restorative work such as fillings); preventative dental and sight check-ups
• Cosmetic surgery (enhancement)	• Cosmetic surgery (reconstructive)
• Medicines for non-complex conditions (e.g. headaches, hay fever)	• Fertility treatments

Source: New B, Le Grand J. *Rationing in the NHS*. London: King's Fund, 1996, p.53.

outlined in more detail elsewhere, and a summary of where this line of reasoning leads is provided in Table 4.[19]

The central point is that we need to shift from understanding 'health' in everyday terms, and instead think about what makes a service relevant to a universally subsidised state-run agency, provided free regardless of income. Many things which do us good, and which indirectly are vital to health, are not provided in this way – think of food or clothing. No one suggests they should be universally provided. The boundary of the NHS is not clear, however, and it needs to be made clearer, both to improve geographical equity in what we can expect from the Service, but also to provide a reminder that the NHS should not provide services merely because they are beneficial.

References and notes

1. Merrison A (chair). *Royal Commission on the National Health Service*, Cmnd 7615. London: HMSO, 1979.
2. The case of prescription charges is not considered here as it raises a different set of issues – the distinction should become clear in the course of the article. The principal point is that a prescription charge is levied not with reference to a particular service – all drugs are charged regardless of the type of benefit provided – but in relation to a particular form of provision: i.e. the dispensing of drugs in a community setting.
3. Taylor D. Dental health care in the 1990s: fewer pickings in healthier teeth? *Health Care UK 1991*. London: King's Fund Institute, 1992.
4. Brearley P *et al. The Social Context of Health Care*. Oxford: Blackwell, 1978.
5. Webster C. *The Health Services since the War: Volume I*. London: HMSO, 1988.
6. Taylor D. Improved vision? British Optical Services for the 1990s. *Health Care UK 1990*. London: Policy Journals/King's Fund Institute, 1990.
7. Health Service Guidance, HSG (97) 44. NHS Executive, 1997.
8. *Royal Commission on the NHS*, op.cit.
9. NHS Executive. *Feet First*. Leeds: NHSE, 1994.
10. Redmayne S, Klein R. Rationing in practice: the case of in vitro fertilisation. *BMJ* 1993; 306:1521–4.
11. Klein R, Day P, Redmayne S. *Managing Scarcity*. Buckingham: Open University Press, 1996, p.77.
12. National Audit Office. *NHS: Patient Transport Services*. London: NAO, 1990.
13. NHS Management Executive. *Ambulance and Other Patient Transport Services: Operation, use and performance standards*. London: DoH, 1992.

14. Chapman R. *Review of Ambulance Performance Standards: final report of steering group.* Leeds: NHS Executive, 1996, p.14.

15. Day P, Klein R. Residential care for the elderly: a billion-pound experiment in policy-making. *Public Money* 1987; March:19–24. Audit Commission. *Making a Reality of Community Care.* London: Audit Commission, 1986.

16. National Audit Office. *NHS residential health care for elderly people.* London: NAO, 1996.

17. Health Committee. *Long Term Care: NHS responsibilities for meeting continuing health care needs. First report.* 16 November 1995, London: HMSO, 1995, p.xxxviii.

18. Clinical Standards Advisory Group. *Community Health Care for Elderly People.* London: The Stationery Office, 1998.

19. New B, Le Grand J. *Rationing in the NHS: Principles and pragmatism.* London: King's Fund, 1996.

Attitudes towards the NHS and its alternatives, 1983–96

Jo-Ann Mulligan

Health Care UK first took the temperature of the public's mood towards the National Health Service (NHS) in 1985, using data from the first ever British Social Attitudes (BSA) survey held in 1983. Looking back to 1983, public confidence in, and satisfaction with, the NHS were both at a high level, almost irrespective of people's party identities or other characteristics, such as age and class. For example, only 26 per cent of the population were in any way dissatisfied with the overall running of the NHS. However, this survey was undertaken when conflicts over cash limits, human resources ceilings and government commitments to the 'safety' of the NHS had only just begun.

Arguments about future health policy have tended to be presented in terms of increased private – against public – health care. But the BSA surveys have tended to show that respondents do not on the whole see the debate in these terms: perceptions of the private sector have changed little. Instead, support for the principle of State health care and for increased government expenditure has remained firm. However, to understand trends in attitudes towards the NHS (and its possible alternatives), it is useful to sketch

Box 1 British Social Attitudes Survey

Social and Community Planning Research (SCPR) fielded its first survey in 1983. Since then it has been conducted every year with the exception of 1988 and 1992. The broad aim of the series is to supplement the mass of factual and behavioural data about British society. Each year a random sample of approximately 3,500 respondents is selected to answer interview and self-completion questionnaires. Questions cover a wide range of topics, usually including party-political allegiance, aspects of national economic and social policy. The data presented here are mainly taken from the 1996 BSA survey and two published sources.[1,2]

a brief background to the policy debates that have been taking place over the last two decades.

Background to the policy debates

During the first Thatcher Government (1979–1983) there was little evidence of the radicalism that came to be associated with Conservatism in the latter 1980s. There were those who saw the 1979 election victory as an opportunity to promote private health insurance and so limit the appetite of a publicly funded NHS for ever larger injections of cash. However, the average level of annual increase in volume of resources made available to the NHS in the three years before the 1983 General Election was a relatively generous 3.1 per cent. Nevertheless, the seeds of future policy change and political turbulence were sown. It was clear that there was a growing recognition within government that this rate of increase was inconsistent with the broader policy goal of reducing taxation.

The second Thatcher Government was much more willing to apply the spending brakes to the NHS. Consequently, increases in annual spending (with the exception of 1987/88) were much more modest. At the same time, new styles of management were introduced to replace the old culture of 'administration'. As the 1980s drew to a close, there was increasing public concern surrounding the more urgent issue of closures of beds and restrictions of services. Eventually, in response to intense pressure from medical leaders in particular, Mrs Thatcher announced a major review of the NHS which resulted in the publication of the White Paper, *Working for Patients*, in 1989. These reforms largely ignored the growing dilemma of how to align public (and private) expectations of health care with public (and private) willingness to pay for those services. They concentrated instead on promoting competition between providers, and later purchasers, in order to improve efficiency within the health care system. Since the Government was urged by a desire to give the reforms the best possible start, the NHS subsequently enjoyed substantial increases in funding during the early 1990s. However, once the Conservatives were settled into their fourth successive election victory, spending began to be reined in. This slowing-down provoked dire warnings, such as that from a group chaired by Sir Duncon Nicol, a former chief executive of the NHS, that a tax-

financed and comprehensive health service was no longer viable.[3]

While the 18 years of Conservative Government saw many changes in health policy and practice which are likely to have influenced public attitudes to the NHS and to spending levels in particular, it is certainly the case that public interest in the financing of the NHS during these years was also fuelled by the growing amount of media attention paid to this topic. Using data from the BSA surveys, we test whether these events have affected people's attitudes towards the Service. To what extent have public attitudes towards the NHS changed since 1983? What sort of people are the strongest advocates of the NHS, what sort of people are most likely to criticise it and what drives these beliefs? Finally, we consider the public's uneasy relationship to alternatives with the NHS and determine the extent to which these opinions are related to satisfaction with the NHS in general and its components. We begin, however, by reporting people's attitudes towards spending priorities.

Public spending, social spending and taxation

In 1996, as in every year of the BSA survey series, respondents were presented with a list of ten areas of government spending and asked to name one as their first priority for extra expenditure. Each year a large majority named 'health' as their first priority, followed by 'education', with the other spending areas a long way behind. As can be seen in Table 1, there was a strikingly large rise between 1983 and 1989 in the proportions naming 'health' as their top priority. During the early 1990s, however, concern about spending on other government programmes – particularly education

Table 1 Health as a first priority for extra public spending, 1983–1996

Priority	1983 (%)	1986 (%)	1989 (%)	1990 (%)	1991 (%)	1993 (%)	1994 (%)	1995 (%)	1996 (%)
Health	37	47	61	56	48	45	44	49	54
Education	24	27	19	24	29	27	30	32	28
Housing	7	7	7	7	8	9	6	5	4
Social security benefits	6	5	5	5	5	5	5	4	3
Help for industry	16	8	2	3	4	6	5	4	4
Police and prisons	3	3	2	2	2	4	5	3	3

Table 2 Percentage naming health as their first priority, by gender and age, 1996

	Total	Men (%)			Women (%)		
		aged 18–34	aged 35–54	aged 55+	aged 18–34	aged 35–54	aged 55+
Health	54	47	50	53	54	57	64

Table 3 'Suppose the Government had to choose between the three options on this card, which do you think it should choose?'

Options	1983 (%)	1990 (%)	1996 (%)
... reduce taxes and spend less on health, education and social benefits	9	3	4
... keep taxes and spending at the same levels as now	54	37	34
... increase taxes and spend more	32	54	59

– also rose. More recently, this trend has reversed again with a 5 per cent year on year increase between 1994 and 1996 in the proportion of people putting 'health' as their first priority. However, it has yet to reach the levels of 1989 and 1990 – the time of the spending crises in the late 1980s.

When responses are broken down into groups, they usually reflect the preoccupations of people at different stages of the life-cycle (see Table 2). For example, social security benefits are especially likely to be named by those aged 65 and over. However, differences in respect of health spending tend not to be as marked. That said, men do appear to attach a lower priority to health spending than women. In particular older women attach the highest priority to health (64 per cent in 1996). These results concur with the fact that older people make greater use of the Health Service than younger people, and women make greater use than men.

When we turn to the question of public expenditure and taxation, a more general and dramatic change has taken place. The BSA survey asks respondents a question which highlights the tension between low tax levels and high public expenditure (see Table 3).

Table 4 Taxation versus social spending and party allegiance, 1996

Options	Conservative (%)	Labour (%)	Lib Dem (%)
... reduce taxes and spend less on health, education and social benefits	4	3	1
... keep taxes and spending at the same levels as now	44	26	28
... increase taxes and spend more (on social programmes)	49	68	69

Table 5 Satisfaction with the NHS, 1983–1996

Response	1983 (%)	1986 (%)	1989 (%)	1990 (%)	1991 (%)	1993 (%)	1994 (%)	1995 (%)	1996 (%)
Satisfied	55	40	37	37	40	44	44	37	36
Neither satisfied nor dissatisfied	20	19	18	15	19	18	17	18	14
Dissatisfied	26	40	46	47	41	38	38	45	50

The majority of respondents (59 per cent) in 1996 appeared happy for taxes to increase in order to spend more on public services compared with less than a third in 1983. Of course, it is by no means clear that individuals would be happy to see their *own* pockets hit by tax rises and there is evidence to suggest that people are not always prepared to contemplate higher levels of taxation for themselves. Brook *et al.* recently sought to investigate this effect by revising the questions in the 1995 BSA survey as part of a major ESRC* research programme into economic beliefs and behaviour.[4] They found that individual's *private interests* as well as their perceptions of the *national interest* are likely to influence what they might 'like to see' happen to public spending. For most spending programmes, a broadly similar proportion of respondents thought higher spending was both in their own interest and in the interest of the country as a whole. However, in the case of health, a larger proportion of respondents thought higher spending would be good for the country than thought it would be good for themselves. This means that if the tax implications of a rise in

health spending were made explicit, in terms of respondents' own economic circumstances, their support for extra spending might diminish. As we see later, this argument has further ramifications for those who choose to take out private health insurance.

Notwithstanding the above, as we might expect, the question of whether the Government should increase taxes to spend more on health and social services exposes substantial party divisions, with over two-thirds of Labour and Liberal Democrat supporters favouring the idea compared with just under half of Conservative supporters (see Table 4).

Satisfaction with the NHS and its services

We now turn to respondents' satisfaction with the Health Service (see Table 5). The BSA first asks respondents a general question about satisfaction with the overall running of the NHS. This question tends to capture general anxieties about the

* Economic & Social Research Council

Table 6 Age and gender differences in satisfaction with the NHS, 1996

	Satisfied (%)	Neither satisfied nor dissatisfied (%)	Dissatisfied (%)
Men			
18–34	24	18	57
35–54	31	12	57
55+	47	12	42
Women			
18–34	33	15	53
35–54	34	13	53
55+	47	13	41

Service rather than concerns about specific services. We see that dissatisfaction with the overall running of the NHS, after dropping in the early 1990s, has increased to 50 per cent of all respondents: an all time high.

These findings are confirmed by a recent poll undertaken by Gallup which showed that the proportion of respondents citing health as one of 'two most urgent issues facing the country' had risen from 30 per cent in 1993 to 48 per cent in 1998.[5] An article in *Health Care UK 1996/97* showed that increased demand for health spending seemed to be associated with rising dissatisfaction with the Health Service.[6] But the relationship between dissatisfaction with the Service and demands for more health spending is rather more complicated as we see when we break down responses into sub-groups, since it is women and older people who are most *in favour* of extra spending on health, who are also those who are most *satisfied* with the Health Service (see Table 6).

These findings suggest that more than one process is at work. It seems that those who use the Health Service most (women and older adults) are both more grateful for what it does and most concerned that it should be well funded. In other words, as Nick Bosanquet commented in 1994:

> ... answers are based primarily on personal experience, self-interest or both. On the other hand, it seems the fall in satisfaction with the NHS in the late 1980s may largely have been borne of media publicity about alleged failings of the service rather than personal experience. The result was a political demand for greater health spending.[7]

This analysis is, of course, applicable to the 1990s, a decade in which the NHS has rarely been out of the media gaze. Furthermore, others have shown the possible importance of newspaper readership and the media in general in influencing attitudes towards the NHS.[8,9] Table 7 shows the number of stories about health or the NHS which mentioned one or more of the terms 'finance', 'expenditure', or 'spending' and which appeared in the main broadsheet newspapers in England between 1983 and 1996. The number reaches a peak around 1990 where controversies over funding had reached crisis point, though the total in 1996 still stands at around three times the total in 1983.

Table 7 Number of media stories on health, 1983–1996

Newspaper	1983	1985	1987	1989	1990	1991	1992	1993	1994	1995	1996
Telegraph	82	110	157	408	349	269	240	222	206	246	295
Times	97	170	181	77	318	202	230	216	209	214	268
Guardian	111	153	153	35	331	296	273	287	280	353	362
Independent	0	0	0	300	358	318	270	284	256	299	311
Total (excl. Independent)	290	433	491	520	998	767	743	725	695	813	925
Total (incl. Independent)	290	433	491	820	1356	1085	1013	1009	951	1112	1256

Table 8 Satisfaction with GPs and dentists, 1983–1996

	1983 (%)	1986 (%)	1989 (%)	1991 (%)	1993 (%)	1994 (%)	1995 (%)	1996 (%)
Local doctors/GPs								
Satisfied	80	77	80	83	83	80	79	77
Dissatisfied	13	14	12	9	10	11	11	13
NHS dentists								
Satisfied	73	74	70	68	58	57	55	52
Dissatisfied	10	10	11	12	20	22	23	25

Although dissatisfaction with the NHS in general has increased substantially since 1993, people still tend to express more favourable views about the specific services it provides. For example, family doctors continue to enjoy widespread support; in every year since 1983 at least three-quarters of the sample stated that they were satisfied with the service their family doctors provided. On the other hand, while more people were still satisfied rather than dissatisfied with dentists, their popularity has continued to fall quite sharply from the levels they enjoyed in the mid-1980s (see Table 8). Arguably, given the BSA survey does not ask about the overall state of dental services in the UK, it may be that this question has begun to pick up more widespread concerns about access to dental care in general.

For hospital services, however, the pattern is closer to that for the NHS as a whole. When the survey series began in 1983, an impressive three in four people expressed satisfaction with inpatient care and around three in five with outpatient care. By 1990, the levels had dropped sharply. Then, following extra public spending on the NHS, attitudes steadied, only to fall again in the period from 1993 to 1996 (see Table 9). The finding that the proportion of respondents dissatisfied with inpatient care in 1996 is the highest in the history of the survey seems in line with the perception that the tail end of the last Conservative Government marked a period of 'crisis' for the hospital service, particularly over emergency admissions during the winter period.

Table 9 Satisfaction with inpatient and outpatient services, 1983–1996

	1983 (%)	1986 (%)	1990 (%)	1991 (%)	1993 (%)	1996 (%)
Inpatient care						
Satisfied	74	67	63	64	64	53
Dissatisfied	7	13	15	13	14	22
Outpatient care						
Satisfied	61	55	51	52	57	52
Dissatisfied	21	29	28	27	23	25

Table 10 Limiting the NHS to those with lower incomes, 1983–1996

	1983 (%)	1986 (%)	1989 (%)	1990 (%)	1993 (%)	1995 (%)	1996 (%)
Support	29	27	22	22	21	23	21
Oppose	64	67	74	73	75	75	77

A universal or two-tier NHS?

What effects have these changes had on attitudes towards the comprehensiveness of the Service and the role of the private sector? The BSA survey asks a number of questions in relation to this. First, if the public's perceptions of the NHS have changed for the worse, notwithstanding sub-group differences, people do not seem to have changed their views about the principles that should underlie the service. The BSA survey asks:

It has been suggested that the National Health Service should be available only to those with lower incomes. This would mean that contributions and taxes could be lower and most people would take out medical insurance or pay for health care.

Opposition to this proposal remained high throughout the 1980s. However, as concern about the running of the Health Service grew, so also did opposition to any weakening of the principle of universal health care. As Table 10 shows, hostility

to a selective NHS is at its highest level ever: the proportion who favour a selective NHS has *fallen* since the question was first asked in 1983. Then almost 30 per cent of respondents supported the idea of a selective service, compared with around 20 per cent who do so now. So, while concern about the performance of the NHS may have increased, the notion of restricting the NHS to certain sections of the population is not at all popular. Over three-quarters of the population want to retain a universal 'free at source' health service.

In the course of the survey, respondents are asked which political party they support and which they feel closest to. In this and all other tables reporting political allegiance, these two groups are both described as 'supporters'. On this basis, while opposition to a selective NHS is still universally high for the three largest parties in 1996, one in four Conservative supporters remain in favour of a selective NHS compared with just under one in six Labour supporters (see Table 11).

Table 11 Limiting the NHS to those with lower incomes and political allegiance, 1996

	Conservative (%)	Labour (%)	Lib Dem (%)
Support	26	16	21
Oppose	72	83	78

Table 12 Attitudes to universal health care, 1996

	'Same for everyone' (%)	'Able to pay for better health care' (%)
Those opposed to limiting the NHS to those on lower incomes	67	31
Those who support limiting the NHS to those on lower incomes	35	64
Conservative supporters	51	48
Labour supporters	67	32
Lib Dem supporters	55	43
Age 18–34	64	35
Age 35–54	63	36
Age 55+	53	45
Total	60	39

However, although the majority feel that universal free care should be available, they may nevertheless feel that people should have the right to buy better medical care for themselves. The BSA survey asks respondents whether they think that health care should be the 'same for everyone', or 'should people who can afford it be able to pay for better health care'. Table 12 shows that a large proportion of people (60 per cent) would deny the choice to others to buy themselves out of the system. This shows the extent to which the public are committed to a universal service. Yet, nearly one-third of those who claimed to be *opposed* to a two-tier NHS also believed that people *should* have the choice of paying for private health care. Being opposed to restricted access to the NHS does not in itself lead people to deny others the right to opt out of the system. The pattern of public opinion appears once again more complex than that.

We find that people's views are related to their support for the welfare system in general and inevitably to their political views too. For example, in 1996, 48 per cent of Conservative supporters versus 32 per cent of Labour supported the view that one should be allowed to buy better health care. Interestingly, older people also seem more likely than younger people to agree with this statement which may reflect concerns to do with the decreasing availability of NHS-funded long-term care for the elderly.

Private health care

Those who are highly dissatisfied can, if they are rich enough, vote with their feet and seek private

Table 13 Private health insurance, 1983–1996

	1983 (%)	1986 (%)	1989 (%)	1990 (%)	1991 (%)	1993 (%)	1994 (%)	1995 (%)	1996 (%)
Respondents:									
– covered by a private health insurance scheme	11	14	15	17	15	15	15	15	17
– whose employer pays the majority of the cost	6	7	8	9	8	8	8	8	8
Members whose employer pays the majority of the cost	54	52	55	53	53	54	53	51	48

Table 14 Income and access to private health insurance, 1996

Household income quartile	% with private health insurance	% of privately insured whose employer pays the majority of the cost
Lowest	4	28
Next lowest	13	38
Next highest	23	48
Highest	42	60

treatment. We have found that while the public are increasingly dissatisfied with the way the Health Service is run, they still appear firmly committed to the concept of a universal service. However, although the majority favour a comprehensive system, a sizeable minority are in favour of the right to pay for health care outside the NHS if one can afford it.

One might suppose that the rise in support for the principle of universal service in the 1980s was all the more remarkable because it occurred despite an increase in the proportion of the population who take out private health insurance (largely for elective care) from 11 per cent in 1983 to 17 per cent in 1990 (see Table 13). However, it is likely that the expansion in private health insurance was associated with the rapid growth of the economy during the mid-1980s rather than any significant shift in attitudes towards the NHS. The private sector has indeed become steadily more important in both the supply and the

financing of health care. For example, public and private expenditure on private hospital care increased from 9.9 per cent of total acute and long-term health expenditure in 1986 to 19.9 per cent in 1996.[10] Although the trend for private health insurance according to the BSA appeared to plateau at around 15 per cent during the early 1990s, the slight rise in 1996 to 17 per cent suggests, perhaps, that it may be on the increase once more.

As we might expect, certain population groups are much more likely than others to have private cover. There is no doubt that private health insurance tends to be the preserve of the relatively well-off. More than two in five of those in the highest income quartile have access to private health insurance, compared with just 1 in 25 of those in the bottom quartile. The better-off are also more likely to have their health insurance paid for by their employer (see Table 14). Adults, at the height of their earning capacity, rather than

Table 15 Age and private health insurance, 1996

	% with private health insurance
aged 18–34	17
aged 35–54	22
aged 55+	12

Table 16 Membership of private scheme and satisfaction with the NHS, 1986 and 1996

	Satisfied (%)		Neither/Nor (%)		Dissatisfied (%)	
	1996	*1986*	*1996*	*1986*	*1996*	*1986*
All	**36**	40	**14**	19	**50**	40
Has private insurance	**35**	37	**15**	19	**50**	37
Employer pays	**32**	36	**18**	26	**50**	38
Employer does not pay	**38**	39	**13**	23	**49**	36

Table 17 Private health insurance and satisfaction with NHS hospital services, 1996

	Inpatient care (%)			Outpatient care (%)		
	Satisfied	Neither/Nor	Dissatisfied	Satisfied	Neither/Nor	Dissatisfied
All	53	17	22	52	18	25
Has private insurance	43	22	25	42	21	31
No insurance	55	16	20	54	17	24

elderly people who have greatest demand for health care, are also more likely to have private health cover. As many as one in five of those aged between 35 and 54 take out private health insurance compared with one in six of 18–34 year olds and one in eight of those aged 55 and over (see Table 15).

Membership of a scheme, however, does not automatically go with strong feelings of dissatisfaction. Strikingly, in both 1986 and 1996 those paying for their own care were no more dissatisfied than the sample overall (see Table 16). Furthermore, there seem to be few differences, in terms of dissatisfaction, between those who paid themselves and those for whom the employer

paid. It appears that those who had moved into the private system were not showing a very strong aversion to the system they had left.

However, if there appears to be little association between private health insurance and dissatisfaction with the NHS in general, is the same true of hospital services? Table 17 shows that the privately insured are indeed less satisfied with inpatient and outpatient care than the sample as a whole in 1996. But the results in Table 16 and Table 17 are not particularly contradictory. As we argued earlier, people who say they are dissatisfied with the overall running of the NHS are not necessarily saying that they are dissatisfied with specific NHS services. Private health insurance is a way by which individuals can *selectively* isolate themselves from parts of the NHS system and seems more likely to be pursued by those who are dissatisfied with specific services.

The picture alters slightly when we turn to the question of private health insurance and support for greater spending on the NHS. The proportion of respondents with private health insurance who supported extra spending on the Health Service was again similar to that for the sample as a whole (53 per cent and 54 per cent, respectively). This latter result is not that surprising if, as we saw before, respondents answer this question in terms of the *national interest* (see Box 2 for details). Using data from the revised tax questions in the 1995 BSA survey, Brook *et al.* found that when the tax implications were made clear, those with private health insurance were *less* inclined to see higher public health spending as in their own interests: 54 per cent supported higher spending, compared with 67 per cent of those without private health insurance.[4] These respondents may see themselves as paying twice for health and thus may be more likely to resist increasing health spending. This implies that a growing private sector will eventually undermine support for the NHS. But an increase in private insurance could result in more pressure for lower spending and hence deeper reductions in service quality. This suggests the possibility of a downward spiral in which support for the NHS is eventually eroded. Yet, looking back over the past 20 years the evidence for this is lacking. The private sector has indeed become steadily more important in both financing and supplying health care, but this has not threatened the founding principles of the NHS. The proportion of respondents in 1996 who support the principle of a health service for all has increased, since 1983, to 77 per cent, one of the highest levels ever.

Box 2 What drives support for higher public spending?

Brook *et al.*[4] argue that there are at least two factors which might influence the public's attitudes towards increased spending on public services:

❑ *Self-interest versus national interest*
The BSA survey normally asks respondents what they would 'like to see' happen to each of a range of government spending programmes. This, however, does not spell out clearly the considerations to be taken into account when responding. Both individuals' private interests and their perception of the national interest are likely to influence what they might 'like to see' happen. Since individuals may weigh the importance of the two considerations differently, Brook *et al.* separated out these two influences on attitudes towards public spending in their revised questions for the BSA survey.

❑ *The size and form of the tax changes required*
The BSA survey hints that choosing 'much higher spending' might lead to tax rises – but it is not clear what the size of these tax changes would be, or who would be asked to pay for them. Brook *et al.* revised the questions in the BSA to explicitly link increases or reductions in public spending to specified changes in household tax bills in the form of either a change in the basic rate of income tax (a penny in the pound, up or down) or a flat-rate £35 charge or rebate per adult living in the household.

After controlling for the above, Brook *et al.* found that the use of private alternatives to the NHS *reduced* support for higher state spending in health. They concluded, however, that the private sector appeared to have less impact on perceptions of national interest in expanded public provision than on perceptions of self-interest.

Conclusion

The financing and organisational structure of the NHS has risen in political prominence during the 1980s and 1990s, gaining in the process a high and sustained media interest. The level of dissatisfaction with the NHS fluctuated during the early 1990s but then rose to its highest level ever in 1996. The latest available evidence from Gallup shows that health is the most urgent issue facing the Labour Government. However, our analysis shows that, despite growing dissatisfaction with the NHS and the growth in the supply of private health care, still only a relatively small proportion of the public either wish to, or can afford to, abandon the NHS in favour of private health provision.

So what of the future? While there is clear public support for a comprehensive service, a substantial minority still favour the right to opt out, albeit selectively, to the private sector. Although it is likely that the private sector will continue to grow and a more mixed economy of care will develop, the present Government is still firmly committed to the NHS and, given the outcome of the latest comprehensive spending review, is prepared to raise the share of GDP on public spending in general and on health in particular. At the same time, the evidence suggests that the UK can continue to support increased spending on the NHS through taxation, if it chooses.[11] This is not to say that the current compromise between public expectations and private interests can or will be sustained. Recent policy developments may well lead to a radically different balance of public and private finance and insurance. Our findings indicate, however, that radical moves in the direction of promoting private health insurance or of restricting access to health care to certain social groups would risk offending public opinion at large and Labour supporters in particular.

References

1. Bryson C. *Trends in attitudes in health-care: 1983–1995*. London: Social and Community Planning Research, 1996.
2. Judge K, Mulligan J, New B. The NHS: new prescriptions needed? In: Jowell R *et al.* (eds). *British Social Attitudes: the 14th report*. Aldershot: Ashgate Publishing, 1997.
3. Healthcare 2000. *UK Health and Healthcare Services. Challenges and policy options*. London: Healthcare 2000, 1995.
4. Brook L, Preston I, Hall J. What drives support for higher public spending. In: Taylor-Gooby P (ed). *Choice and Public Policy: The limits to welfare markets*. Basingstoke: Macmillan Press Ltd, 1998.
5. King A. Voters' fears over health of NHS. *Daily Telegraph*, 5 June 1998, p.14.
6. Mulligan J, Judge K. Public opinion and the NHS. In: Harrison A (ed). *Health Care UK 1996/97*. London: King's Fund, 1997.
7. Bosanquet N. Improving health. In: Jowell R, Curtice J, Brook L, Ahrendt D (eds). *British Social Attitudes 11th Report*. Aldershot: Dartmouth Publishing Company, 1994.
8. Preston I, Ridge M. Demand for local public spending: evidence from the British Social Attitudes Survey. *Economic Journal* 1995;105: 644–60.
9. Judge K, Solomon M, Miller D, Philo G. Public opinion, the NHS and the media: changing patterns and perspectives. *BMJ* 1992; 304: 892–5.
10. Mays N, Keen J. Will the fudge on equity sustain the NHS into the next millennium? *BMJ* 1998; 317:66–9.
11. Hills J. *The Future of Welfare: A guide to the debate*. Rev ed. York: Joseph Rowntree Foundation, 1997.

The NHS is not an island

Public–private relations in UK health care

Justin Keen and Nicholas Mays

The majority of accounts of health care in the UK deal with the NHS and the private health care sector as separate entities. Many ignore the private sector altogether and deal with the NHS as a closed universe – and in doing so are in line with the current Government, which appears to be indifferent to private medicine. Even among the small group of analysts interested in public–private relations, most attention over the last few years has focused on particular issues, such as the behaviour of consultants, who may maintain private practices alongside their NHS work, relations with the pharmaceutical industry, and on the use of the Private Finance Initiative (PFI) for capital projects.[1,2] The logic of these positions is that we cannot ignore the private sector, even if we are principally interested in NHS matters.

Indeed, if one looks at policy debates in other developed countries, the UK stands out in paying little attention to the interactions between public and private sectors, and regulation and incentive mechanisms across health care as a whole. While systems in other EU countries can more readily be described as having mixed financing and provision, the UK is typically deemed to have a 'socialised' system. But this perception is outdated, and of itself constrains our thinking: we have a mixed system, albeit one in which the public component is dominant.

Two main arguments following from this observation are advanced here. The first is that a 'mapping' of the nature and extent of public–private relations leads to useful insights for policy analysis and, ultimately, for policy-making. The mapping exercise highlights specific trends, including the withdrawal of the NHS in the 1990s from direct provision of substantial elements of some psychiatric services, and the increase in income from user charges, particularly for dentistry. When one puts such trends together, the extent of private sector activity, and the interdependences between public and private realms, come into focus.

The second argument is that the distinction between public and private sectors is not clear-cut. It is important to understand the true nature of public–private relations if one is to devise sensible policies for regulating health care as a whole. Many relationships involve actors whose status is not well described by the simple opposition of 'public' and 'private', such as the status of GPs as independent contractors rather than salaried employees, and the provision of NHS-funded services by private firms. There are of course clear distinctions to be made – the NHS and Glaxo Wellcome are not easily confused with one another, even by policy analysts – but these are part of a larger web of subtle and complex relationships.

Mapping public–private relations

We start here with the familiar distinctions between public and private financing and provision of services.[3,4] The top left quadrant in Table 1 shows services which are both financed and provided publicly, which still account for some 86 per cent of expenditure on health care in the UK.[5] It is still the norm for us to see our GP, go into an NHS hospital and be visited by a community nurse, with the care provided free at the point of delivery by public sector staff. It is interesting to note, though, that the percentage of total UK health care expenditure financed and provided by the NHS has been declining slowly but surely over the last 20–30 years.

The bottom right quadrant of Table 1 includes services which are privately financed and

provided. Expenditure on private health care in the UK was approximately £2.35bn in 1996,[6] the large majority of which was paid for through private medical insurance, with much of the rest being paid by individuals directly from their own pockets. Williams and Nicholl[7] reported that 12 per cent of private treatment episodes were self-financed in 1992–93. Personal expenditure, notably self-medication with over-the-counter medicines, and payment for complementary therapies such as osteopathy also belong in this quadrant. Again, the situation here is not quite clear-cut, with some complementary therapy paid for by the NHS.

Anecdotal evidence suggests that the proportion may have risen significantly in the last five years, but reliable current figures are not available. Far from being an outlier at the lower end of international comparisons of public–private expenditure, the UK at around 14 per cent private health care expenditure is now located in the middle of the range of OECD countries.[5]

In the UK people who have private health insurance have double cover: they insure for services on top of their payment of tax monies that support the NHS. This contrasts with EU countries with social insurance-based systems,

Table 1 Public and private financing and provision of health care

	Public financing	Private financing
Public provision	NHS services	NHS pay beds, NHS user charges
Private provision	Some 'waiting list surgery', some mental health services	Services provided in the private health sector, and financed through out-of-pocket payment, loans or private medical insurance. Also contributory schemes for dental and other services.

such as The Netherlands and Germany, which require people to choose between schemes rather than pay twice.

NHS expenditure on private health services is found in the bottom left quadrant. GP fundholders were encouraged to refer people to private services by the last Government, but in the event the extent of referrals was modest. However, the NHS as a whole spent £252m on private acute health care in 1995–96, which meant that it formed a 14.8 per cent 'share' of that market.[6] Perhaps the most interesting development in recent years is the withdrawal of the NHS from provision of some services, including certain psychiatric inpatient services, partly funded through extra-contractual referrals to private hospitals, and the provision of services to people who have left the old long-stay hospitals and now live in private or not-for-profit accommodation.

The final, top right, quadrant in Table 1 is private finance/public provision. NHS pay beds are located here: while relatively small in number – some 1400 beds in 77 units – compared with NHS provision, they make up a significant proportion of the total available private beds. Expenditure from private sources was some £200m in 1996. This quadrant also contains user charges for NHS services including dentistry, prescriptions and eye tests, which raised over £900m in 1996.[6]

Two general points can be made about Table 1. The first is that the private sector is already important – it is just that we do not recognise this point often enough. Those who are concerned to maintain global coverage of health care within the NHS, or who call for a greater private role in health care, may not realise that the horse is out of its stable, even if it has not yet bolted.

A slightly different type of calculation highlights the importance of private activity in health care. Combining figures for the independent supply and private funding of health care, including private sector provision, nursing home places (some £2bn in 1996) and the supply of pharmaceuticals and medical equipment (£3bn in 1996), Laing[6] estimated that the total came to 19.9 per cent of total UK health care expenditure. This figure helps to shift the public/private financing debate away from an 'NHS vs private' debate, to one about managing an already present public–private mix.

Some more complex relationships

While versions of Table 1 appear in many places,[3,4] many relationships do not fall easily into one or other quadrant. One example of such an inter-relationship is NHS pay beds. Pay beds appear in Table 1, but when one looks at them closely, placing them is not straightforward.

Pay beds were created as part of the 1946 settlement with the medical profession at the founding of the NHS. In return for agreeing to work as salaried doctors in NHS hospitals, consultants were allowed to practise privately alongside their NHS work, and to treat patients in private beds located within NHS hospitals, and to bill for treatment provided in pay bed units. Part of the rationale for pay beds is that it is possible to use NHS theatres and other facilities, which are charged for, and included in pay bed prices, emphasising the interdependence of public and private services. Pay beds are an anomaly, then, islands of private practice within the NHS, yet having access to NHS facilities. They embody the tensions inherent in current public–private relations: they are attractive to trusts because they provide income and keep consultants on site, and presumably attractive also to consultants because they provide convenient access to private practice, but they permit two-tier access to health services within the NHS.

Pay beds are not the only places where public and private treatment are related. People who have access to private health care, through insurance or direct payment, can move advantageously between the NHS and private treatment – for example, by seeing a consultant rapidly as a private outpatient and there receiving a referral for NHS inpatient treatment.[8] Figures are not available on the extent to which this occurs, but there are anecdotal accounts of people moving seamlessly between NHS and private treatment for specialist services, including cancer services, where some services are available only in the NHS – radiotherapy being an example. In such cases patients who are otherwise 'private', therefore, need access to the NHS for part of their treatment. For these patients, the NHS–private boundary may be all but invisible at times.

A related issue is the freedom of consultants to maintain NHS and private practice in parallel. The majority of consultants do little or no private work, but a minority – perhaps 1500 out of some 16,000[9] – have substantial private practices, of two or more sessions each week. Yates[1] has used analyses of data on treatment rates and waiting lists to suggest that consultants with extensive private practices tend to have longer NHS waiting lists than colleagues with less or no private work. The amount of work undertaken in one sector may therefore directly affect the amount in the other. It may also be the case that private practice affects the motivation of consultants to work as hard in the public sector as they otherwise might. The conduct of decisive studies in this area is hampered by the difficulty of

obtaining relevant and reliable data from *both* the NHS and private sector – and implicitly also by the reservations of research funding bodies to address such a sensitive issue.

Another example again relates to doctors, but this time GPs. Salter[3] notes the presence of private work within the NHS, and argues that GPs should also be viewed as being in the private sector rather than the NHS, on the basis of their independent contractor status (see Table 2). That is, there is a difference between their legal status and the public's perceptions of their role within the NHS.

One possible response to Salter's arguments is that the status of GPs looks different when looked at from different angles: they are neither quite public nor private. If one examines the legal status of GPs, then they are independent contractors, and typically own their practice premises, and so not strictly part of the NHS. Yet they are in the NHS pension scheme, and earn over 95 per cent of their income from the NHS, which suggests otherwise. (Note that the Inland Revenue does

Table 2 Salter's ledger of expenditure on the NHS: 1992

	£m	%
Private sector	13,987	52
GPs	2,257	
Pharmaceutical	2,938	
General dental	1,246	
General ophthalmic	141	
Supplies, equipment, services	7,171	
Agency staff	234	48
Public sector	12,967	
Salaries and wages of NHS staff	12,328	
Other (e.g. admin)	639	
Total	**26,954**	**100**

Source: Salter B. The private sector and the NHS: redefining the welfare state. *Policy and Politics* 1995; 23:17–30

not now allow people to be self-employed if they have a continuing contract with a single organisation.) The status of GPs is therefore highly anomalous. And, if we visit a GP as a patient, then it seems for all the world that they are part of the NHS: indeed, to many people GPs *are* the NHS.

Table 2 does not reflect capital services, and in particular the development since 1992 which has led to many capital projects being financed within the framework of PFI. The resulting relationships blur the public–private boundary and, because they last so long and involve complex formal contracts, make the identification of the costs and benefits to the NHS inherently difficult.

The overall picture, then, is of a selectively permeable boundary between the NHS and the private health care sector. At some points, and for some people – including clinicians, with the inclination and in the right specialty, and those patients with private medical insurance or the ability to pay out of pocket – the boundary is easily crossed. At other points it is not permeable, and people stay within the NHS: patients who do not have the ability to pay depend on the NHS, and services such as radiotherapy are NHS-only. Sometimes the barrier is as much cultural as legal or financial: it is not difficult to imagine the opprobrium that might fall on a GP who developed and marketed services to her patients alongside her NHS practice. Yet this, in effect, is what an NHS trust with a private patient's wing is doing. More important, though, is the observation that the boundary cannot be easily drawn: it is a complex phenomenon and the NHS itself is on both sides.

Institutional inter-dependences

The examples in the last section raise questions about the nature of relationships between the NHS and private financing, including individual payment and provision of health care. However, there are other public–private relationships, including those between the NHS and industry (e.g. the pharmaceutical, medical devices and computer industries).

The role of the pharmaceutical industry in NHS affairs has a number of elements. The NHS is the main UK marketplace for the sale of pharmaceutical products. It is an environment that provides expertise that can be tapped, in the sense that the NHS trains and employs people on whom the pharmaceutical industry can draw for information and advice, and it is a place where trials can be conducted. The Pharmaceutical Price Regulation Scheme allows the State to exert some influence over pharmaceutical prices. Each of these has attracted comment over the years, but the key point here is that the relationship emphasises the inter-dependence of each on the other.

The training of doctors presents another example of complex relationships. The Royal Colleges, which are private organisations, can specify the nature of the training for doctors, which takes place within the NHS. Those doctors can, if they become consultants, then practise in the private sector. Even here, then, in the training of its own workforce the NHS has complex relationships with other bodies.

Public and private regulation

The final part of the mapping concerns the regulators – using the term broadly – of public and private work. The situation in the NHS has long been complicated and resembles a tangle of rules and procedures: there has not been an explicit, designed internal regulatory system for the public provision of care. One of the main themes of *The New NHS* White Paper is to strengthen governance and accountability, and this may in time result in a more clearly delineated regulatory framework. It remains unclear, though, how the new arrangements for inspection of clinical work under the Commission for Health Improvement and the performance management framework will actually work, save to say that they betray a centralising tendency.

In the private sector the regulatory map looks quite different. There are two major private medical insurance firms (BUPA and PPP), which have a 70 per cent share of the market between them,[10] and a number of smaller ones, including relatively recent entrants such as Norwich Union and Legal and General. Medical insurance companies, along with other insurers, are regulated by the Insurance Directorate, formerly part of the Department of Trade and Industry, but now a section of the Financial Services Authority. The Directorate monitors the ability of firms to write all forms of insurance, and can withdraw licences if necessary. There is, in addition, a degree of self-regulation specifically for private medical insurance products: the Association of British Insurers acts as the industry regulator, and has developed a code of practice.

In addition to these ongoing monitoring activities, the Office of Fair Trading[11] (OFT) and the Monopolies and Mergers Commission[9] can choose to conduct investigations, and indeed both have done so in recent years. One of the issues that medical insurance companies are currently dealing with is the transparency of their products (that is, the ease with which potential customers can understand them), in response to criticism from the Director General of Fair Trading, who argued that customers can not readily compare policies and prices because of the way in which promotional literature is presented.

The Government has not given any indication that it has plans to change this regulatory regime but it may change the arrangements for regulation of private acute and longer-stay hospitals. There are three major players in this sector, General Healthcare (which recently merged with BMI), BUPA and Nuffield Hospitals, and a number of smaller organisations, which are inspected under the same rules as those that apply to nursing homes (the 1984 Registered Homes Act). The responsibility for inspection is delegated to health authorities. These inspections are reported to be uneven across the country, since consistent and unambiguous inspection criteria are lacking. This is an example of regulation of private sector activity – but note that the regulator is not independent, since the NHS is itself a provider of health care.

It is a moot point how well these arrangements for insurers and private hospitals are working: there is very little information available. There is a useful test currently taking place, however, in the call by the OFT for a re-design of the selling of insurance products. The Director General has set a deadline of the end of 1998 for concrete evidence of a response from the industry.

The general point which emerges from this brief review is that there are few obvious parallels between the regulatory regimes in the NHS and private sector. They have grown up separately and reflect the structures of each one. The main exception to this picture is the General Medical Council (GMC), the self-regulating body for the medical profession, which has responsibility for the work of doctors wherever they practise. Hitherto, the GMC has tended to concentrate on disciplinary measures in relation to serious allegations against doctors, rather than on monitoring and regulation of the routine activity of doctors. This may change in the future, in a climate that now favours much clearer governance and accountability arrangements for the medical profession.

Blurring the boundaries

The discussion so far has emphasised the interactions between the public and private arena and the resulting lack of clarity about the nature of the costs and benefits which result.

One example is provided by NHS-pharmaceutical company relations. As in any relationship, one can reasonably ask what each side can – and should – expect from it. While some aspects of the relationship are mutually beneficial – cost-effective drugs which are produced cheaply and sold at affordable prices – there are also costs. For example, it is not clear who should be responsible for the evaluation of 'orphan' drugs – those drugs which do not have patents and whose production is not controlled by any one firm – or for promotion (in the best sense of the term) of such drugs to clinicians and patients, which hints that there are opportunities still to be grasped. Should the NHS pay the research and development costs for these drugs, or should the costs at least be shared?

Indeed, one might ask about the balance of costs and benefits – defining these terms broadly – in

any of the relationships described earlier. For example, is it always sensible for the NHS to provide streams of patients free of charge for drug trials? Does it make sense for the public purse to support the training of doctors and other clinicians, some of whom then move into the private sector, which has not contributed to the costs of training? Is the provision of an 'escape valve' for some consultants to run private practices, and perhaps thereby keep salaries down within the NHS, worth any effects it might have on speed and equity of access to NHS services?

It is not necessary to restrict the assessment to costs and benefits: one can also ask what consonance of interests might be at work in these relationships. We have outlined elsewhere[12] the argument that the 1946 settlement, still largely in place after 50 years, could be viewed as a brilliant reading of the politics of UK health care. The settlement enabled each of the key parties to come away having achieved something for themselves while still binding them into the State system.

Many of the current public–private relationships can be viewed in this light. For example, the ability of patients to move between NHS and private practice may suit patients in gaining access to services and also enable clinicians to provide a timely service. These patients have after all paid their taxes, so one cannot easily question their right to use NHS services: but one might ask whether they should not wait for their turn to access outpatient services along with everyone else, if they wish to use the NHS later on. Other countries have adopted clear policies on this issue: in The Netherlands, for example, the regulatory regime is expressly designed to prevent people with private medical insurance gaining preferential access to treatment.

Health care in context

Fudges and working solutions, rather than elegant models, are not unique to health care systems: they are the way of things, particularly in a historically pragmatic nation. But the health system does stand out from other areas of the public sector in the extent to which the fudges have dominated policy-making in the last decade. The NHS has a tangle of inconsistent rules and procedures, a mix of top-down management, regulation and now performance management.

In some parts of the public sector, Next Steps Agencies have been established 'at arm's length' from central government departments and work within an explicit framework of 'contracts' and 'performance measures'. In others, such as the privatised utilities and railways, there are regulators working within a defined statutory framework. This does not necessarily mean that monitoring and accountability are more effective in these areas, but does mean that the regulatory/performance framework is easier to understand and assess. The NHS is also out of step with other countries, many of which have to deal with their health care systems as a whole. In other words, the fudge between public and private provision initiated in 1946 has led to the growth of two separate systems, which are regulated in quite different ways, but also closely intertwined.

In part, the fudge has been exaggerated recently by the New Public Management, that is policy-making driven by a belief in the virtues of private sector practices, of ever-greater drives for cost reduction, and a progressive blurring of the boundaries between public and private funding and provision.[13] The implementation of policies inspired by these ideas, initially associated with the Conservatives, appears likely to continue under Labour. For example, in the NHS it may be that one set of private sector ideas – about firms and markets – is simply being replaced by the current Government with another, to do with incentives and performance *within* firms. The details may change, but the broad thrust of developments stays the same.

This analysis takes us away from the simple 'public vs private' dichotomy towards an assessment of the merits to the NHS, patients and others of particular forms of relationship. There are several reasons why such an assessment is required.

First, as shown above, the private sector is more important than ever, because of its scale and the complexity of the relationships between the NHS and private firms. We cannot go on ignoring the issue. To give just one example: it is odd, to say the least, that most discussion of clinical governance has been about the situation in the NHS, as if the performance of doctors and other clinicians in the private sector is somehow *ultra vires*. A stress on the NHS does not exclude attending to wider issues.

Second, the current Government is in fact supporting the use of private finance by promoting PFI, and so is not presenting a consistent policy on public– private relations. PFI seems bound to have the effect of making an already complex boundary more complex still, and the possible consequences of this increasing complexity need early scrutiny.

Third, there are always prescriptions for change in the air. On the issue of financing alone this year there have been suggestions from a former General Secretary of the Fabian Society, John Willman, that user charges should be employed far more widely than at present[14] and a call from Michael Portillo, former Conservative minister, for greater use of private insurance and provision.[15] The debates such contributions arouse tend to become polarised between pro- or anti-NHS, and pro- or anti-private sector, camps. This means that it is difficult to move beyond statements informed by beliefs, however sincerely held. It is perfectly reasonable to want to preserve the NHS as a matter of general principle – but this position by itself is not sophisticated enough to inform debates about the complex web of relationships in UK health care today, and whether they are efficient or equitable. We need to be clear about what we want to preserve or change, and why.

Towards a new debate

We conclude with some general comments about monitoring and regulation of public–private relations. These relations usefully serve to highlight a number of important policy issues, and it is at the very least worth asking who gains and loses in the current arrangements. The nature of many relationships is far from clear-cut, and there is a frustrating lack of data about the divide, which prohibits estimation of the (costs and) benefits that might accrue from effective regulation. There are, however, opportunities to understand better how the boundary works and where necessary begin to iron out inconsistencies, such as differential access to secondary NHS services for those with private medical insurance.

This leads us to consideration of strategies for changing individual and organisational behaviour. The range of examples cited earlier makes it clear that there is no single object of regulation, and indeed no single group whose interests need to be promoted or protected.

Broadly, though, regulation should aim to protect the interests of both patients and citizens as distinct groups. A clear focus on patient interests leads to examination of the work of clinicians, particularly doctors. A focus on citizen interests would lead us to look at the work of those who commission services – health authorities, and in time perhaps also Primary Care Groups. Regulation should also seek to maximise the 'returns' from the UK health care sector as a whole: this might not mean a single regulatory framework for the whole sector, but in the first instance would surely involve 'beating the bounds' of the NHS to gather more data and better understand the issues. There would be tricky balances to be struck here, to be sure, but even *thinking* about better co-ordination of services would be a useful start.

There would, then, be at least three main foci of regulation:

1. Regulation of *activity* that crosses the public–private boundary so that, for example, there would be equal rights and responsibilities for patients, doctors and others on both sides
2. Regulation of *commissioning*, to promote better commissioning and monitoring of activity in public and private settings
3. Regulation of *institutional relationships*, so that *inter alia* there is a more consistent basis for the treatment of industries. At present, for example, the pharmaceutical industry has the Pharmaceutical Price Regulation Scheme but relationships with the computer and telecommunications industries are not formally regulated.

A development of this nature would involve substantial change within the NHS – it is not just a matter of bringing the private sector in line with the NHS. There would of course be winners and losers in such a regime, but it is worth considering the argument that patients need proper safeguards wherever they go for care or treatment – for example, it is a striking feature of the NHS that some of the most vulnerable NHS patients are now cared for in private settings. Assuming that private health care is here to stay, it seems sensible to be consistent about all of the environments where health care is provided.

The arguments pursued here might appear to go against the grain of current Government thinking on the NHS, because it has set out its stall to enhance the NHS, and has chosen to do so without reference to the private health care sector: there is no mention of it in *The New NHS*. Given the experiences of some previous Labour Governments in their dealings with the medical profession and the failed attempt to remove NHS pay beds, and the current administration's strong pro-NHS platform before the last Election, this is perhaps understandable. But in practice incentives, public–private partnerships and other ideas are still 'in', and if one looks across public services as a whole, they do not seem so very out of place. Our essentially straightforward analysis leads to different policy prescriptions from those currently on offer, when compared with NHS-only analyses. The current Government has concentrated attention on its own public–private vehicle, the PFI, yet it cannot avert its gaze from wider public–private relations if it expects to create successful health policies.

References

1. Yates J. *Private Eye, Heart and Hip*. Edinburgh: Churchill Livingstone, 1995.
2. Pollock A, Gaffney D, Dunnigan M. Public health and private finance initiative (Editorial). *Journal of Public Health Medicine* 1998; 20:1–2.
3. Salter B. The private sector and the NHS: redefining the welfare state. *Policy and Politics* 1995; 23:17–30.
4. Propper C. *Who pays for and who gets health care*. Nuffield Occasional Papers, Health Economics Series No. 5. London: Nuffield Provincial Hospitals Trust, 1998.
5. McGuigan S. *OHE – Compendium of Health Statistics*. 10th edn. London: OHE, 1997.
6. Laing W. *Laing's Directory of Private Health Care*. London: Laing and Buisson, 1997.
7. Williams B, Nicholl J. Patient characteristics and clinical caseload of short stay independent hospitals in England and Wales, 1992–3. *British Medical Journal* 1994; 308:1699–1701.
8. Calnan M, Cant C, Gabe J. *Going Private*. Buckingham: Open University Press, 1993.
9. Monopolies and Mergers Commission. *Private medical services*. London: HMSO, 1994.
10. *ABI General Business Code of Practice*. London: ABI, undated.
11. Office of Fair Trading. *Health Insurance (Second Report)*. London: OFT, 1998.
12. Mays N, Keen J. Will the equity fudge sustain the NHS into the next millennium? *British Medical Journal* 1998; 317:66–69.
13. Hood C. A management for all seasons? *Public Administration* 1991; 69:3–19.
14. Willman J. *A better state of health: a prescription for the NHS*. London: Profile Books, 1998.
15. Portillo M. The Bevan Legacy. *British Medical Journal* 1998; 317:37–40.

Devolution and health: dynamics of change in the post-devolution health services

Robert Hazell and Paul Jervis

The Labour Government which was returned to power in May 1997 was committed both to reforming the NHS and to introducing a greater measure of devolved government, through devolution to Scotland, Wales and – to a lesser extent – London and the English regions. The processes of policy change stemming from these commitments have proceeded in parallel. Because of the existing constitutional and governance arrangements, the NHS reforms, which have been announced in a series of White and Green Papers, have been introduced through the existing system of *administrative devolution* to Scotland and Wales. The proposals are broadly similar in the three countries, although minor differences of substance and slightly greater differences of style are apparent in the documents.

Much of the implementation of these reforms, and subsequent policy developments, will take place under the post-devolution arrangements. What impact will devolution have on the health agenda? Will it aid or hinder the process of reform? Our purpose here is to explore how the interplay between the 'devolution agenda' and the 'health policy agenda' may evolve over the next few years, and to identify the potential pressure points which may be experienced by those

In Autumn 1997 the Nuffield Trust commissioned a report to explore the issues arising for the UK National Health Service, and for the health services in Scotland, Wales and England, that may result from political devolution to Scotland and Wales.[1] The report focuses mainly on the prospects for policy divergence and experimentation in those two countries. It draws on research, carried out between late September 1997 and the end of March 1998, which involved a series of interviews with representatives of Government (central and local), NHS professionals and managers, academics and other members of the 'policy formation/ influencing' communities; official publications; and discussions at four seminars held to debate the interim conclusions. The majority of the interviews were carried out in Scotland and Wales, with additional discussions in London and two of the English regions. The research examined the early stages of a complex and interrelated set of changes which still have a long way to run. Many further developments will have happened before this article appears in print.

operating in the health services of Scotland, Wales and England. By so doing we may provide, at least in outline, a 'road-map' of the way ahead.

Given the communitarian nature of the societies in Wales and, particularly, Scotland, issues such as health and education are seen as being a major priority for the new Parliament and Assembly, and a 'test-bed' for the exercise of their new powers. There is, of course, a crucial difference between a focus on *health care* and a focus on *health*. The determination to tackle health inequalities and to address the wider determinants of health is common to Scotland, Wales and England and is demonstrated by the green papers on public health which each country has published.

As we shall show below, health inequalities exist within Scotland and Wales, as well as between the two countries and England. It has been argued that, in general terms, health status in Wales is worse than in most of England, and Scotland's health is significantly worse. For example, the Welsh White Paper comments that:

> *Health in Wales is poorer than in the UK as a whole and than in many other Western European countries. Life expectancy is about one year less than in England; the death rate from heart disease in Wales is about 18 per cent higher, and the rates of cancer are about 10 per cent higher.*

In making comparisons of health status between the three countries, the presence of the Home Counties causes a major distorting effect. If they are removed from the comparisons, in general terms the health profiles of the different parts of the UK are broadly similar. But areas of deprivation and poor health status occur throughout the UK, and there can be marked variations between localities as small as electoral wards. One of the features in Scotland is the extreme variation in health status that can exist within a very small geographical area, with wards with some of the best health indicators found adjacent to wards with the worst. Wales contains areas – the former mining valleys – where health status is

particularly poor. And in England too there are areas where health status is far below the average, largely although not entirely in inner city areas.

The devolution proposals

Scotland and Wales

A common saying, usually attributed to the Secretary of State for Wales, is that 'devolution is a process not an event.' Yet the evidence we found suggested that, initially at least, much more effort has been devoted to the event (the devolution legislation and the establishment of the new Parliament and Assembly) than the process (how are we going to work the system post-devolution?).

Scotland and Wales already enjoy a considerable degree of *administrative devolution*. Their health services are run by the Scottish Office and Welsh Office, not by the Department of Health in London. This has enabled Wales, for example, to develop independent initiatives on learning disabilities, breast cancer screening and continuing medical education; and neither Scotland nor Wales has implemented every policy diktat coming from London. But while they have been linked to the Government in London, Scottish and Welsh policies have needed to remain broadly the same. This will change with *political devolution*. The Scottish Parliament and Welsh Assembly, both directly elected, will come under local democratic control and may owe little or no loyalty to London. The Scottish Parliament will have significant law-making powers which will include health generally, the education and training of health professionals and the terms and conditions of service of NHS staff and general practitioners.

Financially, the Scottish Parliament will have little room to increase *total* public expenditure.

It will be dependent on block funding from London, and will inherit the same total budget as the Scottish Office (£14bn), with annual changes set by a population-based formula related to changes in spending in England (the Barnett formula). The Scottish Parliament will have power to vary the basic rate of income tax by up to 3 per cent. However, even if it used these powers it would only raise around £450m of additional revenue.

The Welsh Assembly will not have law making powers, nor will it have power to raise additional revenue. It will allocate the £7bn budget currently assigned to the Welsh Office, will set policies and standards for the public services in Wales, and make orders and regulation through secondary legislation, within the overall legislative framework laid down by Westminster. The Assembly will take over the Secretary of State's responsibilities for the NHS and for the health of people in Wales. It will be able to decide the scale of financial resources for health from within its overall budget; monitor the health of the Welsh population, promote health and tackle ill health; and promote good practice in health services and hold NHS bodies in Wales to account for their performance.

In the legislation enabling devolution, the UK Government proposes to reserve to Westminster certain matters. These consist of regulation of certain professions, primarily where these are currently dealt with under UK statutes, including medical, dental, nursing and other health professions, and some other matters presently subject to UK or GB regulation or operation. The latter include the UK research councils, nuclear safety, the control and safety of medicines, and reciprocal health agreements. Further, a number of matters in the health arena, including abortion, human fertilisation and embryology, genetics, xeno-transplantation and vivisection will be reserved in view of the need for a common approach.

The English Regions and London

Plans for the possible development of regional government in England are much less far advanced, and are currently limited to a Bill to establish regional development agencies (RDAs) which will be responsible for promoting inward investment, helping small businesses and coordinating regional economic development. The RDAs will 'promote sustainable economic development and social and physical regeneration and co-ordinate the work of regional and local partners in areas such as training, investment, regeneration and business support'. Health is not one of the RDAs' core functions but they will have 'a major consultative and advisory role' in a number of 'non core' areas which include public health.

These regional economic development bodies already see the NHS bodies in their regions as essential partners in their activities, both for the contributions that they can bring to improving the health of regional workforces, but also as major regional employers in their own right. We expect that the NHS will come under increasing pressure from the RDAs to engage fully in the regional development agenda. The objectives of the public health Green Paper are likely to be furthered if the NHS is an active participant in the development of regional regeneration and economic development strategies.

The Government's consultation paper on a new Greater London Authority and directly elected mayor for London does not propose that its functions include health, but envisages that the Assembly would have power to scrutinise other public services, including health services for Londoners.

The role of the 'centre' in the devolved system

Given the devolution proposals, what role will be left for the UK 'centre' in terms of health policy? For the Department of Health in formal terms relatively little will change. It will continue to be responsible for a mix of England-only functions and others where it has a wider role within the UK. In terms of what the public understand by the NHS, the Department of Health is already the Department of Health for England only. But it also represents UK health policy interests in the European Union and through relevant international organisations, and supports UK-based health care and pharmaceutical industries. These matters will not change post-devolution. What is administratively devolved now will remain devolved, but will be subject to tighter democratic scrutiny in Edinburgh and Cardiff. What is administratively retained at the centre in London will remain at the centre and will be subject to scrutiny through the traditional mechanism of ministerial accountability to the Westminster Parliament.

In the Westminster Parliament, little will change save that Scottish Ministers will largely disappear, as will the Scottish Grand, Select and Standing Committees. The Select Committee on Health will focus mainly on health issues in England; although it may continue to inquire into the Department of Health's all-UK functions. Scrutiny of legislative and other proposals from the EC will continue to be carried out by Parliament and, given the tight timescales often involved and the lead role for UK ministers, it will be difficult to insert a strong role for the devolved

assemblies except in terms of retrospective scrutiny.

Although expectations are running high in Scotland and Wales that devolution will give them a stronger voice in Europe, the member state will continue to be the UK, and Scotland and Wales will be represented only through the UK delegation. This will not prevent Scotland and Wales forming closer links with the Commission, building on the influence they already have through their listening posts in Brussels (Scotland Europa and the Wales European Centre) and through their membership of the Committee of the Regions. But it will be an increase in influence in lobbying power rather than formal political power; and in an area where the EU's impact so far has been limited.

What else will keep the NHS 'national'?

A major factor that will continue to ensure the 'National' nature of the NHS is that it will continue to be nationally funded through an all-UK tax, income tax, raised by central government and distributed by the Treasury. This distribution is calculated using the Barnett formula, which means that annual adjustments in spending will technically be determined by changes in *English* spending– although with England making up 85 per cent of the whole, the UK Government will effectively be deciding what proportion of the national finances to spend on health on an all-UK basis. But the devolved Governments will be free to vire within their total budgets and the Scots will be free to raise up to 3 per cent additional revenue by raising the rate of income tax.

Another fundamental unlikely to be challenged by devolution is the concept of equity, which leads citizens throughout the UK to expect the same basic levels of public service. This is reinforced by both the national media, which in the UK are particularly strong at national level, and performance measurement and national standards.

Political and professional considerations also serve to moderate diversity. Politically, solidarity between Governments of the same party, so long as Labour rules in London, Edinburgh and Cardiff, will be a force for a common approach. The medical and health care professions, which are unified in England and Wales, and even when technically separate in Scotland observe the same training, professional techniques and standards, also serve as a unifying force.

The Health Service reforms

The UK Labour Government was elected in May 1997 on a manifesto which committed it to 'a fundamental aim: to restore the National Health Service as a public service working cooperatively for patients, not a commercial business driven by competition'.[2] Central to this aim was the removal of the internal market introduced by the previous Government. As noted on page 4, there have been separate White Papers for each part of the UK. These have been developed under the existing system of administrative devolution and the Scottish and Welsh Papers both prepare the ground for when the Parliament and Assembly take responsibility for their nation's health, and their health services.

There are considerable similarities between all three Papers. These include the values and principles underlying the reforms, many of the objectives and a number of the organisational reforms proposed. All three Papers stress the need for improved partnership:

- between different parts of the Health Services, replacing the competition encouraged by the internal market;
- between the Health Services and other organisations, particularly local government;
- between patients and the NHS.

Each Paper proposes to end the internal market by replacing the annual contracting process between health authorities or boards and NHS trusts, and to end GP fundholding. There are also proposals to amend the governance processes to increase public accountability and transparency and to increase clinical efficiency and effectiveness through the use of evidence-based medicine. Improving the information base of the NHS, both for those working within it and for patients, forms part of each Paper.

As well as the similarities, there are some differences in terminology and differences in presentation and emphasis. While, for the most part, these are relatively minor, some of the organisational arrangements do differ and might be the source of divergence in future. Thus, while Wales will be 'party to the establishment and management' of the National Institute for Clinical Excellence and Commission for Health Improvement proposed in the English White Paper, Scotland will establish the Scottish Health Technology Assessment Centre to advise on the cost-effectiveness of interventions. Scottish trusts are expected to publish a set of clinical performance indicators and these may not be the same as those used in England and Wales. Such differences may have implications for the professions and for the development of policies towards clinical governance.

How do these proposals relate to the aspirations and concerns of those working in the Health Service, in Scotland, Wales and England?

Devolution in health – opportunities and threats

In Scotland and Wales, 'making devolution in health work' is envisaged as much as a political process as a professional/medical one. It means taking ownership for the national health systems of Scotland and Wales, and producing something that fits the culture, traditions and aspirations of those countries. Although devolution brings few new freedoms in health policy terms, it is expected to make a difference. As a Scottish respondent commented, *'Devolution doesn't mean anything unless you do things differently – otherwise why have it?'*

People in London, or with 'London-facing' roles, share the aims of raising health status and addressing inequalities. However, we found a strong undercurrent in their views that such objectives are best achieved by maintaining a unified National Health Service, and thus of resisting any divergence of the health systems in Scotland and Wales. The tensions between those who see the need to resist divergence and those who see devolution as the chance to be different are likely to be an important feature of the 'bedding-down' of the post-devolution UK health system.

When health is debated, and decisions are made, on the floor of the Scottish Parliament or Welsh Assembly, the dynamics of policy formation and implementation will change. The way the Scottish Parliament and Welsh Assembly provide leadership for health policy will be crucial. The need is for them to adopt a strategic

orientation, but there is scope for an audit and scrutiny 'explosion' and for 'turf wars' with local government and other parts of the public sector. The background, experience and character of the leading members, and the supporting/influencing roles of the civil servants, will be critical in setting the tone and style of these bodies and realising the potential for strategic leadership. But given the right strategic leadership, the 'return' of the Health Services to what is seen as local *democratic* control is expected by those interviewed in Scotland and Wales to lead to an improvement in working relationships between the Health Services and local government. Also, the smaller-scale and easier communications in Scotland and Wales are expected to make cross-departmental and cross-functional working easier.

Funding is likely to be an area of difficulty. The Barnett formula delivers more favourable per capita funding to both Health Services compared to England. Whether this additional funding (approximately 20 per cent for Scotland and 10 per cent for Wales) is justified by the poorer health status of their populations is a matter for considerable debate. Understandably, both Scots and Welsh insist on the need to preserve the Barnett formula, and currently the UK Government refutes any suggestion that the basis of resource allocation will change. But the use of the formula is already being challenged within some of the English regions, and this pressure is unlikely to go away. Both Scotland and Wales may find public expectations raised by devolution coinciding with periods of increased financial pressure.

The setting of professional standards and the regulation of the medical professions will remain all-UK issues. A possible topic of dispute might be planning the supply of trained medical personnel.

Currently, Scotland is a net exporter of qualified medical staff. But if there are significant pressures on public expenditure, some in the Scottish Parliament may wish to challenge this use of resources. And in parts of both England and Wales there are aspirations to create new medical schools. It is not clear, post-devolution, how decisions affecting the supply of medical graduates might be resolved. A UK-level planning approach would be seen as inappropriate, but a degree of co-operation may be in the interests of all countries.

The medical professions mainly operate on an all-UK basis, with important networks within the professions, and between the professions and Government. Currently, those in Scotland and Wales have full access to these networks, but there are fears that they could become excluded from networks in which previously they would have participated. If devolution led to a fragmentation of professional networks, this would lessen their value for the English as well as disenfranchise Scotland and Wales.

Formal representation with Europe will be a matter for the UK, and will be managed by the International Unit of the Department of Health. But Scotland and Wales will wish to develop further their links with international bodies such as the EU and the WHO, and to forge bilateral links with individual countries. This area is a potential source of conflict post-devolution.

Managing policy in the devolved system

Given the pressures and constraints described above, if any policy divergence comes, it will be initially through changes at the margins, either through experimentation in Scotland and Wales or through England introducing changes that Scotland and Wales do not want to adopt. For example, Scotland and England might take different approaches to the GP role in controlling/influencing the allocation of resources for secondary care. There are already indications that approaches to 'managed care' may integrate primary and secondary care in a different way in Scotland from those in England and Wales. Other more radical steps which the Scots might take are the abolition of trusts, or the adoption of a different approach to the control of prescribing within the Health Service.

If devolution in health is to 'work', it must be able to address opportunities and threats such as those described. It must be supported not merely by systems and structures, but by a sound understanding of the roles and the relationships between the decision-making bodies at the different levels. Three models can be used to explore these roles and relationships, which can be termed 'corporate', 'collaborative' and 'federal'.

The *corporate* model is one based on ownership and control, with the 'centre' determining the objectives for each of the operating units. In the *collaborative* model organisations are independent bodies with full control over their strategies and resources. They may decide voluntarily to collaborate, by pooling scarce resources, co-ordinating activities, or making mutual arrangements which yield scale economies. Collaboration is voluntary and reversible. A *federal* model shares some of the characteristics of the first two. In this, members yield power over some issues to the 'Federation', which develops at its core the competences to deal with them. What is a 'federal' issue and what is a 'state' issue is usually clear-cut, and this model differs from the corporate one in that the 'Federation' cannot collect more power to itself unilaterally.

Legally and constitutionally the devolution relationship will be a corporate one. The Government's devolution White Papers emphasise the continuing sovereignty of the Westminster Parliament, which will retain the power to override the devolved assemblies or to amend the terms of the devolution settlement. This is in contrast to the attitude of those we interviewed in Scotland and Wales, few of whom would accept a corporate model as an appropriate analogy for the relationship between the Scottish and Welsh Health Services and the UK NHS. They thought more in terms of collaborative or federal models.

A further source of tension lies in the Department of Health's mixture of all-UK and England-only roles. The danger is that the needs of England (the 85 per cent of the population) will drive structures and systems that are less than ideal for Wales and Scotland; *and* the separate interests of England may at times be submerged by the UK-level agenda.

The effect of devolution will be to return the Scottish and Welsh Health Services more to local democratic control. The 'policy village' effect in Scotland and Wales will strengthen this but will the new forms of governance advance or retard the performance of the Scottish and Welsh Health Services? Tighter democratic scrutiny could lead to increased emphasis on accountability which, while important, if it becomes too dominant a theme could detract from the strategic leadership required to improve health status and reduce inequalities. The style of leadership, and the expertise provided by the members, of the

Welsh Assembly and Scottish Parliament will be crucial in striking the correct balance between focuses on accountability and performance.

Organisational 'separations' of various sorts are often followed by a period in which former colleagues behave in a surprisingly hostile manner. It seems part of the process of gaining and exercising independence that relationships become more adversarial as people test out their new freedoms and push against the boundaries of their new roles. The same may happen in the Health Services after devolution. Managing through any such period will require skill and sensitivity in Edinburgh, Cardiff and especially Whitehall.

Two alternative scenarios: little change, or growing divergence?

Will the health systems of Scotland, Wales and England diverge after devolution, or will their close similarity be maintained? At present it is too early to tell. There is a set of factors which tends to suggest a little change scenario, and another which might suggest that there will be rather greater divergence among the three Health Services. Both sets of factors contain political, professional, technical and attitudinal elements.

Factors suggesting that there is likely to be relatively little change include the following.

- *Political constraints*, which reflect the fact that devolution offers the Health Services in Scotland and Wales few 'new' freedoms, and existing freedoms have not been used. In part this is because the Scottish and Welsh Labour Parties may feel constrained not to undermine the policies of the Labour Government in London.

- *Professional constraints* stemming from the dominant influence of the (mostly UK/GB) professional bodies which desire to maintain conformity in standards covering clinical practice, education, terms and conditions of service, etc.
- *Technical constraints*, including the high levels of fixed costs, the monopoly power of acute service providers, limited supply and skill-mix of qualified staff, etc. plus continuing or increasing funding constraints.
- *Attitude constraints*, which include the unwillingness or inability of local politicians to break away from managing services to adopt a more strategic role, the predominance of short-term and crisis management, lack of imagination or 'croneyism' in board appointments by local politicians and expectations of equity, reinforced in Wales by the dominance of the national (UK) media.

Factors suggesting that there may be a more rapid divergence include the following.

- *Political factors* which include the belief that local politicians will develop a strategic view, through closer access to health professions, and have more legitimacy to introduce change. The more vigorous democratic scrutiny should lead to improved performance. The pent-up resentment against 'English' health care reforms will lead to pressures on the Scottish Parliament and Welsh Assembly to show instant results.
- *Professional factors* such as the eagerness of many health and other professionals to provide leadership in developing new, appropriate, approaches to health and health care.
- *Technical factors*, such as the existence of 'policy villages', tight groupings of political and professional networks which can make for quicker and easier agreement over policy and strategy. Therefore health gain policies, which require co-ordinated action across departments, should be easier to operationalise in Scotland and Wales.
- *Attitude factors*, such as the greater respect for, and acceptance of, professional expertise in Scotland (and possibly Wales), which may mean that politicians and citizens are more inclined to accept technocratic solutions.

The future evolution of the three Health Services will be determined by the interplay of these factors. It is too early to say which will win out in the longer term; but probably the most important single factor which will influence the outcome is the quality of the new political leadership in Scotland and Wales.

Problem areas post-devolution

We inferred from our discussions that there was the potential for a significant amount of friction as the devolution settlement beds down. The extent of this will be affected as much by the style and culture adopted within the different health communities as by the substantive policy content of service operations. Devolution will require a different mind-set to apply in many areas of the Health Services, that is those in the centre in Whitehall and in the UK professional bodies, as well as in Scotland and Wales.

Contentious issues are likely to include the following.

- Possible differences of opinion over *human resource issues*, such as the consultants' contract and the GPs' contract, and over aspects of regulation, such as prescribing policy and relationships with the pharmaceutical industry. But this is what devolution is about. Countries must have the freedom to change. Maintaining 'inclusive' professional policy and advisory networks will maximise the potential for collaboration and for avoiding policy decisions that cause problems for other countries, but the problem is inherent to devolution!

- Agreeing the mechanisms for *determining the funding of health services,* if the settlement delivered by the Barnett formula is inadequate to address the aspirations of the Scottish and Welsh Health Services or if the formula breaks down. A possible response would be to agree to a fresh, needs-based assessment of the basis for public expenditure, conducted by an independent commission the members of which are appointed jointly by the respective Governments.

- The strong desire in both Scotland and Wales to *form direct health policy links with international bodies,* such as the European Union and the World Health Organization. This may pose a significant challenge for the operation of UK-level 'international health policy'. Scotland and Wales will be unable to change the formal mechanisms or challenge UK-level representation. The answer is to ensure that effective consultative machinery exists so UK delegations are briefed on national view, and to include Scottish and Welsh representatives in delegations. Effective information dissemination and communication will be crucial in creating a culture of inclusion in UK policy matters.

- The manner in which those *health policy matters reserved for decision and action at the UK level* are conducted. This needs to take account of the Scottish and Welsh Health Services' desire for greater freedom and influence in such matters. Here too the solution lies mainly in negotiating and consultative machinery. There may need to be a UK Health Consultative Committee, in which the Health Ministers from England, Scotland, Wales and Northern Ireland come together to discuss such matters; accepting that the English Minister is also the Minister for the UK, who will have to defend the policy to Scottish and Welsh MPs in the Westminster Parliament.

- *The need to collaborate in areas such as education and training,* where the number of medical schools and the output of graduates is determined by the three countries but where a degree of co-ordination over supply and demand may be appropriate. No form of UK-level ' planning' is likely to be acceptable in such areas. The three countries must negotiate appropriate solutions among themselves, and individual countries must retain the right to 'go it alone' if they wish.

- *The* modus operandi *of many of the UK-wide professional bodies,* the ways they relate to their memberships in England, Scotland and Wales, and the way they relate to the three countries' Health Services. This is a matter for the professional bodies themselves. They will need to review their governance, communication and consultation mechanisms in the light of the changed atmosphere and expectations that will result post-devolution. Many bodies are already addressing this agenda.

The need for health policy communities

To support health policy development, Scotland and Wales would benefit from strong health policy communities to provide independent analysis, generate fresh ideas and support more effective policies and practices. At present the UK health policy community is largely focused on Whitehall, and mostly based in England. Initiatives are already being taken to stimulate the development of greater policy capacity in Scotland and Wales, but there is probably scope for more to be done. Any strengthened policy capacity should have strong links to the Health Services and user communities, feature extensive 'practitioner' involvement (practitioners being policy-makers, politicians/members of governance bodies and managers as well as medical practitioners) and focus on policy analysis, policy evaluation and policy implementation rather than basic research.

What will be the outcomes? Will health status improve?

The desire in Scotland and Wales is to make the improvement of the nations' health a central focus of the work of the Parliament and Assembly respectively, to tackle health inequalities and to work for health gain. Will the new strategies adopted in Scotland and Wales differ significantly from those to be adopted in England, and will they prove more effective in improving health gain and addressing health inequalities? As yet we cannot answer this question. But it is important to establish clear performance measures that will indicate what is happening. The consultations on the English, Welsh and Scottish public health Green Papers are a start to this process.

We suggest that possible measures might include the following.

- *Reduction of inequalities in public health*, assessed by improvement over time and against the rest of the UK, in standardised mortality rates, limiting long-term illness, etc.
- *maximisation of the population's health gain*, measured by absolute health gain and health gain relative to the rest of the UK.
- *equality of access to health care facilities*, judged by the take-up of services by different socio-economic groups, waiting lists, etc.
- *more rigorous monitoring of outcomes* through the development and use of outcome measures for standard interventions, with results made publicly available.
- *'democratisation'*, measured, for example, by opinion poll evidence of public satisfaction with the health services and attitudes revealed by media coverage; indications of public acceptability of governance arrangements; increased effectiveness of local government/ Health Services joint working.
- *innovation and experimentation*, judged by the rate of innovation in the Scottish and Welsh Health Services and the uptake of new technology, techniques and organisational approaches, and the implementation of evidence-based medicine, protocols, etc.

Establishing a more definitive set of indicators and monitoring performance against them might be an early task for the newly invigorated health policy communities in Scotland and Wales. An impartial assessment of performance is crucial; and it may also encourage politicians to think and plan long term – because few public health interventions deliver results in the short term.

Conclusion

We have outlined above the constitutional frameworks within which the post-devolution Health Services will operate. We have identified some of the pressure points which may cause tension in the new devolved system. These include decision-making over medical education, financing of the NHS, terms and conditions of staff, relationships with the European Union and other international issues. Whether these potential problems will arise, and if so how they will be resolved, will depend as much on the way the different health departments and Health Services of England, Scotland and Wales work together as with the content of health policies *per se*.

If by a 'National Health Service' is meant a commitment to a particular set of core values and principles, we see little prospect of radically different Health Services in Scotland, Wales and England. But if the discussion turns to matters of organisation and management, there is room for much greater experimentation and divergence in the new devolved system. Appropriate investment at this stage in the design of some 'tracking studies' which could capture the lessons of innovation and change would be extremely valuable. Northern Ireland has a different system for health and social care, but there have been few attempts to learn systematically from this experience. There is significant potential for shared learning from the array of constitutional and policy innovations on which the UK, Scotland, Wales, Northern Ireland and England are all now embarking. Who will 'hold the ring' and encourage this learning to happen?

References

1. Hazell R, Jervis P. *Devolution and Health*. London: Nuffield Trust, 1998.
2. Donald Dewar, in the Foreword to *Designed to Care – Renewing the National Health Service in Scotland*.

The Conservatives and the NHS during the 1990s

Anthony Harrison

With the very title of its first White Paper, *The New NHS*, Labour intended to suggest a fresh start, although it is frank enough to acknowledge that it has built on some of the achievements of the Government that preceded it. But what exactly are those achievements?

Naturally, the White Paper does not attempt systematically to identify them. More surprising, it seems that the Conservatives were not too sure themselves. Their final White Paper, *A Service with Ambitions*,[1] touched only lightly on those policies which reflected their definition of a new NHS: the purchaser/provider split, fundholding and competition between free-standing provider trusts. Instead, it set out five strategic objectives: a well-informed public, a seamless service, knowledge-based decision-making, a highly trained and skilled workforce, and a responsive service. It went on to emphasise the need for the development of primary care, better handling of information, professional development and managing for quality.

This emphasis on human resources and service development – albeit in the most general of terms – could be seen simply as part of the White Paper's overall strategy of trying to move away from unpopular policies. By ignoring them, the Conservatives' last White Paper implicitly acknowledged that there was no electoral benefit to be had from being associated with them. Nevertheless, the 1990 changes were at the time perceived as being the most significant reform of the NHS since its foundation. If they were not successful, it is important to understand why.

In the first part of this overview, therefore, we have drawn on work by the King's Fund and others which focuses on the evaluation of the particular policy interventions associated with the 1990 reforms. In the second, we take some of the key tasks that any health care system must tackle, looking at provision and demand management, and then at tasks which in a system such as the NHS fall to the central organisations, the NHS Executive and/or the Department of Health. In the final section we look at some general characteristics that any health care system should embody and consider whether or not the Conservatives' policies promoted them.

The 1990 reforms

The 1990 reforms were designed to create a market in the provision of health care services. This required the structural division of the existing NHS into purchasers and providers and the creation of new forms of organisation in respect of each of these two functions – health authorities and GP fundholders, on the one hand, and trusts, on the other.

Learning from the NHS Internal Market: a review of the evidence [2] considers all the available evidence bearing on these three elements as well as the market as a whole. The authors attempt to assess whether the changes have made a difference in respect of the five widely used criteria: efficiency, equity, quality, choice and responsiveness, and accountability.

The central conclusion of this survey is that there has been little measurable change, even in areas where there were good reasons for expecting there to be some. For example, fundholders should have achieved a great deal which non-fundholders had not. The authors recognise that there has been cultural change, e.g. in GPs' standing within the overall NHS and a general increase in cost-consciousness, but evidence for specific impacts such as reductions in emergency admissions or prescribing costs, or lower unit costs of care, are hard to find. Even evidence of the impact of the purchaser–provider split, which appeared to open the way for fundamental change in the way that services were provided, proves hard to detect.

In the words of Julian Le Grand, Nick Mays and Jo-Ann Mulligan in the final chapter of the above-cited review:

Perhaps the most striking conclusion to arise from this survey of the evidence is how little overall measurable change there seems to have been related to the core structures and mechanisms of the internal market. Indeed, in some areas where significant changes might have been expected, there were none. For instance, there seems to have been no difference between fundholders and non-fundholders in referral rates for elective surgery despite the fact that one set of GPs was making referrals from a fixed budget for which they were responsible and the other set were not. (p.129)

One conclusion which might be drawn from these findings is that the new institutions were never allowed to work in a distinctive way and indeed never could do so within a system as tightly controlled as the NHS. Whatever the merits of competition, they could not be realised in a system which allowed virtually no spare capacity and moreover was not prepared politically to deal with the consequences of rapid change. As Le Grand *et al.* put it: 'the incentives were too weak and the constraints too strong.' (p.130) They go on to point out that:

Trusts not only had limited opportunities to compete with one another; they had little incentive to do so ... both HAs and trusts were not really treated as independent agents, but viewed more as partially decentralised instruments of central government policy. (p.131)

As this conclusion suggests, one way of looking at the review's findings is to set them in the wider policy context. The 1990 reforms and the new structures which embodied them were only one set of policies introduced in the early 1990s. The Government pursued a vast range of other policies which, as successive issues of *Health Care UK* have argued, did have an impact on the Service by routes other than the market mechanism which the 1990 Act appeared to intend to create. In some ways they subverted the internal market – for example, through the imposition of targets for efficiency gains, waiting-list initiatives and other aspects of the Patient's Charter – with centrally determined service delivery targets. In other ways, such as through *The Health of the Nation*, they attempted to make changes which the market mechanism was not designed for.

Furthermore, there was a rapid turnover in jobs and personnel as new organisations were created or old ones reorganised at national and local level. The reforms and the other policy changes generated a vast amount of activity which was not only unproductive but also diverted attention from the core tasks they were designed to address. In these ways, the will to change, at the level of the system and the level of the individual, was sapped by both the weight of the constraints imposed by the centre and the pressure of other activities and demands on time.

An alternative though complementary view is that the changes to purchasing and providing structures were both off-target, that is they were not aimed at the central tasks which the NHS has to perform, nor did they bear on the vast number of decisions which those working in the NHS at all levels actually have to make. The NHS comprises several hundred thousand professionals who, to a greater or lesser extent, are free to act independently and to make their own personal responses to the circumstances in which they find themselves. A study of speech therapists by Nick Mays and Catherine Pope[3] found, for example, that most had continued to practise more or less independently of change in the organisational framework surrounding them.

This insight into a relatively small profession has not been matched by similar studies for the mass of NHS staff. But it is obvious enough that, during the 1990s, the NHS changed a great deal in ways unrelated to the 1990 Act structures. The Service received significant increases in funding, regular increases in medical staff and, outside hospitals, nursing staff as well. It also did more work as measured by all the usual indicators – outpatient visits, GP consultations, hospital episodes and A&E attendances – and, where measures are available, they suggest it was done more cost-effectively.

There were major changes in the way that hospital services were provided, such as the shift to day surgery; and a wide range of technical innovations, including new surgical procedures and new drugs, were introduced. Similarly, general practice rapidly expanded the quantity and range of skills and services available at local level and specific services such as those for people with serious mental illness were modified by the availability of more effective drugs.

There is no general yardstick to judge whether these changes might have been more rapid under a different set of institutions or incentives. In particular instances, such as the introduction of keyhole surgery, the rate of change appears to have been too fast – which would suggest that individual clinicians were not sluggish in adapting to new ways of operating. In other cases, such as day surgery, or the application of anti-thrombolytics, too slow.

Despite the vast amount of monitoring of the NHS from external bodies such as the National Audit Office, the Audit Commission and the Clinical Standards Advisory Group, as well as internal audit, no overview has been attempted inside or outside of the NHS or the Department of Health which would help identify where change during the 1990s had been beneficial and where not, or where performance would have been better under a different set of policies.

Particular instances can be cited, such as the commissioning of care for elderly people, where performance has been poor, as the evidence cited in Section 1.2 of the Health Policy Review indicates. In the case of cancer screening there has been sustained progress, marred by significant lapses in some areas (see Section 1.3). In both cases, failures have been linked to the way the 1990 reforms splintered the Service by creating free-standing organisations, i.e. trusts accountable for their own performance, not that of the NHS as a whole. In both cases, however, the story is more complicated than that: in both, there had been highly critical reports of the overall organisation of the Service in the mid-1980s – the first by the Audit Commission,[4] the second by the National Audit Office[5] – both of which revealed substantial weaknesses in the central direction and management of policies towards these two specific services.

To review all such evidence and attempt to find explanations for good and bad developments is beyond the scope of this article. Instead, we take a different and selective approach. In the next section we consider three of the key tasks which any health service must perform:

- managing demand, i.e. scarcity;

- delivering services;
- system governance.

Although these are the fundamental tasks which must be discharged in any health care system, the first two were virtually ignored in the 1990 reforms. Purchasers were to determine how resources were to be used: how these decisions might be related to the decisions of users to access the Service was ignored. Similarly, the creation of trusts as new forms for organising provision did not rest on any analysis or even description of the forces making for change in either hospital or primary care or indeed where the existing system was failing for institutional reasons, e.g. where the scale of provision might be uneconomic or unsustainable. The third element, system management, was subsequently considered but, as we shall see, the analysis on which proposals for change were made was a misguided one.

Managing demand

The central challenge which faces the NHS is to accommodate the demands falling on it within the available resources. It cannot meet all of them to the highest possible quality: it must manage the resulting scarcity. This has also been so but the external environment within which the Service must meet this challenge has been changing, noticeably so in the period considered here, making the central task more difficult.:

- patients are more informed and have higher expectations of what the NHS should provide. This has implications both for pressure on services and their manner of delivery and for professional roles;
- the media are quick to focus on failures;
- those working in the NHS, influenced by

wider trends in society, wish to modify the nature of their working commitment;

- technical change increases the scope for effective interventions, news of which quickly becomes common knowledge.

Demand management in a service which is largely free at the point of use requires a range of measures, including:

- ensuring that people are routed to the most cost-effective options;
- encouraging and supporting self-care where this is appropriate;
- controlling professionals' demands, particularly for new and expensive procedures.

For most of the life of the NHS, the management of scarcity has been carried out implicitly, mainly at local level by individual clinicians. This process was accepted by the public largely because it was not understood. But during the 1980s and 1990s the forces set out above and some of the measures taken by the previous Government began to change that. On the one hand, specific central requirements, particularly *The Patient's Charter*, encouraged users to see themselves as consumers with rights. On the other, the development of an explicit, largely non-clinical purchasing function brought the issues out into the open.

Overall, these changes made the task of managing scarcity more difficult. So the 1990 reforms should have been accompanied by measures to make the management of scarcity more effective by, for example, supporting clinicians in their rationing role. The main thrust of policy during the 1980s and 1990s, however, was to attempt to get more output out of the given quantum of resources, through a series of measures designed to improve

efficiency in the way that NHS resources were used. Moreover, the emphasis on efficiency was complemented by an emphasis on extra activity in its own right, in ministers' statements on the impact of the reforms and through the purchaser efficiency index. As the Health Policy Review in *Health Care UK 1995/96*[6] noted, trusts were deemed a success by the Conservative Government precisely because they were associated with an increase in activity.

At national level, the emphasis on primary care, which typified Government rhetoric during much of the period, could be seen as part of a strategy of trying to move the Service away from high-cost secondary care interventions towards low-cost primary ones. But the hospital service was used more, rather than less, for outpatient consultations and emergencies as well as elective care.

The reasons for this are complex but one partial explanation is that GPs are demand-identifiers as well as gatekeepers. In other words, the increase might be attributed to better primary care services identifying more need for hospital treatment and hospitals themselves being able to do more for particular groups of the population, such as the very young and the elderly.

But while the observed increase might have been justifiable in terms of benefits to patients, it might also be attributable to a failure to link budgets to decisions at local level. The Conservatives implicitly recognised the need for this link to be strengthened in their gradual expansion of the scope of fundholding. The total purchasing pilots effectively put the burden on GPs of reconciling the forces for demand diversion and demand creation. By the end of their period of office, however, the pilots had just begun. As the results of the National Evaluation of Total Purchasing Pilot Projects[7] show, there were no major changes to record, but in some areas a start had been made in implementing change through the introduction of lower cost, community-based alternatives to hospital services.

The potential for self-care was recognised but not pursued. *The Health of the Nation* White Paper[7] referred to the importance of fostering individual responsibility for health and subsequent ministerial statements[8] in relation to the availability of over-the-counter drugs made the same point. In 1996, the Patient Partnership scheme[9] was announced, designed to promote a new relationship between patients and professionals based on better information. By 1997 its impact had been minimal.

Some contribution to controlling professional demands, however, was made through the health technology assessment programme of new forms of treatment, introduced in 1993. As EL(95)105, *Improving the effectiveness of clinical services*,[10] puts it:

> Sometimes new health technologies become available before we have a complete picture of their application and cost effectiveness ... **Any further investment on [sic] these services should be in the context of ... recognised assessments, and not as part of routine care.** (p.2)

Similarly, the emphasis on clinical effectiveness of existing treatments evidenced in the creation of the Cochrane Centres and other similar initiatives began to lead to explicit calls for reduction of some interventions and caution about the use of others. In respect of drugs and new surgical procedures, control was still weak in

1997. Licensing conditions for drugs remained essentially the same and no formal mechanisms were put in place for surgical procedures.

Moreover, these were internal technical improvements which did nothing to help the public understand the issues. This helps to explain why, when ambulance standards were reviewed, the Government failed to take the chance to manage demand downwards, to less expensive services. The opportunity to divert demand away from the NHS was presented by the professionally executed *Review of Ambulance Standards*.[11] The recommendation of a category of call which would not have necessarily merited an ambulance response was rejected by the Government, fearful that it would appear to be making yet another cut. Instead, it went for higher performance standards. Not surprisingly, the demand for ambulance services has been rising faster than for any other major service and continues to do so.

Relations with the media and the public remained poor. In part, this was no fault of Conservative health ministers, who could never shake off the association between the general policies of the Government towards public provision and the Health Service in particular. This perhaps goes some way to explaining why virtually no political effort was made to explain to the public the case for more effective control over the introduction of new drugs and procedures. As was predicted at the time of their establishment, the creation of health authorities with an explicit purchasing function revealed what had before been implicit, and also in itself led to explicit decisions – for example, on whether or not to pay for a new drug – which had never been made in that way before. Attempts by health authorities to manage scarcity within their own patch appeared to be inequitable and also to reflect a breakdown in the universal nature of the Service.

Overall, therefore, the previous Government did not manage scarcity well: indeed they made no systematic effort to do so across the Service as a whole. Not surprisingly, by the end of the Conservatives' period of office, the apparent pressures on the Service were greater than ever: all indicators of use were up as well as waiting lists. These increases occurred even though what evidence exists, e.g. reported morbidity in the General Household Survey, does not suggest that the population was becoming less healthy. Nevertheless, despite a considerable increase in resources and in measured efficiency, the feeling of pressure on the Service when the Conservatives left office was as great as in 1988, the events of which gave rise to the review which, in turn, led to the 1990 reforms. In these simple terms, the period 1990–1997 could be seen as a complete failure.

Delivering services

Although the NHS is largely a care delivery organisation, it does not have a list or menu of the individual services which it provides. Providers have had little discretion over the patients they have to treat but they have had almost complete discretion as to how they respond to and treat patients approaching the Service, i.e. how they design and deliver services and determine which resources, particularly the human resources, they require to do so.

The NHS – or the educational system on its behalf – does of course incur massive expenditures training its workforce, but however good individual clinicians are, at whatever they are trained to do, that does not guarantee an effective and efficient service. There is a vast range of issues affecting clinician performance which greater professional competence alone cannot resolve. To take one example, the case for the district general hospital (DGH) made over 30 years ago turned in part on the benefits of what were then judged to be the right size of clinical teams to handle the workload generated by a district. Equally, it was recognised that the DGH would need to be supported by the resources of more specialised centres as well as local hospitals for simpler procedures. The concept of the DGH also recognised that clinical quality had to be balanced against considerations of cost and access, i.e. non-clinical factors.

Equally, the design of services for specific patient groups, be they emergency cases or those with rare cancers, requires a range of analytic and management skills. Thus while the NHS as a clinical service undoubtedly needs well-trained clinicians in the right numbers and with the requisite mix of skills, it also requires, not at the sharp end of service delivery but in close support, the complementary skills which ensure that the service as a whole works well.

After the enthusiasm of the 1960s, the notion of planning the way that services are provided within the NHS has never, taking the broad span of services, taken hold. In particular, areas such as the creation of the DGH network and the location of so-called specialised services, regions did have a planning role often by virtue of their control over access to capital funding, but in general services developed in a heterogeneous manner largely as a result of the initiative of individual clinicians.

At one level, this decentralised approach may work well since it allows individuals or teams the scope to innovate and experiment. It will not work well, however, where change requires the co-ordinated action of a large number of clinicians, particularly where services run across the boundaries of different organisations. In such circumstances, there is a need for a mechanism which allows a broader view to emerge and be implemented – in other words, a capacity for service design.

Designing services

The introduction of the 1990 Act led to a reduction in the limited capacity that existed to take a broad, i.e. national or regional, view. Moreover, as the King's Fund review cited above concluded, the nature of the institutions of the internal market made it harder to effect considered change where that change involved more than one provider. Implicitly, therefore, the task of service planning was shifted down from the centre or region to the local level, either to trusts or to purchasers.

However, it has become clear during the 1990s that many service issues straddle individual trusts and purchasers. The 1990 definition of trust and purchaser boundaries paid no attention to factors making for change in the way that hospital services were organised. Growing specialisation, new technology and changes to doctors' training created pressures for larger hospitals and for services to be designed over larger catchment areas.

Under the 1990 arrangements, health authorities were encouraged to combine into consortia and/or to agree on lead purchasers. As noted in Section 1.1 of the Health Policy Review, the Audit

Commission found in its 1997 report, *Higher Purchase*,[12] that these arrangements did not work. In this respect the 1990 Act's structure proved a failure.

Furthermore even at local level, the capacity to plan and design services has been poor, particularly where this involves combining elements from different organisations. In *Health Care UK 1995/96* we cited evidence from the Health Advisory Service,[13] in relation to patients with acquired brain damage. This year's Review cites the Clinical Standards Advisory Group's report on community health services for elderly people,[14] which reached similar conclusions to the Audit Commission 1997 report, *The Coming of Age*.[15] Both found gaps in provision, be it of rehabilitation services or alternatives to hospital admission, which meant that the Service as a whole did not work effectively in terms of cost or quality.

Our conclusion is that the capacity of the NHS to plan and design services probably declined during the 1990s and in any case did not match up to the new challenges that emerged during that period. While in principle the new purchasing structure should have led to improvements at local level, in practice it did not do so. There was no compensating increase at regional or national level, rather the reverse. During the whole period of the Conservative administration, the centre produced no analysis on the hospital service as a whole. Individual regions such as South East Thames did[16] but this capacity, too, came to be dispersed.

The Calman-Hine report on cancer care[17] was an exception. Its starting premise was that cancer care in the UK did not perform as well as other countries, and that the service as a whole, from general practice to specialist centre, had to be consciously designed. As we have argued elsewhere,[18] the report was deficient in a number of ways. In particular:

- it failed to take resources into account;
- it did not deal with training;
- it did not take the impact of its proposals on the rest of the Service into account;
- the evidence base was weak and the hoped-for benefits therefore unclear.

However, it did represent the first significant step in the 1990s towards considering systematically, at national level, how a major service such as cancer care should be delivered. But by the same token, it underlined the need for and the lack of such a structured approach for other services, as well as the lack of a suitable evidence and information base for this task.

Planning the workforce

Workforce planning was, if anything, slower to take hold than service planning. In respect of doctors, the central departments have always had the final say by virtue of their financial control over medical training. However, although the Medical Workforce Advisory Committee – the latest in a series of bodies charged with the task of forecasting the need for doctors – has attempted to improve the methodology for estimating how many doctors are 'needed', the criticisms made 20 years ago by Alan Walker and Alan Maynard[19] still largely stand.

The two persistent areas of omission have been the systematic consideration of the scope for substitution by other professions and the implications of further specialisation. More

recently, other factors have come to the fore, particularly changes in the way that doctors view their careers. Increasingly, they are looking for new career patterns, which means that their lifelong adherence to the NHS, at least in the way it is currently organised, cannot be taken for granted.

The three reports issued by the Medical Workforce Advisory Committee which appeared during the 1990s show awareness of these issues. Moreover, the Committee commissioned for its second report a major study of the factors bearing on the demand for doctors. However, it is hard to discern any measurable improvement in their capacity to tackle the issues facing them, in part because of the inherent difficulty of estimating the nature of the service requirements many years in advance and in part because to do so requires a reconsideration of the nature of the professional roles for which doctors are trained. By the end of the Conservatives' period of office, there were signs in professional publications, such as *Future Patterns of Care by General and Specialist Physicians*,[20] that these issues were being considered but with no evident impact on official policy-making.

In respect of other professional requirements, the Conservatives made a major change with the establishment of regional education consortia and their local counterparts, which were intended to emphasise the needs of employers rather than the independent 'needs' of the professions. By 1997, these had scarcely begun to be effective but the change was in the right direction of linking training requirements to service needs.

But the requisite knowledge base for the new organisations was weak. The amount of research available, for example, on the nursing requirements of whole hospitals and the comparative performance of hospitals staffed in different ways remained as tiny as it was when the Conservatives came to power. Furthermore, no strategic approach or central lead of the kind that the IHSM 1996 report, *The Future Healthcare Workforce*,[21] called for, emerged before their time in office came to an end.

Our overall conclusion is that as far as the capacity to plan and deliver health services is concerned, the 1990s saw only very modest improvement in some areas and losses in others. There was a virtually complete failure to relate or bring together effectively the various factors making for change in the way health care is delivered. This was particularly true of hospitals where the Government did begin to tackle seriously the number of hours worked by junior doctors and also, partly as a result of European pressures, to change postgraduate training. But it made no attempt to estimate the impact of those policies on hospital costs or capacity.

During the whole of the period, moreover, there was no significant central capacity to plan for, or even reflect on, the broad issues posed to the way services are delivered by changes in technology, medical staffing and quality considerations or to relate effectively the various factors making for change to the role of the hospital or in the roles of individual professions.

System governance

We turn next to tasks which fall almost entirely to the NHS Executive and the Department of Health – termed here 'the centre'. These are tasks which are concerned with the management of the system as a whole, both policy-making, i.e. making the 'rules', and also monitoring whether or not the 'rules' are being kept to.

Policy-making

What counts as 'good' policy-making in such a politically contentious area as health is in itself contentious. The view we take here is that policy-making for the health care sector is, politics aside, particularly difficult because of the scale of the sector, its complexity and the factors making for change in the broader environment. Accordingly, there is a *prima facie* case for experiments or pilots and learning by doing. But whether policy change is piloted or implemented across the board, the various elements should be consistent, i.e. not working against each other.

The policies introduced by the 1990 Act were highly unpopular in some quarters not simply because of their content but also because of the way they were introduced and the basis on which they were justified. The changes were largely an act of faith – there was no substantial body of knowledge either in the UK or from overseas on which to base them. The notion of trying out the idea of an internal market in parts of the country was explicitly rejected.

However some aspects of the 1990 system were taken more slowly – particularly, the development of fundholding and its variants. Here new ways of working were allowed to emerge as a result of local initiative. Furthermore in the 1997 Primary Care Act, the notion of piloting became entrenched in legislation. Thus towards the end of the Conservatives' time in office, a more defensible style was emerging.

As far as consistency is concerned, it is hard to discern any improvement during the 1990s. The most persistent failure was that between health and social care where policies during the 1990s moved in opposite directions, with the former emphasising rapid turnover and the latter working to the slower tempo of lifetime care. The differences between the two became ever more apparent at the interface between hospital discharge and post-operative care through the bed blockages that resulted.

Within the NHS itself, the main inconsistencies, at strategic level, lay in the balance between primary and secondary care. As noted above, the real relationships between the two were never worked out. As a result, the financial framework was not aligned to allowing any significant shift between the two. Furthermore, while Government rhetoric emphasised the scope for shifting care away from hospitals, centrally directed policies promoted more care within them.

Managing the system

One of the major developments of the 1980s and 1990s has been an increasing central role not only in introducing new policies but also attempting in a number of areas actively to manage the Service. The creation of the NHS Management Executive in the 1980s reflected the then Government's belief that the NHS required a more active style of management at central as well as local level. The NHS market was supposed to some degree to be self-regulating; central management would be able to exercise, in the words of the Functions and Management Review,[22] 'a light touch'. As successive issues of Health Care UK have demonstrated, that is not how things have worked out.

During the 1990s, the management grip of the centre grew. The abolition of the regional health authorities and the creation of regional offices with no effective independence created an enforcement machine for central imperatives such as Patient's Charter requirements and the purchaser efficiency index.

In last year's Health Care UK, Robert Maxwell,[23] looking back over 30 years or so concluded that:

> What is depressing 30 years later is to recognise that, despite much more sophisticated management now than then, my confidence in the NHS is in some ways less. It is not that standards of medical and nursing skill are lower or that the inefficiencies of the NHS are greater. Rather it is, I think, that because of the dramatic expansion of what is medically possible – expansion at a pace much greater than the increases in NHS funding – the job we are trying to do has become harder. (p.247)

The foundation of this perception is the mismatch between ambition and performance. The centre found itself taking on more, but knowing less. The reasons for that lie with the central mistake of the 1990 system, that it could lead to a smaller central (and regional) role. The reviews of the role of the Department and the Executive and the subsequent policy of cutting management costs in all parts of the Service, combined with the churning of people in senior management posts, meant that much of the 'wisdom' of the Service was lost, at the same time as the resources available for analysis and reflection were systematically reduced.

In these circumstances it is not surprising that the Government resorted to simple measures of control. The purchaser efficiency index and the trust regime with its emphasis on effective local management of resources both had good effects in promoting efficiency and local initiative. But they also had bad ones in terms of the incentives they introduced to increase activity, regardless of the wider implications and ignoring the connections between the various elements which make up a service for a specific care group.

Given the broad-brush nature of the efficiency index, this is scarcely surprising. Towards the end of its period of office the Conservative Government began to use financial incentives in a different way, i.e. through special, nationally controlled funds to target specific issues such as mental health, the health–social divide and winter pressures. This was a natural progression for a more active centre to take. But it was not developed sufficiently to represent a worked-out style of management different from that adopted in the wake of the 1990s reforms.

Overall, as far as the central roles are concerned, we conclude, with Robert Maxwell, that there was a deterioration rather than an improvement. The reasons lie not simply with the growth in what the Service can do, in a technical sense. They also lie in the growing concern of the centre actively to steer it in particular directions. While the task of managing the NHS became more difficult, the implications of that were not recognised: central and particularly regional capacity to monitor and understand the NHS was reduced rather than strengthened.

General characteristics

The defining characteristic of any health care system is its knowledge base. Traditionally, that has been assumed to mean that its professionals are highly trained but, as knowledge and the investment required to produce it have grown, that simple definition has become increasingly obsolete. The growth in clinical knowledge is just one of many factors making for change in the way that health services are provided. Economic,

social and political forces are compelling change in the way that care is delivered.

As a consequence, any health care system must be flexible and adaptable to changing circumstances, which in turn implies an ability to innovate and experiment not simply in respect of specific clinical interventions but also in terms of policies.

In the rest of this section we consider these two broad characteristics.

Developing the knowledge base

By 1998, the notion that the delivery of care, not to mention policy-making, should be evidence-based had become a cliché. In this area, there was little progress during the 1980s but the 1990 regime was genuinely innovative. As far as research is concerned the initial trigger was the 1988 House of Lords report on Medical Research,[24] which recommended major changes in the way that research was commissioned, particularly in non-clinical areas. Subsequently, the appointment of Michael Peckham as Director of R&D led to a major effort to develop an R&D programme relevant to the needs of the NHS. With the implementation of the Culyer task force proposals on the financing and commissioning of research carried out within the NHS, the way was opened up for more effective direction of their content.

The R&D initiative was rightly presented at the time as a major new development which no other country could match. It, together with the changes introduced following the Culyer report, is moving the generation of knowledge within the NHS in the right direction. Moreover, initially as a support for purchasers and then as a support for clinicians, a large number of steps were taken during the 1990s to assess the significance of existing knowledge and to encourage its application in practice. Furthermore, the various initiatives such as the York Centre for Reviews and Dissemination and the Cochrane Centres are increasing the capacity of the NHS to absorb knowledge from all sources.

Nevertheless, the balance of the effort continues to reflect clinical priorities rather than the wider needs of the Service. In each of the key tasks discussed above there are major gaps in knowledge and understanding. The critical failure over the whole history of the NHS has been to take the management of the Service, including the central role, seriously. Instead, the vast majority of publicly financed research and nearly all privately financed research have been on specific clinical interventions rather than the effective development of broad services, such as secondary care, and their management. The R&D initiative, though focused on the 'needs of the Service', continued with the same bias. By 1997, no programme had been developed specifically on the organisation and delivery of care and within the Policy Programme the same bias persisted. Only one major piece of policy monitoring, that into total purchasing, was begun.

The major weakness of the new approach is that it did not go far enough in redressing the imbalance the House of Lords identified in its 1988 report to the needs of managing and developing the Service, as they came to be identified during the 1990s.[24] The balance of effort and the style of research support has remained heavily focused on the specific clinical intervention rather than systems of care. In effect, the publicly financed system of research funding has reproduced the failings of the private.

System issues blend clinical and managerial considerations, as well as technology. Furthermore, neither private nor publicly funded research has shed much light on fundamental issues of clinical organisation, such as the balance between specialisms and generalists, or the wide range of speculative issues, or on major structural change, i.e. the underlying factors making for change in service delivery.

The knowledge the Service needs may be generated by means other than formal research. If new forms of service delivery are to be tried out, however, learning can only take place if suitable monitoring arrangements are in place and the capacity for the knowledge and experience gained can be exchanged. The developments in fundholding and the pilot schemes emerging from the 1997 Act represent a major gain.

Nevertheless, the record here too is mixed. The assessment of the evaluation carried out in the London Implementation Zone[25] suggested that the preparation of projects had been too hasty and the subsequent assessment skimped. Furthermore, very little nationally directed piloting was done within secondary care – the North Staffs Trauma Centre and the hospital re-engineering schemes at King's College Hospital and at Leicester Royal Infirmary are two exceptions.

The second strand, organised diffusion of what is known, can also be seen as an important innovation which can arguably be attributed to the creation of the free-standing purchasing role. Although, as Gifford Batstone and Mary Edwards argued in last year's Health Care UK,[26] the way the policies have been implemented could be criticised for not relating effectively to the concerns of practising clinicians, it was clearly aimed at the right target – the effective use of existing knowledge.

The 1990 Act provided for the general introduction of medical, later clinical, audit. Here too the process of implementation and its cost can be criticised: it is impossible to demonstrate that it was worth the investment made in it as the National Audit Office report[27] and the subsequent Public Accounts Committee hearings demonstrated. However, whatever their faults, these initiatives did serve to establish the importance of evidence and effective monitoring of performance and in this sense provided the essential basis for subsequent developments.

A final development was that of external audit, in particular the role of the Clinical Standards Advisory Group and the Audit Commission which, together with the National Audit Office and the Health Advisory Service, provided a much more effective assessment of how the Service was performing than had been available in previous years.

In particular instances, such as cancer screening, the series of National Audit Office reports and the subsequent hearings before the Public Accounts Committee did lead more or less directly to a better system for managing the Service. In other areas, such as purchase of supplies, successive reports from the National Audit Office have found, despite substantial change, that major weaknesses remain. There has been no systematic attempt to estimate the impact of reports such as these across the Service as a whole, but at least it can be said that the Service's knowledge base has been vastly strengthened.

Overall

We conclude that the process of providing the NHS with the knowledge base it needs was effectively begun in the 1990s. However, the R&D programme has not been designed to counter adequately the existing biases in research and has therefore produced virtually nothing which bears on the issues of service configuration that is now facing the Service in many parts of the country nor on the requirements of managing the Service. However, more information and general intelligence has become available in other ways: it is hard, however, to show whether effective use has been made of them.

Flexibility and adaptability

Against the background of change and uncertainty set out above, any health care system must be flexible and adaptable. The NHS pre-reforms was typified by an administrative hierarchical structure, changed every so often according to nationally determined policies. The 1990 Act encouraged flexibility by reducing the significance of geographical boundaries in service provision and, particularly, in primary care through GP fundholding, by allowing new ways of providing services to emerge, albeit slowly.

However, the 1990 structure had the effect of hardening the boundaries between different parts of the NHS and creating incentives to keep work locally. The trust regime, combined with the efficiency index, probably reduced flexibility in respect of changing the way that services were provided, particularly across the hospital–community boundary.

Another source of inflexibility was finance. In fact, compared to other parts of the public sector, NHS finance has always enjoyed a high degree of flexibility since very little of it has been tied to specific activities: with HCHS, health authorities enjoyed virtually complete financial freedom to allocate resources between competing uses. But at the boundary of primary and secondary care, the division between HCHS and FHS proved an obstacle to shifting services from hospital to community settings. With the 1997 Act, the first steps were taken to remove this impediment to change, albeit on a pilot basis.

In contrast to finance, professional boundaries within the NHS have always presented formidable barriers to change. Some progress was made during the 1990s towards removing the obstacles they presented. The review of the Act governing the professions allied to medicine[28] suggested a large number of changes which would have increased flexibility, though no action had followed by the end of the previous Government's time in office. In the case of nurse-prescribing, which the Government did support, progress with pilot schemes was painfully slow. Within hospitals, pressure on the Service meant that innovation was 'forced' and a number of new roles developed, particularly for nurses. Within primary care, the potential of nurse practitioners started to be realised, largely as a result of developments within nursing.

More generally the professions themselves began to recognise the needs for change. One example is the joint statement, *In the Patient's Interest*,[29] from the Standing Medical and Nursing & Midwifery Advisory Committees, the result of a working group established at the behest of the Government. In some cases, the initiative appears to come from within the professions, e.g. the BMA's *Towards Tomorrow*,[30] an attempt to define the future of the hospital consultant, or the GMC's *Good Medical Practice*.[31]

Here too the 1997 Act represented a step forward, since it allowed for general practice to be provided in different ways, involving different combinations of clinical skills. What was missing, however, was the kind of root-and-branch approach proposed in *The Future Healthcare Workforce*,[21] a study supported by the Institute of Health Services Management. This called for professional boundaries to be tackled across the board, rather than the piece-by-piece approach exemplified above, a call, however, to which there was no response in the period under review.

Overall

The NHS in 1997 was a more flexible institution than in 1990. The idea of change and the need for flexibility had become effectively embedded in it. Fundholding in its variants could be seen as a series of attempts to the best way forward in a field, that of local purchasing, in which there was virtually no relevant experience. The 1997 Act, passed at the eleventh hour of the Conservatives' period of office, opened the way for experiment and innovation across financial, organisational and professional boundaries. Both encouraged the notion that change should be locally driven, and that the centre had to create the conditions in which it might occur. But nationally some of the most important boundaries constraining change such as those surrounding the professions and finance, had only been addressed in a tentative way by the time the Conservatives left office.

Conclusion

The research findings cited at the beginning of this article suggested that the previous Government had little to show for what appeared at the time to be highly radical policies. Our own analysis suggests that the Conservatives also failed to tackle effectively some of the central tasks that any health service must discharge.

Most important of all, for all their general scepticism about the value of throwing money at problems, they continued to do so within the NHS. The central task of managing demand continued to be ducked. So too did the planning of services and the requirements of good management of the system as a whole. While the first systematic attempt was made to develop a knowledge base for the NHS – a major achievement – that initiative fell short of what the NHS required.

Underlying the radicalism of the 1990 Act was the notion that a health care system cannot simply be assumed to deliver high-quality, cost-effective services. Instead, a conscious effort must be made to try to find the best set of institutions, roles and incentives to ensure that it does. The specific measures the Conservatives took may with the benefit of hindsight appear misguided. But they were right in believing that change was required. Arguably, therefore, the most important legacy of the 1990 reforms was the very idea of reform itself.

References

1. Secretary of State for Health. *The National Health Service: a service with ambitions*. London: Stationery Office, 1997. (Cmnd 3425.)
2. Le Grand J, Mays N, Mulligan J. *Learning from the NHS Internal Market: a review of the evidence*. London: King's Fund, 1998.
3. Mays N, Pope C. *Speech and language therapy services and management in the internal market: a national survey*. London: King's Fund in association with the Royal College of Speech and Language Therapists, 1997.
4. Audit Commission. *Making a Reality of Community Care*. London: Audit Commission, 1986.
5. National Audit Office. *Cervical and breast screening in England*. London: HMSO, 1992.
6. Harrison A (ed). *Health Care UK 1995/96*. London: King's Fund, 1996.
7. Secretary of State for Health. *The Health of the Nation*. London: HMSO, 1991.
8. Harrison A (ed). *Health Care UK 1994/95*. London: King's Fund, 1996.
9. NHS Executive. *Patient Partnership: building a collaborative strategy*. Leeds: NHS Executive, 1996.
10. NHS Executive. *Improving the effectiveness of clinical services*. EL(95)105. Leeds: NHS Executive, 1995.
11. Department of Health. *Review of Ambulance Standards*. London: Department of Health, 1996.
12. Audit Commission. *Higher Purchase: Commissioning specialised services in the NHS*. London: Audit Commission, 1997.
13. Health Advisory Service. *Mental health services*. Williams R (ed). London: Stationery Office, 1996.
14. Clinical Standards Advisory Groups. *Community Health Services for Elderly People*. London: Clinical Standards Advisory Groups,1998.
15. Audit Commission. *Coming of Age*. London: Audit Commission, 1998.
16. South East Thames Regional Health Authority. *Shaping the Future: a review of acute services*. London: SETRHA, 1995.
17. Department of Health. *A Policy Framework for Commissioning Cancer Services: A report by the expert advisory group on cancer (Calman/Hine)*. London: Department of Health, 1995.
18. Harrison A. *National Service Frameworks*. In: Klein R (ed). *Implementing the White Paper*. London: King's Fund, 1998.
19. Maynard A, Walker A. *Doctor Manpower 1975–2000*. London: HMSO, 1978.
20. Royal College of Physicians. *Future Patterns of Care by General and Specialist Physicians*. London: RCP, 1996.
21. Institute of Health Services Management. *The Future Healthcare Workforce*. Manchester: University of Manchester, 1996.
22. Department of Health. *Managing the New NHS: functions and responsibilities in the new NHS*. Leeds: Department of Health, 1994.

23. Maxwell R. *A View from the Touchline*. In: Harrison A (ed). *Health Care UK 1996/97*. London: King's Fund, 1997.

24. House of Lords. Select Committee on Science and Technology. Priorities in medical research. London: HMSO, 1998.

25. Mays N *et al*. *Evaluating Primary Care Development*. London: King's Fund, 1997.

26. Batstone G, Edwards M. *Challenges in promoting clinical effectiveness and the use of evidence*. In: Harrison A (ed). *Health Care UK 1996/97*. London: King's Fund, 1997.

27. National Audit Office. *NHS England: Clinical Audit*. London: NAO, 1995.

28. JM Consulting. *The Regulation of the Health Professions*. Bristol: JM Consulting, 1996.

29. Standing Medical and Nursing & Midwifery Advisory Committees. *In the Patient's Interest*. London: Department of Health, 1996.

30. BMA. *Towards Tomorrow: The role of the consultant*. London: BMA, 1996.

31. General Medical Council. *Duties of a Doctor*. London: GMC, 1995.